P9-EDF-969

GUIDE TO REVISION

ab	abbreviations
adv	adverb
agr	agreement
ap	apostrophe
cap	capitalization
coh	coherence
coll	colloquial
CS, CF	comma splice
d	diction
dev	development
div	division
DM	dangling modifier
emp	emphasis
frag	sentence fragment
FP, ‖	faulty parallelism
gl	glossary
gr	grammar
id	idiom
k, awk	awkward
lc	lower case
MM	misplaced modifier
P	punctuation
¶	new paragraph
no ¶	no paragraph
ref	reference
rep	repetition
st	sentence structure
sub	subordination
shift	shift in perspective
sl	slang
sp	spelling
t	tense
trans	transition
w	wordiness
x	error
∧	omission
"/, ?/, -/, etc.	

CONCISE ENGLISH HANDBOOK

SECOND EDITION

CONCISE ENGLISH HANDBOOK

Check for abbreviations that should be spelled out (221-222)
Use adverb form to modify verbs and other modifiers (46)
Check agreement of subject and verb, pronoun and antecedent (17, 33)
Check for omission or misuse of apostrophe (236-238)
Check for words that should be capitalized (241)
Strengthen sequence of ideas; show relevance of detail (148, 161, 169)
Expression is too colloquial for its context (93)
Use semicolon or period between independent clauses (254)
Check for awkward, inaccurate, inappropriate wording (75)
Develop your point more fully—support, explain, illustrate (151, 161)
Check dictionary for syllabication of the word (220)
Rewrite the sentence to indicate what the modifier modifies (51)
Check for unemphatic, anticlimactic diction or organization (123, 139, 171)
Do not punctuate as a sentence—lacks an independent clause (248)
Put items joined by "and," "but," "or" in same grammatical category (63-66)
Check standing of debatable usage in glossary (346)
Check for unsatisfactory forms or constructions (1)
Check for unidiomatic, un-English expression (81)
Rewrite the sentence to make it clearer or more natural (124, 137)
Check for faulty or unnecessary capitalization (241)
Shift modifier into more appropriate position or rewrite sentence (49-50)
Check for omission or misuse of punctuation (245)
Break up into paragraphs that reflect organization (147)
Avoid confusing or unnecessary paragraph break (147)
Check reference of pronouns (33-37)
Avoid unnecessary or awkward repetition (138)
Check faulty predication, incomplete or mixed construction (54)
Check for inadequate or inappropriate subordination (132)
Check for shift in time or use of pronouns, shift to passive (67-72)
Expression is too slangy for its context (95-96)
Check for spelling errors (224)
Use appropriate tense of verb (27-28, 67)
Strengthen transition from point to point (149, 197)
Remove deadwood (107, 134)
Correct obvious error
Correct obvious omission
Use punctuation mark indicated (see reference chart, 244)

HANS P. GUTH
SAN JOSE STATE COLLEGE

WADSWORTH PUBLISHING COMPANY, INC.
BELMONT, CALIFORNIA

Hans P. Guth

Concise English Handbook, Second Edition

First edition: five printings

© 1961, 1965 by Wadsworth Publishing Company, Inc., Belmont, California. All rights reserved. No part of this book may be reproduced in any form, by mimeograph or any other means, without permission in writing from the publisher.

L.C. Cat. Card No.: 65-12527

Printed in the United States of America

Third printing:
AUGUST 1966

PREFACE

The *Concise English Handbook* makes available the handbook sections of *Words and Ideas* for use as a compact guide to written English. In this revised edition, the material has been thoroughly reworked in order to simplify its organization and to make the book throughout more consistent and more succinct. The section on grammar presents essential terminology and deals with basic problems of correctness. The sections on diction and sentence style concentrate on accurate, effective, and economical use of language. The sections on the paragraph, the whole theme, and the research paper present and illustrate essential principles of composition and rhetoric. Sections 6 and 7 offer a concise review of mechanics; the glossaries provide brief discussions of points of usage and definitions of grammatical terms. The student using the book as a reference guide in theme writing and theme correction will find every section and subsection a self-contained unit.

Given the present state of indecision and rapid development in the teaching of grammar, I have tried to find solid common ground. With minor variations, the terminology used in the book is that familiar to both teacher and student. At times, I have preferred a common-sense equivalent to a term unprofitably or confusingly technical. Occasionally I have used a term from the new linguistics that seemed apt or useful. Extensive trial use suggests the conclusion that the student finds these materials accessible, intelligible, and relevant to his needs.

Like the original version of the book, this second edition owes much to the criticisms of interested colleagues. I repeat my thanks to the readers of the original manuscript: Dudley Bailey, T. A. Barnhart, Robert W. Dent, Jack Fink, Hans Gottschalk, Harold Kane, and Paul Roberts. In the preparation of the present version, I have profited greatly from the comments of Whitney F. Bolton, University of California; Pascal Covici, Southern Methodist University; Emil Dillard, Adelphi College; Philip Durham, University of California at Los Angeles; Gerhard Joseph, Georgetown University; James Lill, Portland State College; C. F. Main, Rutgers University; and Floyd C. Watkins, Emory University.

CONTENTS

ACKNOWLEDGMENTS

I am indebted to the following for permission to reprint copyrighted material:

George Allen & Unwin Ltd. for permission to use a passage from Bertrand Russell, *Mysticism and Logic*.

The American Scholar for permission to use passages from articles by Joseph Wood Krutch, Donald J. Lloyd, and Philip M. Wagner.

Maxwell Anderson for permission to use a passage from his article "It Comes with the Set," *New York Herald Tribune*, September 6, 1957.

Appleton-Century-Crofts, Inc., for permission to use a passage from *A History of the English Language*, second edition, by Albert C. Baugh. Copyright © 1957, Appleton-Century-Crofts, Inc.

The Atlantic Monthly for permission to use passages from articles by Laird Bell, Saul Bellow, Paul Brooks, Curtis Cate, John K. Galbraith, Erle Stanley Gardner, Oscar Handlin, Gerald W. Johnson, Alfred Kazin, Walter Lippmann, T. S. Matthews, Charles W. Morton, Vance Packard, Leslie C. Stevens, Joseph Wechsberg, and Edward Weeks.

Bantam Books, Inc., for permission to use a passage from Clancy Carlile, "The Animal Fair," *New Campus Writing No. 2*, published by Bantam Books, Inc.

James B. Conant for permission to use a passage from *The American High School Today*.

Doubleday & Company, Inc., for permission to use passages from *The Summing Up* by W. Somerset Maugham, copyright 1938 by W. Somerset Maugham, reprinted by permission of Doubleday & Co., Inc.; and from "Whistling Dick's Christmas Stocking" in *Roads of Destiny* by O. Henry, Doubleday & Co., Inc.

E. P. Dutton & Co., Inc., for permission to use a passage from *Education and Freedom* by H. G. Rickover.

Clifton Fadiman for use of a passage reprinted by special permission from *Holiday,* copyright © 1957 by The Curtis Publishing Company.

Fortune for permission to use passages from articles by Adlai E. Stevenson (October 1955) and William H. Whyte (November 1950).

Harcourt, Brace & World, Inc., for permission to use a passage from Alfred Kazin, *A Walker in the City* (Harcourt, Brace & World, Inc.).

Harper & Row for permission to use passages from E. B. White, *One Man's Meat;* and from articles by Bruce Bliven, Heywood Broun, Robert Brustein, Miriam Chapin, John Fischer, John W. Gardner, Robert L. Heilbroner, Jane Jacobs, Marion K. Sanders, C. P. Snow, Dr. Ian Stevenson, Philip M. Wagner, and William S. White.

Harvard University Press for use of a passage reprinted by permission of the publishers from Joseph Hudnut, *Architecture and the Spirit of Man,* Cambridge, Mass.: Harvard University Press, copyright 1949 by The President and Fellows of Harvard College.

Howard Mumford Jones for permission to use a passage from an article in the *Saturday Evening Post.*

Alfred A. Knopf, Inc., for permission to use passages from Bruce Bliven, *Preview for Tomorrow,* copyright 1953; from Alistair Cooke, *One Man's America,* copyright 1951, 1952; from Julian Huxley, *Essays of a Biologist,* copyright 1923; and from H. L. Mencken, *A Mencken Chrestomathy,* copyright 1949.

Little, Brown & Company for permission to use passages from Walter Lippmann, *The Public Philosophy.*

The Macmillan Company for permission to use a passage from Arthur M. Schlesinger, *Paths to the Present,* copyright 1949.

Scott Meredith Literary Agency, Inc., for use of a passage from an article by Arthur C. Clarke in *Holiday,* reprinted by permission of the author and the author's agent, Scott Meredith Literary Agency, Inc.

Arthur Miller for permission to use passages from articles in *Holiday.*

The New Yorker for permission to use a passage from James Thurber, Copr. © 1955, The New Yorker Magazine, Inc.

Oxford University Press, Inc., for permission to use a passage from Rachel L. Carson, *The Sea Around Us.*

Queen's Quarterly for permission to use a passage from an article by K. W. Maurer.

Random House, Inc., for permission to use a passage from Jonathan Norton Leonard, *Flight into Space,* copyright 1953 by Jonathan Norton Leonard; and for permission to reproduce entries taken from *The American College Dictionary* (Copyright 1947, © Copyright 1962) and reprinted by permission of Random House, Inc.

The Reporter for permission to use passages from articles by Robert Bendiner, Marya Mannes, and William Lee Miller; and additional passages from articles by Michael Harrington, Lois Phillips Hudson, Ken Macrorie, Marya Mannes, William Lee Miller, George Steiner, copyright 1962 and 1963 by The Reporter Magazine Company.

Virginia Rice for permission to use passages from Paul Horgan, "Pages from a Rio Grande Notebook," *The New York Times Book Review,* copyright © 1955 by Paul Horgan.

Rinehart & Company for use of a passage from Lionel Trilling's introduction to *The Adventures of Huckleberry Finn,* by Mark Twain, in Rinehart Editions (New York: Rinehart & Company, Inc., 1948), copyright 1948, 1950, by Lionel Trilling. Reprinted by permission of Rinehart & Company, Inc., Publishers.

Saturday Review for permission to use passages from articles by Frederick Lewis Allen, John Mason Brown, Henry Steele Commager, Elmer Davis, John Van Druten, James A. Michener, Ashley Montague, Edith M. Stern, and William H. Whyte, Jr.; and additional passages from articles by Malcolm Cowley, James K. Feibleman, Claude M. Fuess, Arthur Mayer, Liston Pope, Bertrand Russell, Hartzell Spence, Albert Szent-Gyorgyi, Harold Taylor, and Richard L. Tobin.

Charles Scribner's Sons for use of passages from "The Golden Honeymoon" by Ring Lardner, copyright 1922, 1950 by Ellis A. Lardner (*How to Write Short Stories*), reprinted by permission of the publishers, Charles Scribner's Sons.

Time for use of passages reprinted courtesy of *Time*, copyright Time Inc. 1958.

The University of North Carolina Press for permission to use a passage from Norman Foerster, *The Humanities and the Common Man,* Chapel Hill: University of North Carolina Press, 1946.

University of Oklahoma Press for use of a passage reprinted from *Is the Common Man Too Common?* by Joseph Wood Krutch and others, copyright 1954 by University of Oklahoma Press and used by permission.

The Viking Press, Inc., for permission to use passages from Harrison Brown, *The Challenge of Man's Future;* John Steinbeck, *The Grapes of Wrath;* and Lionel Trilling, *The Liberal Imagination.*

The World Publishing Company for permission to reproduce entries from *Webster's New World Dictionary of the American Language,* College Edition, copyright 1958 by The World Publishing Company.

Yale University Press for permission to quote from David Riesman, *The Lonely Crowd.*

1

GRAMMAR

When a child begins to talk, he learns not only to name things but also to work the names of things into complicated patterns. Soon he is able to say "Suzie won't give me my ball back" or "Johnny says there isn't any Santa Claus." He has evidently mastered the major principles of **grammar**; that is, the *system by which words combine into larger units to convey ideas and information.*

G 1 Grammar and Usage

The study of grammar can help a writer make appropriate and mature use of the resources of the language.

The student in high school and college must learn to adapt the grammatical patterns he learned as a child to changing needs. The language that the educated adult uses in serious conversation and in writing differs to some extent from the language he uses when not on his best behavior. A student learns early that often he should say "is not" rather than "ain't," "can hardly wait" rather than "can't hardly wait," and "this kind of car" rather than "these kind of cars." Such differences are often discussed under the heading of **usage** rather than of grammar. While grammar concerns itself with generally applicable principles, the study of usage investigates our *choices among alternative words, word forms, and constructions.* Usage varies, at least to some extent, from period to period, from area to area, from social group to social group, and from one kind of writing to another.

G 1a Standard and Nonstandard. *Serious writing employs the kind of English that enjoys social and cultural prestige.* **Standard** usage is the language of education, journalism, and other white-collar occupations. You will use it in your written work except when you record or deliberately imitate illiterate or **nonstandard** speech. Nonstandard speakers have usually had relatively little formal education. Their jobs often require little reading of instructions and little writing of reports. They may have few dealings with teachers, lawyers, newspapermen, and other presumably highly literate persons.

Here are some of the distinctive forms and constructions of nonstandard English: [1]

VERB FORMS:	he *don't,* you *was,* I *says; knowed, growed;* I *seen* him
PRONOUN FORMS:	*hisself, theirself; this here* book, *that there* car; *them* boys
CONNECTIVES:	*without* you pay the rent; *on account of* he was sick; *being as* she couldn't come
DOUBLE NEGATIVES:	we *don't* have *no* time; a little rain *never* hurt *no* one

G 1b Formal and Informal. *Different kinds of standard English are appropriate to different occasions.* Relatively **informal** usages are found primarily in casual conversation, but also in writing designed to sound chatty or familiar. Relatively **formal** usages are characteristic of the language of scholarly studies, books on serious subjects, articles in serious magazines. Though more characteristic of written than of spoken English, these usages are also found in formal lectures, speeches, and discussions.

Here are some characteristic features of informal English:

[1] See the Glossary of Usage for further examples.

CONTRACTIONS:	*don't, doesn't, isn't, won't, can't; I'm, you've, they're*
CONVERSATIONAL TAGS:	*well, . . .; why, . . .; now, . . .*
PRONOUN FORMS:	it's *me,* that's *him; who* did you invite
PRONOUN REFERENCE:	everybody took *theirs;* somebody left *their* gloves
INTENSIFIERS:	*so* glad, *such a* surprise; *real* miserable, *awful* fast

The line between informal and formal English is not easy to draw. It is a matter not only of forms and constructions but also of word choice, sentence style, and organization.[2] The difference is often a matter of degree, with some expressions sounding more easygoing than others. At one extreme, the term **colloquial**, used in this book mainly in reference to word choice, describes the *usages most clearly suggestive of informal, improvised speech.* At the other extreme is usage so punctiliously formal as to be stilted or affected. As used in this book, the term *formal* describes usage generally appropriate to the discussion of serious issues.

Most college writing requires a knowledge of formal usage. Even if you are content to have your writing sound casual and relaxed, you have to be able to use a more formal style when the situation clearly demands it.

G 1c Sentence Construction. *A writer's language patterns need to grow in accuracy, scope, and flexibility.* Learning to choose between alternative usages is not all there is to grammar—let alone to effective writing. As a college student, you are exploring new areas of knowledge and learning to digest complicated and unfamiliar ideas. You must learn to use your linguistic resources to meet new and varied demands:

[2] For a discussion of formal and informal diction, see D 3.

(1) *You must learn how new words or phrases fit into sentences.* A child, when first introduced to the idea of freezing, learns to say "it froze" rather than "it freezed." Similarly, the high school student who is introduced to the word *criteria* learns to write "*These* criteria *are* unreliable" rather than "*This* criteria *is* a phony."

(2) *You must make relationships between words reflect relationships between ideas.* In a first draft, you may put down disjointed odds and ends: "My father bought a store in Oakland. Soon afterward property values went up. He sold the store at a handsome profit." In the finished paper, you may want the information about his making a profit to stand out as the main point. You will then arrange the material accordingly:

My father, who had bought a store in Oakland, sold it at a handsome profit when property values went up soon afterward.

Notice how the more complex version of the following passage emphasizes the point that the word discussed has many different meanings:

SIMPLE: The term *democracy* originated in ancient Greece. Different people have used it to describe quite different political systems. Usually the person who uses the word thinks it has only one meaning.

COMPLEX: *Democracy,* a term that originated in ancient Greece, has been used to describe quite different political systems, though the person who uses it usually thinks it has only one meaning.

If you have had little training in stating complicated ideas, you may produce sentences that are in various ways garbled or confused. They may suffer from scrambled word order, with major elements arranged upside-down. They may have a chopped-off effect because they start a pattern and leave it incomplete. They may be shaky because of inconsistent construction, combining patterns that do not go together. Through grammatical analysis you can sort out such sentences, identifying the various familiar speech patterns they contain.

EXERCISE

How successful are the following attempts to reproduce in writing the characteristic forms and constructions of nonstandard speech? Which features of nonstandard usage do you recognize?

1. I be dog iffen there wadden more folks there. Coming by wagon and foot and car, they was. Brother Slynum, he was standing at the entrance in his preaching suit just a-waving and helloing to everybody. The women was in their print dresses and sunbonnets. The men folks, too, was in their Sunday-go-to-meeting clothes. That ere tent with the sign painted over the door, "Welcome! All Day Singing and Dinner on the Ground," it was sagging in the wind. Outen front was the tables where everybody was putting the victuals: salads, cakes, cornbread, preserves, puddins, and Lord knows what all. At the far end of the table over a stone-built stove they was frying the catfish.

It was a jump-rope day. The spring was all stretched out on the pastures beyond, pretty and a little shy maybe, like a lazy gal waiting for her feller. With buttercups for freckles. But that ere spring didn't have nothing on me, I had more freckles than ere was buttercups. Yep. Mama said I swollered a dollar and it broke out in pennies. But she was just spoofing. I hadden never seen a dollar.—Clancy Carlile, "The Animal Fair," *New Campus Writing*

2. Well, anyway, they come over to help us celebrate the Golden Wedding and it was pretty crimpy weather and the furnace don't seem to heat up no more like it used to and Mother made the remark that she hoped this winter wouldn't be as cold as the last, referring to the winter previous. So Edie said if she was us, and nothing to keep us home, she certainly wouldn't spend no more winters up here and why didn't we just shut off the water and close up the house and go down to Tampa, Florida? You know we was there four winters ago and staid five weeks, but it cost us over three hundred and

fifty dollars for hotel bill alone. So Mother said we wasn't going no place to be robbed. So my son-in-law spoke up and said that Tampa wasn't the only place in the South, and besides we didn't have to stop at no high price hotel but could rent us a couple rooms and board out somewheres, and he had heard that St. Petersburg, Florida, was *the* spot and if we said the word he would write down there and make inquiries. —Ring W. Lardner, "The Golden Honeymoon," *How to Write Short Stories*

G 2 Grammatical Analysis

Grammar is the study of how words work together in a sentence.

Words convey only vague and tentative meanings as long as they are loosely strung together. G.I.'s and tourists abroad can carry on a rudimentary conversation with foreigners after picking up a few isolated words. A foreign visitor to the United States can make at least a dent in the language barrier by taking individual words from a dictionary. "Father—alcohol—baby—crying—beating—doctor—courtroom—jail" tells some kind of a story. However, what makes it broken English rather than standard English is the absence of definite relationships among words.

G 2a Grammatical Devices. *English employs several kinds of grammatical devices to give precise meaning to a succession of words.* In the typical written sentence, inflections, word order, and function words combine to help the reader select among the possible meanings of words and work those words into a meaningful sequence.

(1) **Inflections** are *changes in the form of a word that correspond to differences in grammatical relationships.* Inflections signal the differences in meaning between the sentences in each of the following pairs:

Stop*s* annoy*ed* our passenger.
Stop annoy*ing* our passenger.

The physician studi*ed* burn*s*.
The physician'*s* study burn*ed*.

The endings spelled *s, ed,* and *ing* are the inflections most frequently used in English.

NOTE: Some languages, such as Latin and German, rely heavily on inflections. Originally, English was close to German in number and importance of inflected forms. Through the centuries, however, English has shed many of these. Modern English relies primarily on other grammatical devices.

(2) A second major grammatical device is **word order**. In English, *different arrangements of words in a sentence produce different meanings*. Compare the sentences in the following pairs:

Gentlemen prefer *blondes*.
Blondes prefer *gentlemen*.

A *tramp* called *the mayor a liar*.
A *liar* called *the mayor a tramp*.
The mayor called *a tramp a liar*.

He ate *only* the steak.
He ate the *only* steak.

(3) A third major grammatical device is the use of *words whose main function is to clarify relationships among other words*. Many modern grammarians group these words together as **function words**. Function words account for the differences in meaning in the following pairs:

George set *a* poor example.
George set *the* poor *an* example.

He left the lady his estate.
He left *with* the lady *for* his estate.

The nurse neglected the patient.
The nurse *was* neglected *by* the patient.

G 2b Basic Sentence Elements. *The most important of the basic grammatical categories are those required to make up the various typical sentence patterns.* In analyzing sentences, grammarians assign words to basic categories, or **parts of speech**, according to the functions they perform. The same word may serve different functions, and belong to different grammatical categories, in different sentences. The word *light* performs a different function in each of the following:

Turn off the *light*.
Let's *light* a candle.
She had *light* hair.
The water was *light* blue.

(1) *The basic model of the English sentence consists of only two major elements.* A complete sentence normally has at least a **subject** and a **predicate**:

SUBJECT	PREDICATE
The boy	reads.
A car	stopped.
Dogs	bark.

The most important part of the subject is usually a **noun**: *car, student, bulldog, college, education.* Characteristically, nouns name or classify things, places, people, animals, concepts. The housewife looking up entries in the Sears Roebuck catalogue, the chemist giving names to new plastics, the businessman naming new products—all rely on the naming function of the noun. Nouns occur in such typical noun positions as "*Dogs* bark," "I like *dogs,*" and "for my *dogs.*" Their appearance is often signaled by such noun markers as *a, an,* and *the* (**articles**); *this, these, that,* and *those* (**demonstrative pronouns**); or *my, our,* and *your* (**possessive pronouns**). Most nouns add the inflectional *s* to refer to more than one of a kind (plural): boy*s*, dog*s*, car*s*, idea*s*. Many nouns show noun-forming endings (**suffixes**) like *-acy, -age, -ance, -dom, -hood:* liter*acy*, bond*age*, import*ance*, king*dom*, nation*hood*.

The place of nouns may be taken by **noun equivalents** or noun substitutes, such as the **personal pronouns**:

He reads.
It stopped.
They bark.

The predicate, the second major part of a simple sentence, normally makes some kind of assertion concerning the subject. (Sometimes the predicate asks a question about the subject.) The most important word, or group of words, in the predicate is the **verb**: *reads, stopped, has left, will return, is reprimanded, has been elected*. The verb signals the performance of an action, the occurrence of an event, or the presence of a condition. A noun may *name* an action: *theft, movement, investigation*. A verb refers to present, future, past, possible, or hypothetical performance: *steals, has moved, may investigate*. Verbs occur in typical verb positions: "Let's *eat*," "*Eat* your cereal," and "Big fishes *eat* little fishes." Most verbs change from the plain form to the plain form plus *s* after *he* or *she* (third person singular): "He eat*s*," "She write*s*," "He investigate*s*." Typical verb-forming suffixes are *-ize* and *-en:* organ*ize*, sharp*en*, redd*en*.

In verb forms consisting of several words, a limited number of **auxiliaries** recur:

I *am* eating	you *should* eat
he *has* eaten	we *may* eat
she *had* eaten	he *has been* eating
they *will* eat	it *must be* eaten

(2) *Several typical sentence patterns are expansions of the basic subject-predicate group.* In many sentences, the verb is an

action verb, indicating what the subject does or what happens to the subject. Such an action verb may be followed by one or two **objects**. An object is a noun or a noun equivalent. It may indicate a possible target of an action; it may indicate something that is in some other way affected by or involved in what the subject does.

SUBJECT	ACTION VERB	OBJECT	OBJECT
The student	reads	a book.	
My friend	sent	me	a letter.
Fred	called	his roommate	a liar.

In other sentences, the verb is a **linking verb**, which introduces a description of the subject. A linking verb links the subject to a description that identifies the subject or points out some of its characteristics.

SUBJECT	LINKING VERB	DESCRIPTION
Schnoogle	is	a mailman.
He	may be	your brother.
The price	seemed	reasonable.
The food	tasted	good.

The description following the linking verb is often a noun (*mailman, brother*). It may also be an **adjective**, a word that can point out a quality of a noun (see G 2c). A noun or an adjective used to complete the predicate is called a **complement**.

(3) *Several other typical sentence patterns are important because of the way they modify the usual subject-predicate relationship.* One of them uses the **passive** construction. It reverses the more common actor-action sequence by making the receiver, the target, or the result of the action the subject of the sentence. The passive construction can be recognized by characteristic forms of the verb, using the auxiliary *to be* and the **past participle**. (See G 4a.)

SUBJECT	PASSIVE VERB
A letter	was sent.
Prices	have been raised.
The series	will be discontinued.

The second pattern employs the verb form used in requests and commands (**imperative**) and omits the subject.

VERB	COMPLEMENT
Shut	the door.
Be	a man.
Keep	quiet.

A third pattern, beginning with *there is* or *there are,* postpones the subject:

	VERB	SUBJECT
There	is	hope.
There	was	no time.
There	were	few survivors.

NOTE: In identifying basic sentence elements, you will have to distinguish between verbs and **verbals**. *Verbals are derived from verbs but do not by themselves function as predicates.* The most distinctive and the most important of the verbals are the *to* forms (**infinitives**) and the *ing* forms (**gerunds** and **present participles**). Infinitives and gerunds often serve as subjects or as complements, taking the place of nouns:

Speeding	causes	accidents.
He	refused	*to pay.*
Teachers	discourage	*cheating.*

These verbals do have some important similarities to verbs. For instance, they are often followed by objects:

Studying *grammar*	inspires	me.
Fred	refused	to pay *his dues.*
Courtesy	forbids	calling *a policeman a cop.*

The *ing* forms are called present participles when they function as adjectives. (See G 2c.)

G 2c Modifiers. *The typical sentence contains words, or groups of words, that in various ways develop, restrict, or otherwise modify the meaning of the basic sentence elements.* Such **modifiers** can be roughly divided into two main groups: those that modify nouns or noun equivalents and those that modify other parts of a sentence or the sentence as a whole.

(1) All of the modifiers italicized in the following examples modify the noun *dog* and thus belong in the first group:

A *shaggy* dog barred my way.
A *big, yellow* dog was chewing the rug.
A dog *wearing a muzzle* emerged from the door.
A *police* dog tracked me down.
A dog *with droopy eyes* dozed in the sun.

Of these modifiers, the first three (*shaggy, big, yellow*) have the structural and formal characteristics of adjectives. An **adjective** can be identified as occurring in typical adjective positions: "a *reasonable* price," "The price is *reasonable,*" "a very *reasonable* price." Most adjectives have distinctive forms for use in comparisons: *small—smaller—smallest; good—better—best; reasonable—more reasonable—most reasonable.* Typical suffixes serving to derive adjectives from other words are *-ic, -ish, -ive,* and *-ous:* bas*ic,* fool*ish,* expens*ive,* courage*ous.* In traditional grammar, however, any modifier that modifies a noun or noun equivalent is said to *function* as an adjective.

(2) The second group of modifiers is illustrated in the following sentences:

The bell rang *twice.*
Suddenly the bell rang.
The bell rang *loudly.*
The bell rang *at intervals.*

Twice, suddenly, and *loudly* belong to a class of words known as **adverbs**. Many of these show the distinctive *ly* ending. *At intervals* is not formally an adverb, but in traditional grammar it is said to serve an adverbial function.

NOTE: Combinations introduced by *with, at, on,* and similar words may modify either nouns or other parts of a sentence:

The man *with the ax* opened the door.	(adjective function)
The man opened the door *with the ax.*	(adverbial function)
The girl *from Chicago* disappeared.	(adjective function)
The girl disappeared *from Chicago.*	(adverbial function)

With, at, on, and *from* are **prepositions**. Their most characteristic function is to relate a noun or noun equivalent to the rest of the sentence. Other common prepositions are *about, by, during, in, of, through, to, under, until,* and *without*. A preposition plus the noun it introduces is called a **prepositional phrase**.

G 2d Joining Clauses. *When several subject-predicate groups combine, the individual subject-predicate groups need to be distinguished from the sentence as a whole.* They are traditionally referred to as **clauses**. The following sentences illustrate different ways of joining one clause to another:

My brother proposed to Elvira;	*however,*	she dislikes him.
My brother proposed to Elvira,	*but*	she dislikes him.
My brother proposed to Elvira,	*though*	she dislikes him.
My brother proposed to Elvira,	*who*	dislikes him.

(1) Clauses are called **independent** when they are *self-sufficient enough to stand by themselves,* to be punctuated as

complete sentences. They are still considered independent when they are joined to another independent clause by an adverbial connective or by a coordinating connective.[3] **Adverbial connectives** (often called conjunctive adverbs) are such words as *however, therefore, moreover, nevertheless, besides.* **Coordinating connectives** (often called coordinating conjunctions) are such words as *and, but,* and *for.* A grammatically complete sentence ordinarily contains at least one independent clause. A sentence combining two or more independent clauses is called a **compound sentence.**

(2) Clauses are called **dependent** when they are *subordinated to the clause to which they are joined* by a subordinating connective or by a relative pronoun. **Subordinating connectives** (often called subordinating conjunctions) are words like *if, when, because, though,* and *whereas.* **Relative pronouns** are *who, which,* and *that.* A sentence combining an independent clause with one or more dependent clauses is called a **complex sentence.**

Dependent clauses can be considered as modifiers. Those introduced by subordinating connectives usually, though not always, serve adverbial functions: "The bell rang *when I started to answer.*" Those introduced by relative pronouns usually serve adjective functions: "The bell *that had startled me* had ceased to ring."

(3) A special type of dependent clause, rather than being joined to the main clause, *replaces one of its nouns.* Such a clause-within-a-clause is called a **noun clause**:

NOUN:	*The thief*	returned my documents.
NOUN CLAUSE:	*Whoever stole my wallet*	returned my documents.

NOUN:	He was excited by *the news.*
NOUN CLAUSE:	He was excited by *what he had heard.*

[3] For a full discussion of connectives and their bearing on punctuation, see P 3–4.

That, frequently used as a relative pronoun, is also used to introduce a noun clause:

> Osbert denied *that he had forged the check.*
> *That Osbert forged the check* has not been proved.

NOTE: Dependent clauses are often hard to recognize, because one or more elements of the clause may be missing. Especially in informal writing, *whom, which,* and *that* are often omitted. Supplying the missing element in such constructions often facilitates grammatical analysis:

> The speaker [*whom*] *we had invited* failed to appear.
> The support [*that*] *we received* was inadequate.

After a subordinating connective, the subject and all or part of the verb are often omitted, provided they can be inferred from the context. The resulting clause is sometimes called an **elliptical clause**:

> *When* [*you are*] *in doubt,* consult your dictionary.
> *When* [*he was*] *questioned,* the suspect readily admitted the theft.

EXERCISES

A. Take five groups of three or four words each (for example, *boy—follow—dog*). Arrange each group in five different patterns, using the grammatical devices described in G 2a. Example: *The boy follows the dog. Dogs followed the boy. Follow the boy's dogs. Follow the dog, boys. Dog the following boys.*

B. Collect five groups of words that show the same root taking different suffixes for different parts of speech.

EXAMPLES:	*red*	red*ness*	redd*ish*	redd*en*
	organ	organ*ism*	organ*ic*	organ*ize*

C. Choose three simple subject-predicate sentences that can be expanded and modified so as to illustrate several of the sentence types described in G 2b.

EXAMPLE: John called.
John called me.
John called me rude.
I was called by John.
Call a taxi!
There is John calling.

D. Compose ten simplified sentences illustrating the variations in sentence pattern described in G 2b.

E. From your current reading, select ten short sentences (one clause each) in which typical sentence patterns are complicated by modifiers. Underline all basic sentence elements: subjects, verbs, complements.

F. From your current reading, select ten sentences that illustrate different ways of joining clauses. Underline the basic elements of each clause.

G. In the following sentences, identify the basic elements in each clause. Describe the function and grammatical category of as many other elements as you can. Point out distinctive grammatical features.

> 1. The water in the bowl was purple, and the goldfish were gulping for air. 2. Throughout the length of the valley, the river's course widens and narrows by turns. 3. In recent years, sport parachuting has enjoyed a small boom. 4. The only means of access was to hack one's way through hundreds of miles of jungle. 5. He painted with the suppleness of an artist who wanted a deep union with nature. 6. Many customs were common to both sides of the Rio Grande when the river became a frontier. 7. Recipes for happiness cannot be exported without being modified. 8. Uncle Alfred complained that outboard motors had driven off the fish. 9. Avoiding traffic policemen is easy if they ride in specially marked cars. 10. Fritz annoyed the neighbors by blowing the bugle his father had brought back from France.

H. Analyze the following passage, using the terminology provided in G 2. Identify all basic sentence elements. Describe the function and grammatical category of as many other elements as you can. Point out unusual or difficult grammatical features.

> The rain began with gusty showers, pauses and downpours; and then gradually it settled to a single tempo, small drops and a steady beat, rain that was gray to see through, rain that cut midday light to evening. And at first the dry earth sucked the moisture down and blackened. For two days the earth drank the rain, until the earth was full. Then puddles formed, and in the low places little lakes formed in the fields. The muddy lakes rose higher, and the steady rain whipped the shining water. At last the mountains were full, and the hillsides spilled into the streams, built them to freshets, and sent them roaring down the canyons into the valleys. The rain beat on steadily. And the streams and the little rivers edged up to the bank sides and worked at willows and tree roots, bent the willows deep in the current, cut out the roots of cottonwoods and brought down the trees. The muddy water whirled along the bank sides and crept up the banks until at last it spilled over, into the fields, into the orchards, into the cotton patches where the black stems stood. Level fields became lakes, broad and gray, and the rain whipped up the surfaces. Then the water poured over the highways, and cars moved slowly, cutting the water ahead, and leaving a boiling muddy wake behind.—John Steinbeck, *The Grapes of Wrath*

G 3 Agreement

The subject and the predicate of a sentence are connected by a close reciprocal relationship.

The nouns and pronouns that can make up the main part of the subject usually have two forms, one referring to a single item (**singular**), the other referring to more than one item of the same kind (**plural**). The verbs that make up the main part of the predicate may also have two forms, one to be used when the subject is singular, the other to be used when the subject is plural. When subject and verb are both either singular or plural, they are said to agree in **number**:

SINGULAR	PLURAL
The boy *goes* home.	The boys *go* home.
Love *makes* fools.	Fools *make* love.
My girl friend *was* pleased.	My girl friends *were* pleased.

G 3a Irregular Plurals. *Some nouns borrowed from other languages preserve irregular plurals.* Although most English nouns use the familiar *s* plural (car*s,* building*s,* tree*s,* book*s,* petition*s*), a number of words have difficult, irregular alternative forms.

(1) *Many Greek and Latin words require you to learn irregular plural forms:*

SINGULAR	PLURAL	SINGULAR	PLURAL
crisis	crises	criterion	criteria
thesis	theses	phenomenon	phenomena
analysis	analyses	medium	media
hypothesis	hypotheses		

NOTE: "Dat*a*" *are* items of information, and "bacteri*a*" *are* very small organisms that may cause disease. The singular forms of these two words (*datum* and *bacterium*) are rarely used, with the result that *data* now often occurs as a singular. A boy who graduates from college becomes an "alumn*us,*" a girl an "alumn*a.*" Several male graduates would call themselves "alumn*i,*" several female graduates "alumn*ae.*" (On the other hand, an "alumn*i* organization" may include *both* men and women.)

(2) *Many other Greek and Latin words are shedding their original plurals.* According to recent dictionaries and handbooks of grammar, it is becoming both common and acceptable to say

"curricul*ums*" rather than "curricul*a*," "memorand*ums*" rather than "memorand*a*," and "formul*as*" rather than "formul*ae*." However, many scientists, physicians, and teachers who use Greek and Latin terminology as a matter of daily routine prefer the older forms.

G 3b Confusing Singulars and Plurals. *Agreement problems are caused by a number of everyday expressions that are not clearly either singular or plural.*

(1) *Each, neither, either,* and *everyone* (**indefinite pronouns**) may seem to refer to more than one person or thing, but they are treated as singulars in formal written English:

> Each of the students *is* going to receive a diploma.
> Either of the plans *sounds* all right.

A number of is treated as a plural if it means "several" or "many":

> A number of people *were* standing in the hallway.

(2) *Expressions indicating quantity* may be treated as singulars even when they seem plural in form, provided the sentence is concerned with the whole amount rather than with the individual units:

> In those days two dollars *was* much money.
>
> It is the most imperative social truth of our age that about one-third of the world is rich and two-thirds of the world *is* poor.—C. P. Snow, "On Magnanimity," *Harper's*

(3) Words like *audience, committee, family, group, jury, police,* and *team* may be singular in one sentence and plural in another. We use these **collective nouns** as singulars when we are thinking of the group as a whole; we use them as plurals when we are thinking of the individual members of the group:

SINGULAR: The family *is* a crucial social unit.
PLURAL: The family *were* seated around the dinner table.

SINGULAR: The police *has* many responsibilities.
PLURAL: The police *are* not always helpful.

(4) Words ending in *ics* look like plurals but are often singular. Singular are *aeronautics, mathematics, physics,* and similar words that identify a branch of knowledge or field of study:

Mathematics *is* an indispensable tool of modern science.

Athletics is used most often as a plural but may also occur as a singular: "Athletics *are* said"—could be "*is* said"—"to be good for a boy." Other words ending in *ics* are singular in some senses and plural in others. We say "Statistics *doesn't* appeal to me" when speaking of the science of statistics; we say "Statistics *don't* convince me" when speaking of statistical data.

NOTE: Consult a college dictionary when you are not sure of the different forms of a noun or when you are not sure whether a given form is to be treated as a singular or as a plural.

G 3c Compound Subjects. *Agreement problems occur in sentences that contain more than one subject per clause.* After such a **compound subject**, the verb may appear in the plural form even if each of the subjects is singular when taken by itself:

Tom and Sue *don't* smoke.
Hiking and canoeing *are* fun.

Whereas *and* actually adds one possible subject to another, *or* merely gives us a choice between two possible subjects, each of which may be just one single item. Thus, we say "Both his father and his mother *are* to blame" but "Either his father or his mother *is* to blame."

Some special difficulties should be noted:

(1) *As well as, together with,* and *in addition to* often seem to add one subject to another. Strictly interpreted, however, they merely show that what is said about the subject applies also to other things or persons, or that the subject is accompanied by other things or persons:

> Aunt Martha, together with her six children, *is* leaving town.

NOTE: Some writers use the plural form when the singular seems to fight with the over-all meaning of such a sentence. However, you will be safer from criticism if you revise the sentence, using *and:*

> The president, as well as the deans and department heads, *was* sitting on the platform.
> The president, the deans, and the department heads *were* sitting on the platform.

(2) Sometimes even two nouns joined by *and* do not add up to a plural. They may be merely different parts of the *description of a single thing or person:*

> Pork and beans *is* not one of my favorite dishes.
> My closest friend and associate *was* a cocker spaniel.

(3) In some sentences, an *or,* an *either . . . or,* or a *neither . . . nor* gives the reader a *choice between a singular subject and a plural one.* Make the verb of such a sentence agree with the subject closer to it:

> Either laziness or excessive social obligations *have kept* him from his work.

Either excessive social obligations or just plain laziness *has kept* him from his work.

However, the sentence often sounds more natural if the subjects can be changed so that they are both singular or both plural:

Too much social life or just plain laziness *has kept* him from his work.

G 3d Blind Agreement. *Complicated or unusual word order may lead you to make the verb agree with a word that stands in front of it but that is not its subject.* The result is sometimes called **blind agreement**.

(1) Agreement errors are common when *a plural noun intervenes between a singular subject and its verb.* If most of your friends *were* late and only one of them *was* on time, you should say: "Only one of my friends *was* ready in time"—not "*were* ready in time." Beware of faulty agreement whenever the subject of a sentence is one thing singled out among several, one quality shared by several members of a group, or one action affecting different things or persons:

The usefulness of his remedies *has been* questioned—not "*have been* questioned."
Understanding the opponent's motives *is* important—not "*are* important."

(2) When for some reason *the subject follows the verb,* do not make the verb agree with a stray noun that stands in front of it:

Sleeping in the cradle *were* two rosy-cheeked infants.
(Who was sleeping? The infants *were* sleeping.)
In the very first chapter *occur* several incredible incidents.
(What occurs? Incidents *occur.*)

G 3e Agreement after *There* and *It*. *Special problems occur in sentences starting with "there is," "there are," "it is," and their possible variations.*

(1) *There* is neither a noun nor a pronoun and cannot be the subject of a sentence. After *there,* the verb agrees with the **postponed subject**—that is, with whatever is "there":

SINGULAR: There *was* much work to be done.
PLURAL: There *were* scattered rumblings of dissent.

In formal usage, the plural verb is required even when followed by a compound subject of which each part is singular:

> On the crown of the hill, there *are* a miniature plaza, miniature cathedral, and miniature governor's palace.—Arnold J. Toynbee, "The Mayan Mystery," *Atlantic*

(2) *It* is a pronoun and can occur as a subject. After *it,* the verb is always singular:

It'*s* your last chance.
It *was* the Joneses.

G 3f Agreement after *Who, Which,* and *That*. *A number of agreement problems are caused by relationships between several clauses.* For instance, *who, which,* and *that* often serve as subjects in **adjective clauses**—that is, dependent clauses that modify a noun or pronoun. The verb following the *who, which,* or *that* agrees with the word being modified:

SINGULAR: I hate a man who *stares* at me.
PLURAL: I hate men who *stare* at me.

Formal English requires agreement in combinations like "one of those who does" and "one of those who do." "Jean is the only one of those girls who *goes* to college for an education" means that one girl *goes* to college for an education but that the others don't. "Jean is one of those girls who *go* to college for an education" means that a number of girls *go* to college for an education and that Jean is one of them.

EXERCISES

A. In a college dictionary, look up the plural forms of the following nouns: *antenna, appendix, beau, bureau, cactus, cello, cherub, focus, hippopotamus, index, nucleus, oasis, stadium, stigma, stimulus, vertebra, virus.* Check whether the following forms are singular or plural or both: *addenda, agenda, apparatus, candelabra, deer, dice, Saturnalia, series, species, strata.*

B. Select appropriate forms, paying special attention to irregular plurals.

> 1. Constant crises *(1)has/(2)have* undermined the confidence of the people in their government. 2. For many of us, prestige is one of the most important *(3)criterion/(4)criteria* of success. 3. Jean and Margaret were the only *(5)alumna/(6) alumnae/(7)alumni* present at the ceremony. 4. The college offers more than twenty *(8)curriculum/(9)curricula.* 5. The mass media of communication *(10)has/(11)have* rapidly increased their influence in recent decades. 6. The *(12)analysis/(13)analyses* of such material takes time. 7. The memoranda he sent out *(14)was/(15)were* often unintelligible. 8. These data *(16)invalidates/(17)invalidate* all previous *(18) hypothesis/(19)hypotheses* concerning the origin of life.

C. Select appropriate forms, paying special attention to common sources of faulty agreement.

> 1. In many of my classes the attitude of the students *(1)was/ (2)were* very poor. 2. The benefits that the city has derived from its new industries *(3)is/(4)are* negligible. 3. Cooking, as well as sewing or cleaning, *(5)has/(6)have* always bored me. 4. I was raised in a home where smoking and excessive drinking *(7)was/(8)were* not permitted. 5. Getting along with one's neighbors *(9)is/(10)are* not always easy. 6. The quali-

ties that a girl looks for in a future husband *(11)is/(12)are* determined in part by her family background. 7. The World's Fair dazzled everyone who *(13)was/(14)were* there. 8. The ability to talk about something other than money and children *(15)is/(16)are* important if a marriage is to last. 9. Colleges have to make provision for students who are below average academically but who nevertheless *(17)wants/(18)want* a college education. 10. Using words like *dichotomy* and *schizophrenia (19)is/(20)are* no sign of superior intelligence. 11. She was one of those hostesses who *(21)makes/(22)make* no attempt to entertain the guests. 12. His father felt that five dollars *(23)was/(24)were* more than sufficient as a monthly allowance. 13. According to the judge, neither of the witnesses *(25)was/(26)were* guilty of perjury. 14. We soon realized that our supply of food and fuel *(27)was/(28)were* dangerously low. 15. Weapons like the bow and arrow, the spear, or the knife *(29)was/(30)were* among the first major inventions of man.

G 4 Difficult Verb Forms

A writer must learn to use verb forms appropriate to serious written English.

Verb forms like *knowed* and *growed* are among the most distinctive features of nonstandard English; differences like those between "If I *was*" and "If I *were*" help set apart informal from formal standard English. The most important verb forms are those traditionally grouped together to form the system of tenses. The **tenses** of a verb are the various *forms that indicate primarily, though not exclusively, different relationships of events in time:*

ACTIVE

		Progressive
Present	I ask	(I am asking)
Past	I asked	(I was asking)
Future	I shall (will) ask	(I shall be asking)

Perfect	I have asked	(I have been asking)
Past Perfect	I had asked	(I had been asking)
Future Perfect	I shall (will) have asked	(I shall have been asking)
	PASSIVE	
Present	I am asked	(I am being asked)
Past	I was asked	(I was being asked)
Future	I shall (will) be asked	—
Perfect	I have been asked	—
Past Perfect	I had been asked	—
Future Perfect	I shall (will) have been asked	—

G 4a Regular Basic Forms. *Most English verbs, the regular verbs, have two basic forms* (**principal parts**).

(1) The first form is the plain form of the verb (*consent, smoke, depart, investigate, organize*). Standing by itself, it can form the **present tense**. This "simple" present may indicate that something is actually happening now, but it often indicates that something is done regularly or habitually or that it will take place in the immediate future:

We *consent.*
I *smoke* a pack a day.
They *depart* tonight.

The plain form can combine with *will* or *shall* in the **future tense**:

He *will* talk to you later.[4]

The plain form plus *ing* makes up the present participle, used in the various tenses of the **progressive construction**. The progressive construction normally indicates that at a given time an action or event is actually in progress:

[4] See the Glossary of Usage for discussion of *shall—will, should—would.*

We *are considering* your request.
Her husband *was painting* the house.

(2) The second basic form of a verb can stand by itself as the **past tense**, which indicates that an action took place in the past and came to an end in the past. To form this "simple" past, regular verbs add *ed* or *d* to the plain form:

He *consented.*
We *asked* him.
They *investigated* him thoroughly.

Regular verbs make the *ed* form do double duty as a verbal (past participle) combining with the various forms of *have* to make up the **perfect tenses**. These consider an action as "perfected," in the sense of completed, prior to a given point in time. "I *have considered* your request" describes something that has happened in the fairly recent past and that has a bearing on the present. "I *had considered* his request very carefully" describes something that had already happened when other events in the past took place.[5]

G 4b Irregular Basic Forms. *Irregular verbs often have not two but three basic forms.* These may be either confusingly different or confusingly similar. First, the difference between the simple present and the simple past is not merely a matter of adding a characteristic ending. Instead, there are changes difficult to schematize: *run—ran; know—knew; go—went.* Furthermore, the simple past is often different from the past participle: *run—ran—run; know—knew—known; go—went—gone.*

(1) Pay special attention to verbs whose basic forms are *confusing in spelling or in sound.* Here is a brief list:

[5] See G 12a for sequence of tenses and shifts in tense.

PRESENT	PAST	PERFECT
begin	began	have begun
blow	blew	have blown
break	broke	have broken
bring	brought	have brought
choose	chose	have chosen
come	came	have come
deal	dealt	have dealt
do	did	have done
draw	drew	have drawn
drink	drank	have drunk
drive	drove	have driven
eat	ate	have eaten
fall	fell	have fallen
flee	fled	have fled
fly	flew	have flown
freeze	froze	have frozen
go	went	have gone
grow	grew	have grown
know	knew	have known
lead	led	have led
run	ran	have run
see	saw	have seen
send	sent	have sent
sing	sang	have sung
speak	spoke	have spoken
swim	swam	have swum
take	took	have taken
throw	threw	have thrown
wear	wore	have worn

(2) Sometimes you have a *choice of two acceptable forms:*

They gracefully *dived* (or *dove*) into the pool.
She *dreamed* (or *dreamt*) of a sloe-eyed Arab prince.
He *lighted* (or *lit*) his cigarette.
Your prediction *has proved* (or *has proven*) wrong.
The ship *sank* (or *sunk*) within minutes.
Business *thrived* (or *throve*) as never before.
The sleepers *waked* (or *woke*) refreshed.

(3) In a few cases different forms for the same tense correspond to *differences in context or in meaning*. For instance, it is "The picture was *hung*" but "The prisoners were *hanged*"; "The sun *shone*" but "The boy *shined* my shoes."

NOTE: When in doubt about the basic forms of a verb, consult your dictionary. It lists the basic forms of all irregular verbs in the *choose—chose—chosen, run—ran—run* order.

G 4c Verbs with Confusing Doubles. *Some verbs have doubles just different enough to be confusing.*

(1) *Lie—lay—lain* indicates that somebody or something is situated somewhere. The same basic forms are used in the combination *lie down:*

> On hot days the animals *lie* in the shade.
> A letter *lay* on the floor.
> He *should have lain down.*

Lay—laid—laid indicates that somebody is placing something somewhere. Use it when you can substitute *place* or *put:*

> I wish I *could lay* my hands on him.
> The weary travelers *laid down* their burdens.
> You *should have laid aside* some money for emergencies.

(2) *Sit—sat—sat* indicates that someone is seated. *Sit down* follows the same scheme:

> Though he told me that he seldom *sat* while at work, he *has sat* for an hour exactly where he *sat down* when he looked for a place to *sit.*

Set—set—set, one of the few verbs with only one basic form, belongs with *lay* as a possible substitute for *place* or *put*. You, yourself, *sit,* or *sit down;* you *set,* or *set down,* something else:

> When you *have set* the alarm, *set* it down by the cot I *set* up.

(3) *Rise—rose—risen* means "get up" or "go up." *Raise—raised—raised* refers to lifting something or *making* it go up:

> Since you *rose* this morning, the tax rate *has risen* ten cents.
>
> Though he *is* always *raising* his prices, he *has* not *raised* the salaries of his employees.

G 4d Subjunctive Forms. *One special set of verb forms is disappearing from informal speech and writing but is still often required in formal usage:* "She would call us if she *were*"—not "if she *was*"—"ill." "We demand that he *answer*" —not "that he *answers*"—"the question." *Were* and *answer* here represent special forms that make no distinction between singular and plural. These **subjunctive** forms occur in certain types of clauses that are concerned with possibilities rather than with facts.

(1) After *if, as if,* and *as though,* use *were* instead of *was* if the possibility you have in mind is *contrary to fact or highly improbable:*

> The bird looked as if it *were* a plane.
> If I *were* you, I would try to improve my language habits.
> He acts as if his name *were* John D. Rockefeller.

However, *is* or *was* is required if you are considering a genuine possibility:

> If your brother *was* ill, he should have notified you.
> It looks as if the plane *is* going to be late.

In borderline cases, make sure that the *if-clause* uses a verb form that corresponds to the point of view adopted in the main clause. Use the ordinary or factual form after *if* when the main clause uses a matter-of-fact form like *will, shall, can,* or *may.* Use the subjunctive form when the main clause uses a form suggesting improbability:

FACTUAL: If she *is* wise, he *will* propose.
SUBJUNCTIVE: If she *were* wise, he *would* propose.

NOTE: Do not use *would* in the *if*-clause as a kind of poor man's subjunctive: "If he *were* elected"—not "*would be* elected" —"he would eliminate corruption and graft."

(2) Use subjunctive forms in noun clauses *after verbs indicating that something is desirable or necessary* but has not yet come about. *Were,* for instance, occurs in sentences like the following: "I wish I *were*"—not *"I was"*—"a wise old man." Forms like *answer* instead of *answers, go* instead of *goes* or *went,* and *be* instead of *is* or *was* occur after verbs signaling a suggestion, a request, a command, or a resolution:

His wife insists that he *spend* more time at home.
We demand that he *repay* all his debts.
I move that this question *be* referred to one of our innumerable committees.

(3) In some set phrases (*be* that as it may) and *in writing that is distinctly formal or literary in tone,* the subjunctive expresses ordinary conditions or alternatives:

He was determined to go on, *come* what may.

The artist must have faith in the all-importance of art, and particularly in his own form of art, *be* it painting, sculpture, poetry, drama, fiction, or music.—Malcolm Cowley, "Artists, Conscience, and Censors," *Saturday Review*

EXERCISES

A. Select verb forms appropriate to formal written English.

1. If a teacher *(1)lays/(2)lies* a hand on an unruly student, he is likely to be sued by the student's parents. 2. In discussions touching on religious issues, many perplexing questions can be *(3)raised/(4)risen.* 3. After the class *(5)sat/(6)set* down, Mrs.

Pidnack wanted to know who had *(7)wrote/(8)written* "baloney" on the blackboard. 4. The picture showed two elderly gentlemen *(9)setting/(10)sitting* at a table and playing chess. 5. While the boys *(11)swam/(12)swum* in the clear, cold water, I *(13)sat/(14)set* in the canoe watching them. 6. While *(15)setting/(16)sitting* up a new filing system, we must have *(17)mislaid/(18)mislain* your letter. 7. The report has been *(19)laying/(20)lying* on his desk all summer; at least I saw it *(21)lay/(22)lie* there last week. 8. When I *(23)saw/(24)seen* the deserted entrance, I *(25)knew/(26)knowed* that the performance had already *(27)began/(28)begun.* 9. The Park Department finally *(29)sat up/(30)set up* benches for visitors who might want to *(31)set down/(32)sit down.* 10. Satisfied with the conditions *(33)sat/(34)set* by the negotiators, the rebels last week *(35)laid down/(36)lay down* their arms.

B. Select subjunctive forms where appropriate.

1. If there *(1)is/(2)was/(3)were* another war, untold millions would lose their homes or their lives. 2. I wish grammar *(4)was/(5)were* less complicated than it is. 3. If the Obunga *(6)are/(7)were/(8)would be* vegetarians, why do they have sharply filed teeth? 4. It looks as if there *(9)is/(10)were* just enough gasoline to get us back into town. 5. The ordinance requires that subdivision signs *(11)are/(12)be* kept smaller than the houses they advertise. 6. If the vocationally minded student *(13)was/(14)were/(15)would be* sent to a trade school, high schools could put more emphasis on academic subjects than they do now. 7. If your record *(16)is/(17)were/(18) would be* as clean as you claim, the commission will gladly grant your request. 8. Mariners used to drink rum as if it *(19)is/(20)was/(21)were* water. 9. No one suggested to Raymond that he *(22)read/(23)reads The Brothers Karamazov* rather than *Treasure Island.* 10. These practices would not be tolerated if the founder *(24)is/(25)was/(26)were/(27)would be* still alive.

C. From the current issue of a magazine, select five sentences that illustrate different uses of the subjunctive.

D. (**Review**) Check all verb forms for agreement and for conformity to the conventions of formal usage. Identify each sentence that needs revision.

1. (1) At one time I thought of college as a place where everyone studies hard during the week and then relax during the weekend. (2) Since I came to college I have found my theory to be quite wrong. (3) Sometimes I think I am the only one of the girls in our house who does any homework. (4) A number of them go out almost every night.

2. (5) There are different ways of teaching American history. (6) In grade school and high school, Washington or Jefferson is often presented as if he were a god-like figure. (7) The political-science courses one takes in college often shows that the nation's great men were men with human feelings. (8) Such an approach requires that the student reconsider many familiar notions.

3. (9) In college, maturity and a sense of responsibility begin to make themselves felt. (10) The college girl's ideals and outlook on life broadens. (11) She soon becomes one of those who look for more in a boy than physical appearance. (12) She demands that her future husband be ambitious and reliable.

4. (13) Advertisers are often unfairly accused of insincerity or outright fraud. (14) It is true that there are misleading advertisements and commercials. (15) But the number of advertisers who practice deliberate deception are relatively small. (16) Many well-established business firms value their reputations too highly to join the ranks of those who mislead their customers.

5. (17) The significance of many of the words used by Shakespeare are hard to understand. (18) The language and especially its vocabulary have changed since he wrote his plays. (19) *Rede* is used for "advice," *husbandry* means "economy," and a porcupine is called a "porpentine." (20) These examples are taken from just a few pages of *Hamlet*.

G 5 Reference of Pronouns

To make a pronoun stand for the right noun, you have to place the right pronoun in the right position.

When you use *he, it,* or *this,* it should be clear to your reader who or what *he, it,* or *this* is. A pronoun has to refer clearly to its **antecedent**, the thing or person for which the pronoun is a substitute.

G 5a Ambiguous Reference. *A pronoun should not point to more than one possible antecedent.* Look at the use of *she* and *her* in the following example: "Mary was friendly to my sister because *she* wanted *her* to be *her* bridesmaid." The reader here has no way of knowing which of the two girls was getting married and which was going to be a bridesmaid. The sentence is **ambiguous**; it confuses the reader because of an unintended double meaning.

(1) If the substitute could refer to more than one antecedent, you may have to repeat the noun itself: "When Tom was talking to Jim's brother, *Jim's* girl friend smiled at *Jim's brother* from across the street." However, you will often do better to *shuffle the different parts of the sentence* until the pronoun is preceded by only one possible antecedent:

AMBIGUOUS: After *Father* brought *Junior* back from the game, we took pictures of *him*.

CLEAR: We took pictures of *Father* after *he* brought *Junior* back from the game.

CLEAR: We took pictures of *Junior* after *Father* brought *him* back from the game.

(2) The pronouns that most often cause ambiguity have distinctive forms for singular and plural antecedents: the singular *he, she,* or *it,* as against the plural *they*. If a *they* is preceded by two plural nouns, you can sometimes avoid ambiguity by *making one of them singular:*

AMBIGUOUS: *Students* like *science teachers* because *they* are realistic and practical.

CLEAR: A *student* usually likes his *science teachers* because *they* are realistic and practical.
(*They* can no longer be mistakenly referred to *students.*)

Similarly, one of two possible singular antecedents might be changed into a plural:

A *writer* must necessarily talk to his *readers*—better than "to his *reader*"—in simple language if *his* vocabulary is limited.
(The singular *reader* would leave it doubtful whose vocabulary is assumed to be limited.)

G 5b Reference to Modifiers. *Pronouns are usually taken to refer to one of the basic elements of a sentence rather than to a modifier.* The following sentence would sound absurd: "During the summer, Grandfather worked on a river boat, but in the winter *it* usually froze over." The *it* seems to refer to the boat, but boats do not freeze over. Similarly absurd sentences may result when a pronoun is expected to refer to a **possessive**:

AMBIGUOUS: I reached for the horse's bridle, but *it* ran away. (The bridle seems to be running away.)

CLEAR: The horse ran away after I reached for *its* bridle. (The possessive has been made into a pronoun and the noun put where it is needed to prevent confusion.)

NOTE: Reference to a possessive accounts for the awkwardness of sentences like the following: "In *John Steinbeck's* novel *The Grapes of Wrath,* he describes the plight of the marginal farmer"—better "In *his* novel . . . *John Steinbeck* describes . . ."

G 5c Vague *This* and *Which*. *Idea reference frequently causes ambiguous sentences.* **Idea reference** results when a *this* or *which* refers to the over-all idea expressed in the preceding statement. Students often write sentences like the following: "I knew that Bob was cheating, but the other students were not aware of *this*." The *this* may refer either to Bob's cheating or to the writer's knowing it.

AMBIGUOUS: She spent her time getting special help for her English course, *which* her roommates considered unfair. (What did her roommates consider unfair—the English course, her getting special help, her spending her time this way?)

A vague *this* can be easily supplemented by a noun indicating the idea referred to: "this fact," "this assumption," "this outrage." A vague *which* is more difficult to improve. Often you will find it easier to do without it. Suppose you say: "I have received only one letter, *which* frightens me." If you mean that you were frightened not by the letter itself but by receiving only one, it would be clearer to say:

CLEAR: Receiving only one letter frightened me.

G 5d Implied Antecedents. *To make a sentence acceptable in formal English, we may have to eliminate indirect reference.*

(1) In informal conversation, we often make a pronoun refer to an antecedent that we have not actually mentioned, though we *expect its identity to be understood.* We say, "In London, *they* have a great deal of fog" without explaining that the *they* means "Londoners" or "the people living in London." We say, "I like *Life* magazine, because *they* print many interesting articles." The implied antecedent of *they* is not the magazine itself but its editors or its publishers.

REVISED: London has much fog.
REVISED: *Life* magazine prints many interesting articles.

(2) A special problem in student writing is the orphaned *it,* the use of *it* to refer to an *implied idea* in a sentence like the following: "My mother was a teacher; therefore, I have also chosen *it* as my profession." The *it* stands not for "teacher" but apparently for "teaching":

REVISED: My mother was a teacher; therefore, I have also chosen *teaching* as my profession.

Equally objectionable is the orphaned *they:* "The prisoner's hands were manacled to a chain around his waist, but *they* were removed at the courtroom door." What was removed? The prisoner's hands? Apparently "the manacles":

REVISED: The prisoner's hands were manacled to a chain around his waist, but *the manacles* were removed at the courtroom door.

G 5e Indefinite Antecedents. *In formal usage, indefinite pronouns are treated as singular antecedents.* Formal English thus avoids an inconsistency that occurs in the everyday use of **indefinite pronouns** like *everybody, somebody, anybody,* or *nobody*. Everyday language uses a singular verb after these words but then sometimes switches to a plural pronoun.

FORMAL: Someone left *his* gloves—not "*their* gloves."

FORMAL: After hours everybody does as *he* pleases—not "as *they* please."

FORMAL: Nobody should meddle in affairs that are none of *his* business—not "none of *their* business."

One and *a person* belong in the same category:

One must honor *his* (or *one's*) obligations—not "*their* obligations."

One can never be too careful about *his* language—not "*their* language."

None started as the equivalent of "no one," but today either singular or plural forms after it are acceptable:

None of the students *has his* books ready—or "*have their* books ready."

NOTE: When we use *everybody, a person,* or *none,* we are often thinking of both men and women. However, "Everybody ate *his or her* lunch" would sound clumsy. *His* can do double duty in such cases.

EXERCISES

A. Of the numbered pronouns in each passage, identify the one that is vague, ambiguous, or misleading.

1. No one (1) who has ever been at a horse race can forget (2) his excitement at seeing (3) them come down the home stretch. 2. On the far side of the town, (4) they are clearing land for a housing project, (5) which is to be completed before next July. 3. When leading newspapers have (6) their top correspondents write stories accusing (7) our government of being corrupt, steps should be taken to correct (8) this. 4. We finally bought Uncle Peter a power lawnmower, but (9) he rarely cuts (10) it more than once every three or four weeks. 5. Gophers have been eating our geraniums. (11) This annoys my father, (12) who has been trying to get rid of (13) them for a long time. 6. A good secretary does not discuss business matters with (14) her friends unless (15) they are generally known or unless (16) she has the permission of (17) her employer. 7. While the little boy's father read (18) his newspaper, (19) he kept reaching for (20) it and crying "Daddy!" 8. The public often discovers that (21) it has been deprived of important information, (22) which goes counter to the traditional policy of (23) our government. 9. When Elizabeth came home, (24) she told (25) her grandmother that the cost of (26) her new permanent alone was enough to curl a woman's hair. 10. (27) My history instructor announced to the students in (28) his class that (29) they would write a paper on the fall of Constantinople. (30) This was a major catastrophe.

B. Check all pronouns for clarity of reference. Identify each sentence that needs revision.

1. (1) The hedgehog is the English version of its cousin, the porcupine. (2) English gypsies used to prepare hedgehogs by

baking them whole in a thick coat of clay. (3) The spines and the outer skin would come off together with the clay, which had become brickhard. (4) They are said to make good eating.

2. (5) Dr. Bain has made a name for himself by a column devoted to popularized psychology. (6) Occasionally my friends and I agree with him. (7) Last week, for instance, he said that a person should not be unrealistic in what they expect of their future mate. (8) On the whole, however, I object to his treating all psychological problems as if they could be solved with a stamped, self-addressed envelope.

3. (9) As a long-time admirer of Walt Sidney, I like his treating cartoon animals as if they were people, but I object to his making people as simple as cartoon animals. (10) One of his motion pictures tells the story of a white boy whom Indians take from his parents and who grows up as the adopted son of an Indian chief. (11) Later the boy is returned to his true parents as the result of a peace treaty, which raises the problem of how he will adjust to civilized surroundings. (12) As you no doubt suspect, blood and the pure love of a white girl finally triumph over the savage ways of his childhood.

G 6 Pronoun Forms

Pronoun forms are among the most easily applied touchstones of formal written English.

Pronouns have alternative forms, used depending on the function of the pronoun in the sentence. *I* and *he* are **subject-forms**, identifying the person that the predicate says something about. *Me* and *him* are **object-forms**, identifying the object of a verb. Only half a dozen pronouns have a distinct object-form: *I—me; we—us; he—him; she—her; they—them; who—whom.* The subject- and object-forms of pronouns are grouped with the possessive of nouns as forms indicating grammatical **case**.

A third possible form typically indicates that the object of an action is identical with the performer. *Himself, themselves, myself, ourselves,* and similar forms are called **reflexive forms**:

> He cut *himself.*
> They asked *themselves* what had gone wrong.

They are also used as **intensives** reidentifying something for emphasis:

> The dean told me so *himself.*
> We should also weigh the testimony of the accused men *themselves.*

NOTE: Formal English avoids the use of the reflexive forms as indiscriminate substitutes for the plain subject- or object-forms:

> My friend and *I*—not "and *myself*"—were the last ones to leave.
> I asked both his wife and *him*—not "and *himself*"—to come over after dinner.

G 6a Inappropriate Subject- and Object-Forms. *The conventions governing the use of subject- and object-forms in written English differ from those of informal and nonstandard speech.*

(1) Choose the standard form when a pronoun is *one of several subjects or objects in a clause:*

> My brother and *I*—not "*me* and my brother"—were reading comic books.
> (Who was reading? *I* was reading.)
>
> She asked my brother and *me*—not "my brother and *I*"—to dry the dishes.
> (Whom did she ask? She asked *me.*)

Since nouns make no distinction between subject- and object-forms, be careful with pronoun-noun combinations like *we Americans—us Americans* or *we girls—us girls.*

> *We boy scouts* are always eager to help.
> He told *us boy scouts* to keep up the good work.

(2) In formal usage, subject-forms are required *after linking verbs,* which introduce not an object of an action but a description of the subject:

> The only ones not invited were *she* and a girl with measles.

The need for this use of the subject-form seldom arises except after "it is," "it was," "it must be," and so on. (See the Glossary of Usage for *it's me/it is I.*)

(3) Object-forms are required *after prepositions* (with *her;* because of *him;* for *me*). Make sure to use object-forms for pronouns that are not the first but the second or third object in a prepositional phrase:

> This kind of thing can happen to you and *me*—not "to you and *I.*"
> I knew there was something between you and *her*—not "between you and *she.*"

(4) *As* and *than* are often treated as connectives even when most of the clause they presumably introduce is missing. To decide whether they should be followed by the subject- or the object-form of a pronoun, you may have to reconstruct the missing clause:

> He is as tall as *I* (am).
> I owe you as much as (I owe) *them.*
> Her sister was smarter than *she* (was).
> I like her better than (I like) *him.*

G 6b Who and Whom. Who *and* whom *are easily confused because their function in a sentence is not always obvious.* Furthermore, *who* is increasingly replacing *whom* in speech:

SPOKEN: Tell me *who you are thinking of.*

WRITTEN: It is good for the sanity of all of us to have *someone whom we continue to think of* as Mister even though we address him by his given name.—Philip M. Wagner, "Mencken Remembered," *The American Scholar*

An inappropriate *who* may sound too informal for its context; an inappropriate *whom* may sound ignorant and forced.

(1) When *who* or *whom* occurs *at the beginning of a question, who,* the subject-form, asks a question about the subject. *He, she, we,* and *they* would be possible answers: *Who* did it? *He* did. *Whom,* the object-form, asks a question about an object. *Him, her, us,* and *them* would be possible answers: *Whom* did you meet? I met *him. Whom* also serves as the object of a preposition: To *whom* should I write? To *him.* The pronoun remains in the object-form even if the preposition does not precede the pronoun but follows the verb: *Whom* are you looking *for*? I am looking for *him.*

In more complicated questions it may not be obvious whether a *who* inquires about a subject or about an object. However, the *he*-or-*him* test will always work:

Who do you think will win? (I think *he* will win.)
Whom did you expect to come? (I expected *him* to come.)

(2) *Who* and *whom* may *introduce dependent clauses.* They may introduce an indirect question; that is, a question presented not as a request for information but as part of another sentence (**noun clause**). They may link a modifier to the noun or

pronoun being modified (**adjective clause**). In order to apply the *he*-or-*him* test to a dependent clause, separate it from the rest of the sentence:

SUBJECT: Ask her / *who* wrote the letter. (*He* wrote the letter.)
SUBJECT: We approached the man / *who* was waiting. (*He* was waiting.)
SUBJECT: Here is a nickel for / *whoever* gets there first. (*He* gets there first.)

OBJECT: *Whom* we should invite / is a difficult question. (*We* should invite *him.*)
OBJECT: She knew my brother, / *whom* I rarely see. (I rarely see *him.*)
OBJECT: He knew few people / on *whom* he could rely. (He could rely on *them.*)

G 6c ***Who, Which,* and *That*.** *Who* and *whom* refer to persons (the man *whom* I asked), whereas *which* refers to ideas and things (the car *which* I bought). A *who, whom,* or *which* introducing a **restrictive modifier** may be replaced by *that:*

> The man *that* I asked liked the car *that* I bought.

A *whom* or a *which* that is the object in a restrictive modifier is often left out:

> The man [whom] I asked liked the car [which] I bought.

G 6d **Possessives with Verbal Nouns.** *Formal usage prefers a possessive pronoun before a verbal used as a verbal noun.* A combination of a pronoun and a verbal with the *ing* ending may express two different relationships. In the sentence "I saw *him returning* from the library," you actually saw *him*. In the sentence "I object to *his using* my toothbrush," you are not objecting to *him* but merely to one of *his* actions. In the first sentence, the object of the verb is *him,* while *returning* is a **present**

participle modifying the object. In the second sentence, the object of the verb is *using,* while *his* is a **possessive pronoun** indicating *whose* action the speaker has in mind. The verbal here is a **gerund**, or **verbal noun**.

Use *my, our, his, their* instead of *me, us, him, them* when the object of a verb or of a preposition is not the person himself but one of his actions, traits, or experiences: [6]

> We investigated the chances of *his* being elected.
> There is no excuse for *their* not writing sooner.
> I do not like *your* associating with the neighborhood children.

EXERCISES

A. Select pronoun forms appropriate to formal written English.

> 1. Belonging to too many organizations keeps a person away from *(1)his/(2)his or her/(3)their* studies. 2. A child that has real problems is often too embarrassed to discuss them with *(4)his/(5)their* parents. 3. Teen-agers often adopt a new fad as a way of expressing *(6)his/(7)their* rebellion against authority. 4. A newspaper can never satisfy all *(8)its/(9) their* subscribers. 5. The American public enjoys Westerns because they give *(10)it/(11)them* a chance to escape from humdrum reality. 6. Participation in student government is good for the students because it develops an understanding of the institution of which *(12)he is/(13)they are* a part. 7. Sometimes it seems as if nowadays no one has the time to enjoy *(14)himself/(15)themselves.* 8. A number of my friends take more interest in playing golf in a gym class than *(16)he does/(17)they do* in solving mathematical problems. 9. Love stories are popular because love is something that everyone knows or will experience in *(18)his/(19)his or her/ (20)their* lifetime. 10. Much confusion would have been

[6] In formal usage, nouns observe a similar distinction, provided they have a distinctive possessive form. See Glossary of Usage under "possessives."

avoided if each one of them had waited for *(21)his/(22)their* turn.

B. Select pronoun forms appropriate to formal written English.

1. When my mother punished my sister and *(1)I/(2)me/(3) myself,* she always seemed to suffer more than *(4)we/(5)us.* 2. I stopped at Jane's house because I had some letters for her mother and *(6)she/(7)her/(8)herself.* 3. My parents did not mind *(9)me/(10)my* associating with artists as long as I did not imitate their habits. 4. Most of *(11)we girls/(12)us girls* were looking for the tall, handsome athletic star with the winning personality. 5. I recognize the man's face; it was *(13) he/(14)him* who started the riot. 6. My sister is much better than *(15)I/(16)me/(17)myself* at learning foreign languages. 7. In discussing contemporary authors, the lecturer objected to *(18)their/(19)them* painting too gloomy a picture of the American scene. 8. Every year, my father takes my brother and *(20)I/(21)me* camping. 9. Between you and *(22)I/(23) me,* I would rather have a husband in a Ford than a friend in a Jaguar. 10. Space navigators need to protect *(24)them/(25) themselves* against the powerful radiation of the sun to prevent *(26)their/(27)them* dying from acute sunburn.

C. Select *whom* where required by formal usage.

1. No matter *(1)who/(2)whom* I meet, I always in the end have to listen to his problems. 2. I felt more at ease talking to boys *(3)who/(4)whom* had definite ambitions in life than to those *(5)who/(6)whom* lived from football game to football game. 3. As a principal, he knew many parents *(7)who/(8) whom/(9)which* took only a casual interest in their children's education. 4. The man *(10)who/(11)whom* knocked at the door was not the one *(12)who/(13)whom* we expected. 5. After the abortive revolt, the prince surrounded himself with subordinates on *(14)who/(15)whom/(16)which* he could rely. 6. *(17)Who/(18)whom* she corresponds with and *(19)who/(20) whom* is allowed to visit her are jealously guarded mysteries. 7. *(21)Who/(22)whom* do you think was the girl with *(23) who/(24)whom* I saw him? 8. I wonder *(25)who/(26)whom* you expect to believe these fantastic stories.

D. From a local newspaper, select ten sentences using *who* or *whom*. Which of them conform to the conventions of formal usage?

G 7 Forms of Modifiers

A writer must distinguish the two major kinds of modifiers.

Modifiers may be single words. Such single-word modifiers fall into two main categories. *Beautiful, strange,* and *happy* are **adjectives**, whose most characteristic position is that adjacent to a noun. An adjective modifies a noun by identifying it as one of a kind or by pointing out one of its characteristics. *Beautifully, strangely,* and *happily* are **adverbs**. Characteristically an adverb comments on the manner or the circumstances of the action or condition indicated by the verb. (See G 2c.)

G 7a Adverb Forms. *Formal English requires a more frequent use of distinctive adverb forms than everyday conversation.* Most adverbs are distinguished from the corresponding adjectives by the characteristic *ly* ending: *bright—brightly, cheerful—cheerfully, considerable—considerably, frequent—frequently, happy—happily, rapid—rapidly, rare—rarely, single—singly.* However, some adverbs, such as *fast, much, thus,* and *well,* have no distinctive ending. Some words ending in *ly* are not adverbs but adjectives:

a *friendly* talk	a *lonely* life
a *leisurely* drive	a *manly* reply

(1) Formal usage prefers "talks *loudly*" to "talks loud," "go *slowly*" to "go slow," or "come *quickly*" to "come quick," though both the long form and the short form of these adverbs have long been standard English.

(2) *Good* and *bad* used as adverbs are nonstandard. In

standard English, "I don't hear so good" would be "I don't hear *well.*" "I write pretty bad" would be "I write *badly.*" (The adverb *well* may, however, do double duty as an adjective, especially in the sense of "healthy," "not ill.")

G 7b Adjectives with Linking Verbs. *Not every modifier appearing next to a verb is necessarily an adverb.*

(1) Linking verbs link the subject to a description of it, which may be a noun but is often an adjective:

> His habits are *expensive.*
> Most of the bottles were *empty.*
> The speaker seemed *nervous.*

A **predicate adjective**, even though it becomes part of the predicate, points back to the subject. Here are some other verbs that may function as linking verbs:

> Genevieve *turned* pale.
> The heat *grew* oppressive.
> He *became* rich overnight.
> Your fears *will prove* silly.
> The accused *remained* silent.
> Honeysuckle *smells* sweet.
> The soup *tasted* flat.
> His hands *felt* moist.
> Sirens *sound* frightening.
> Your friend *looks* ill.

NOTE: Some verbs may function either as ordinary verbs or as linking verbs. In "The waiter appeared hurriedly," *hurriedly* tells us how the man acted. In "The waiter appeared hurried," *hurried* describes the man himself. In "John slowly looked at me," *slowly* describes John's action. In "John looked slow," *slow* describes John.

(2) In some sentences, a verb and its object are followed by a description of the object. The description, called the **objective complement**, may be either a noun (He called me *a genius*) or an adjective (He called me *lazy*). Notice the difference between adjective and adverb in the following pairs:

He called the meeting accidental.
He called the meeting accidentally.

George called his girl friend eager.
George called his girl friend eagerly.

G 7c Adverbs to Modify Modifiers. *In formal usage, use the distinctive adverb form to modify either an adjective or another adverb.* In "a *poorly* informed American," *poorly* is an adverb modifying the adjective *informed.* The man's supply of information is poor, though he himself may be wealthy.

ADVERB + ADJECTIVE: a surprising*ly* beautiful bird
a hopeless*ly* retarded student
an impressive*ly* versatile actor

ADVERB + ADVERB: You sang admirab*ly* well.
He answered surprising*ly* fast.
She worked incredib*ly* hard.

Many everyday expressions use adjective forms as informal **intensifiers**: "He speaks *awful* fast." "Dean Howard is *real* popular." "I am *dreadful* sorry." In formal English, omit such intensifiers altogether or use a formal intensifier like *very.* Use *fairly* or *rather* to replace the informal *pretty* in "pretty old."

EXERCISES

A. In simplified sample sentences, use each of the following words once as an adjective and once as an adverb: *better, early, fast, hard, just, only, well.*

B. Select the modifier appropriate to formal written English.

1. In the few weeks Judy spent in France, her French improved *(1)considerable/(2)considerably.* 2. Selling Christmas cards, I had to talk fast and *(3)furious/(4)furiously* before the householder could slam the door in my face. 3. Many students who have the ability to do *(5)good/(6)well* in their studies nevertheless lack the incentive. 4. We found that our

visitor had an *(7)amazing/(8)amazingly* knowledge of American literature. 5. No matter what dish Carolyn prepared, it tasted *(9)flat/(10)flatly*. 6. I read the questions as *(11)careful/(12)carefully* as the time allowed. 7. The book contained biographies of people who behaved *(13)noble/(14)nobly* in the face of adversity. 8. The characters in many current motion pictures speak and dress fairly *(15)realistic/(16)realistically* for Hollywood standards. 9. An experienced cryptographer can decipher a simple code very *(17)easy/(18)easily*. 10. As the questions continued, the lecturer sounded more and more *(19)impatient/(20)impatiently*. 11. Most drivers drive too fast and too *(21)careless/(22)carelessly* most of the time. 12. The cabin looked *(23)solid/(24)solidly* and well built. 13. A girl should not plan to become a secretary if she does not spell *(25)good/(26)well*. 14. Falling from the slippery roof, he hurt himself *(27)bad/(28)badly*. 15. The man we had been following turned the corner *(29)hurried/(30)hurriedly*.

G 8 Position of Modifiers

A writer needs to place modifiers in such a way as to prevent misunderstanding or unintended double meanings.[7]

A modifier may modify different things depending on where it is placed in a sentence.

G 8a Only and Almost. *Certain adverbs need to be placed with special care.* A word like *only,* which serves both as an adjective and as an adverb, may appear almost anywhere in a sentence:

Only I asked the man for his pen.
I asked *only* the man for his pen.
I asked the *only* man for his pen.
I asked the man for his *only* pen.
I asked the man for his pen *only*.

[7] See the Glossary of Usage for discussion of the split infinitive.

Almost is another word that needs to be carefully placed:

The car *almost* broke down on every trip we took.
(It never quite did.)
The car broke down on *almost* every trip we took.
(It did quite frequently.)

G 8b Misplaced Prepositional Phrases. *Modifiers may make the reader stumble when they do not occur in the most logical place in the sentence.* One type of easily misplaced modifier is the **prepositional phrase** (*in good faith, with due caution, after the dinner, on all fours, for the good of the country*). Here is an example of a misplaced prepositional phrase: "This picture was described as the best ever painted *by my art teacher*." Did your art teacher paint the picture, or did he describe it as the best ever painted?

(1) Though it is easy to misplace a prepositional phrase, it is usually equally easy to *shift it into a more appropriate position:*

MISPLACED:	He looked at the tree he had felled *with his hands in his pocket.*
REVISED:	*With his hands in his pocket,* he looked at the tree he had felled. (It is hard to fell trees with one's hands in his pocket.)
MISPLACED:	I hate crooks *like the district attorney.*
REVISED:	*Like the district attorney,* I hate crooks. (This revision presupposes that you have no reason to doubt the district attorney's honesty.)

(2) Like pronouns, modifiers point to nouns or pronouns used as major sentence elements in preference to possessives. "*At the age of ten,* my grandfather died" seems to mean that your grandfather died when he was ten years old. To improve

such a sentence, you often need to *spell out the meaning intended by the modifier:*

When I was ten, my grandfather died.

G 8c Misplaced and Dangling Verbals. *Verbals used as modifiers have to be clearly related to what they modify.* In the sentence "*Singing,* the mother cared for the baby," the verbal is placed next to the person who does the singing. In the sentence "*Singing,* the baby was cared for by the mother," the verbal is **misplaced**, unless the baby has learned to sing unusually early. In the sentence "*Singing,* the baby was cared for," the verbal is left **dangling**, because the person who does the singing has disappeared from the sentence.

What applies to verbals applies equally to **verbal phrases**—that is, verbals plus other material which they introduce:

MISPLACED: *Being a naughty little boy,* my father often whipped me.
REVISED: *Being a naughty little boy,* I was often whipped by my father.

DANGLING: *To do well in college,* good grades are essential.
REVISED: *To do well in college,* a student needs good grades.

Misplaced and dangling verbals can create absurd images in the reader's mind: "*Racing across the ocean,* land was sighted" (the land was racing across the ocean); "*Walking down the aisle,* the wedding march began to play" (the wedding march was walking down the aisle); "*While shaving,* the telephone rang" (the telephone was shaving). To revise such a sentence, you may have to replace the verbal with a clause:

As *the ship* was racing across the ocean, one of the crew sighted land.

While *the bride and groom* were walking down the aisle, the organist started to play the wedding march.
While *I was shaving,* the telephone rang.

G 8d Absolute Constructions. *Some verbal phrases are not intended to modify any one part of the main sentence.* These are called **absolute constructions**. The most common ones are the many generally acceptable expressions that *clarify the attitude or intention of the speaker:*

Generally speaking, traffic is getting worse rather than better.
He had numerous children—seven, *to be exact.*
Considering the location, the house is not a bad bargain.

Formal English, more frequently than informal English, uses verbals that *carry their own subjects along with them:*

The air being warm, we left our coats in the car.
Escape being impossible, he prepared for the worst.
Most of his colleagues having left the room, Senator Hoakum decided to omit the last twenty pages of his speech.

EXERCISE

Check the following sentences for confusing or misleading modifiers. Label each sentence *S* (satisfactory), *DM* (unsatisfactory because of a dangling modifier), or *MM* (unsatisfactory because of a misplaced modifier). If your instructor desires, rewrite unsatisfactory sentences.

1. Stopped by a policeman in a 30-mile zone, George Van Meter was given a ticket for doing 42 mph on his bicycle. 2. While riding in pursuit of the bandits, the hero's horse was shot from under him. 3. Being a high school sophomore, Shakespeare meant very little to me. 4. Having lived in India for many years, he knew many of the country's problems from first-hand experience. 5. By assigning question-and-answer problems, students fail to develop the ability to think a prob-

lem through by themselves. 6. The weather being unusually mild, we decided to have supper on the terrace. 7. As a child, my mother used to tell me stories of handsome princes on white chargers and of lovely princesses asleep in charmed castles. 8. Its siren wailing frantically, the ambulance skidded into the stalled sedan. 9. Sharks are a danger when vacationing in tropical waters. 10. Considering his lack of training, his performance has been truly remarkable. 11. The author's critics conducted a running argument in a literary magazine, which lasted for several months. 12. Listening to a live concert, music has a spontaneous quality that no mechanical equipment can reproduce. 13. To speak a language well, one has to know the overtones as well as the dictionary meanings of words. 14. The searching party returned to the camp, all efforts to find the missing girl having been unsuccessful. 15. Sir Malcolm heard the news that an heir had been born with great pleasure.

G 9 Confused Sentences

Many garbled sentences are the result of hasty writing, inaccurate copying, or careless typing.

Even when the reader can make out the intended meaning, he will be annoyed at being temporarily tripped up by a defect that the writer should have caught in revision.

G 9a Omission and Duplication. *Check your sentences for carelessly omitted or duplicated elements.* Make sure you have transcribed each sentence in full, without omitting minor sentence elements like *a, the, has, be,* or *am.* Make sure you have not awkwardly repeated minor elements, especially connectives like *that* or *when:*

> I think *that* because he is ill (*that*) he will not come.
> When school starts in the fall (*that is when*) most parents sigh with relief.

Many hastily written sentences appear on paper before the writer has quite formulated what he was going to say:

HASTY: After my sister moved to Ohio, her little girl contracted polio, but did not cause paralysis.
(It was not *the girl* that didn't cause paralysis, but the disease.)

REVISED: After my sister moved to Ohio, her little girl contracted polio, but fortunately *the disease* did not cause paralysis.

G 9b Mixed Construction. *A writer should not confuse different ways of expressing the same idea.* The experienced writer will try out various possible constructions and select the one that seems to fit best. The inexperienced writer may plunge ahead, confusing the various possibilities. The result is known as **mixed construction**:

CONSISTENT: *Whenever he saw a pretty girl,* he ran after her.
CONSISTENT: Any pretty girl *caused him* to run after her.
MIXED: *Any pretty girl* he ran after her.

CONSISTENT: The department manager *rejected his application.*
CONSISTENT: The department manager *did not want him to be* one of his assistants.
MIXED: The department manager *rejected him to be* one of his assistants.

To unscramble such sentences, you have to consider the alternatives and limit yourself to one of them. Thus, "In case of emergency should be reported to the head office" yields "*In case of emergency, report* to the head office" and "*Emergencies should be reported* to the head office."

NOTE: Confusion of *because* and *because of* is an especially frequent cause of mixed construction. *Because* introduces a clause: "The course was canceled *because not enough students registered.*" *Because of* introduces a prepositional phrase: "The course was canceled *because of insufficient enrollment.*" Disregard of this distinction produces sentences like this one: "The course was canceled *because of not enough students registered.*"

G 9c Faulty Predication. *The predicate of a sentence should not say something about the subject that does not logically apply to the subject.* For instance, a writer may anticipate in the subject all or part of the assertion contained in the predicate. Suppose you say, "*The choice* of our new home *was selected* by my mother." What was actually selected? Not a choice, but a home:

LOGICAL: The choice *was made* by my mother.
LOGICAL: *The home* was selected by my mother.

The idea anticipated in the subject may only partly overlap with that expressed in the predicate: "*The price* of our new cabin cruiser *was* rather *expensive.*" (What was actually expensive? The cabin cruiser, not the price. A price can be high, and the expense can be great, but a price cannot be said to be expensive.)

FAULTY: At the beginning of the year, *the participation* in club activities is always *overcrowded.* (The meetings—not the participation—are overcrowded, though the fact that many people participate is of course the reason for the overcrowding.)

LOGICAL: At the beginning of the year, *our club meetings* are always overcrowded.

G 9d Faulty Equation. *Linking verbs account for a special type of faulty predication.* An *is, was,* or *becomes* should not equate two things that are not equal. Nor should it introduce a description inapplicable to the subject. In informal English, such equations are often loose and illogical. "His job *is*

a mailman" is illogical because a mailman is a person, not a job. Formal English would require "*He* is a mailman" or "His job is *that of* a mailman."

(1) The most common type of faulty equation makes a linking verb introduce not a description of the subject, but an **adverbial clause**. Children, for instance, will say, "A zoo is *when you go to look at animals.*" "When you go to look at animals" is not logically a description of a zoo; normally it would indicate *when* an action takes place or a condition occurs.

FAULTY:	Punishment is *when you are told to stand in the corner.*
SATISFACTORY:	When you are told to stand in the corner, you are being punished.
SATISFACTORY:	One form of punishment is to make the child stand in a corner.
SATISFACTORY:	Punishment is a means of keeping children out of mischief.

Only rarely does an *is-when* or an *is-where* sentence actually describe a time or a place:

> Tuesday *was* [the day] *when* I saw him last.
> Poughkeepsie *is* [the place] *where* I was born.

(2) Linking verbs often cause faulty equation when they introduce **prepositional phrases** that would normally indicate the circumstances of an action:

> Our only hope *is to convince* your parents—not "*is by convincing* your parents."
> Their method of selection *was to question* the candidates carefully—not "*was by questioning* the candidates."

G 9e Faulty Appositives. *Make sure that your appositives can be equated with the nouns they modify.* An **appositive** is a noun placed next to another noun to explain or describe it: "John, *a sophomore,* came to see me." Here, John and the sophomore are identical. However, it does not make sense to say, "There was only *one telephone call, a friend* of yours." A friend can *make* a telephone call, but we would not say that he *is* one.

FAULTY: We have only one *vacancy, a mathematics teacher.* (A teacher is not vacancy, and a vacancy is not a teacher.)

REVISED: We have only one *vacancy,* a *position* for a mathematics teacher. (What is actually vacant is a *position* for a teacher.)

EXERCISE

In the following sentences, point out all instances of hasty writing, mixed construction, faulty predication, and faulty apposition. Label each sentence *S* (satisfactory) or *U* (unsatisfactory). If your instructor desires, revise unsatisfactory sentences.

1. In modern industrial society, the sponsorship of the fine arts is no longer supported by wealthy aristocratic patrons. 2. Amnesia is when a character in a second-rate novel temporarily loses his memory. 3. According to recent statistics, the divorce rate for couples from different racial backgrounds compared with couples of different religion had more success in marriage. 4. The purpose of the reception was to acquaint old-timers with some of the newcomers to the area. 5. A prizefighter is not the kind of profession that offers its devotees economic security. 6. Shirley's husband was unable to support her in the style to which she had become accustomed to. 7. At night, a thousand neon signs hide the shabbiness of the jerry-built stores and offices from the traveler's view. 8. Surrealism was a movement dedicated to artistic expression of the irrational and the subconscious. 9. It is certainly very difficult for a teacher in the social sciences to avoid becoming personally involved than a teacher of chemistry or of physics. 10. I believe that if the government allowed everyone to do as he pleased that our country would not long survive. 11. A flash flood is when a river suddenly

rises over its banks. 12. Sandra was offered her first acting role by the Civic Theater, an amateur group that picked up Broadway plays after everyone else was done with them. 13. Just because a person has a college degree does not mean that he is exceptionally intelligent. 14. Jargon is a kind of language composed mainly of words like *homologous, processual,* and *socializee.* 15. In case of new outbreaks of the disease should be reported to the health authorities immediately. 16. A jurisdictional dispute is where two different agencies claim jurisdiction in a given case. 17. Don's sales technique was to flash a big smile and to call all customers by their first names. 18. Cornelia had always wanted to meet one of the artists of whom she had heard a great deal about. 19. Joe had hardly batted the ball over the fence than we heard a splintering of glass and an anguished yell. 20. I suddenly realized that we were no longer on level ground and that the road was tilting upward on great concrete stilts.

G 10 Incomplete Constructions

Formal English requires a writer to spell out relationships merely implied in various informal constructions.

Formal written English requires accuracy in a number of relationships that, though common, are less central to the basic structure of a sentence than predication and apposition.

G 10a Informal So and Such. *Statements of degree need to be accurately worked out in formal English. So* and *such* often indicate that something has reached a definite point, producing certain characteristic results:

> She was so frightened *that she was unable to speak.*
> There was such an uproar *that the chairman banged his gavel in vain.*

Informal English often omits the characteristic result. *So* and *such* then function as **intensifiers**: "I am *so* glad." "He is *such* a lovely boy." You can make such sentences generally acceptable in two different ways. You can substitute an intensifier like *very* or *extremely:* "I am *very* glad." You can add a characteristic result: "He is such a lovely boy *that all the kindergarten girls are running after him.*"

G 10b Incomplete Comparison. *Formal English frowns on incomplete comparisons.* Normally, *more, better,* and *whiter,* the **comparative forms**, establish a comparison between at least two elements:

> *Carpenters* make more money than *teachers.*
> *Half a loaf* is better than *a slice.*

Most, best, and *whitest,* the **superlative forms,** establish a comparison within a group of at least three elements: [8]

> The annual classic at Le Mans is the most dangerous *automobile race in Europe.*

(1) Formal English gives a writer less leeway than informal English in letting the reader find out for himself *what is being compared with what.* Most obviously informal are incomplete comparisons resulting from the use of *more* and *the most* as intensifiers: "That girl has *more* luck" (than who or than what?). "I had *the most* wonderful experience" (of the day? of the year? of a lifetime?). "I saw *the most* exciting play" (the most exciting play of the season? the most exciting play by this author? the most exciting play ever produced?).

(2) To satisfy demanding readers, state explicitly what is being compared even when the *terms of a comparison can be inferred* from the context:

[8] See the Glossary of Usage for discussion of the double comparative and of the superlative in reference to two.

After I took a course in Remedial Reading, I read twice as fast (*as I had before*).

When we saw the revised estimate, we realized we would have to spend more money (*than we had planned*).

G 10c Illogical and Ambiguous Comparison. Hasty writing often causes comparisons that are absurd or ambiguous.

(1) *Some sentences compare things that are not really comparable:* "The skin of her cheeks was as soft as a child." Actually, her skin was as soft as a *child's* (skin), or as soft as *that* of a child. Check for logical balance in sentences like the following:

LOGICAL: The *teachings of* Horatio Alger reached a wider audience *than those of* Whitman.—Saul Bellow, "The Writer as Moralist," *Atlantic*

Sometimes the absurdity of an illogical comparison is not immediately obvious: "Their fullback was heavier than any man on their team." Their fullback is part of their team, and he cannot be heavier than *any man* on the team, including himself. He can be heavier than *other* men on the team:

LOGICAL: Their fullback was heavier than *any other man* on their team.

(2) *Some comparisons mention three comparable items without making it clear which two are being compared.* "Tom liked Dick better than Harry" may mean two different things:

CLEAR: Tom liked Dick better than Harry *did.*
CLEAR: Tom liked Dick better than *he liked* Harry.

G 10d Contraction of Coordinate Elements. *Telescoping of coordinate elements does not work in formal written English if the forms concerned are merely similar rather than* *identical.* When several items of the same kind are coordinated by a connective like *and* or *but,* we often omit forms that would cause unnecessary duplication. Such omission may cause truncated sentences.

(1) Unsatisfactory telescoping occurs most frequently in *sentences with several predicates.* In "It *can* be done and *will* be done," the *be done* after *can* is identical with that after *will.* We can therefore omit it and say: "It *can and will* be done." However, formal writing would avoid "It *can and has* been done." The complete forms are *can be done* and *has been done. Been* would have to serve as a substitute for an omitted *be.*

If one of several verbs in a sentence appears in a shortened form, fill in the complete forms first to make sure that only identical items are omitted:

INCOMPLETE: Some men never have and never will master the fundamentals of punctuation.

COMPLETE: Some men never have *mastered* and never will *master* the fundamentals of punctuation.

INCOMPLETE: The patient was given an injection and the instruments made ready.

COMPLETE: The patient *was* given an injection, and the instruments *were* made ready.

(2) A special kind of unsatisfactory telescoping occurs in *double-barreled comparisons* of the *as-good-if-not-better* type: "My theme is as good if not better than yours." "English is as important if not more important than courses in how to raise petunias." The complete forms would be *as good as* and *better than,* and *than* cannot substitute for an omitted *as.* Formal English would require "My theme is as good *as,* if not better *than,* yours." Less awkward and equally acceptable is the practice of shifting the second part of the comparison to the end of the sentence:

My theme is as good as yours, *if not better.*
English is as important as courses in how to raise petunias, *if not more so.*

(3) When you coordinate *several prepositional phrases,* guard against omitting prepositions that are not identical but merely express a similar relationship:

SATISFACTORY: I have great *admiration and respect* for him. (Taken up separately, the two prepositions would prove identical: "admiration *for* him" and "respect *for* him.")

UNSATISFACTORY: I have great *respect and faith* in him. (Taken up separately, the two phrases would require different prepositions: "respect *for* him" and "faith *in* him.")

Notice the use of different prepositions in the following examples:

She was jealous *of* but fascinated *by* her rival.
His behavior during the trial adds *to* rather than detracts *from* my admiration for him.

EXERCISE

Check the following sentences for incomplete and ambiguous constructions. Point out unsatisfactory comparisons and unsatisfactory contraction. Label each sentence *S* (satisfactory) or *U* (unsatisfactory). If your instructor desires, revise unsatisfactory sentences.

1. Women on the whole understand children better than men. 2. Roger's stews and sauces were as good as the best restaurant in Paris, if not better. 3. Religion today is receiving a better press and more general attention than it has had for many years. 4. In this district, teachers have always been and will always be hired on the basis of their professional competence alone. 5. In much of Europe, American films are more popular than any other country. 6. The discussion grew so heated that David decided to keep his views

to himself. 7. Children seem to like the so-called "adult" Westerns as much as adults do. 8. Year after year, American colleges produce more physical education teachers than mathematics. 9. The Secretary of State usually attracts more criticism than any member of the President's cabinet. 10. Critics of our schools must realize that they can and are doing great harm by indiscriminate attacks. 11. Unlike a track coach, a history teacher seldom has a newspaper article written about him when his students do exceptional work. 12. The impact of American books, magazines, and comics in Great Britain is much greater than British publications in the United States. 13. We spend about one and one-half times as much on tobacco products each year as we spend on higher education. 14. A good background in the liberal arts is excellent preparation for such practical professions as engineers and lawyers. 15. The United States has more television sets to the square mile than any other country in the world. 16. The ingredients used in the most expensive cosmetics often cost no more than those used in cheap products. 17. Mike never has and never will succeed in making his restaurant something more than a place to eat food. 18. Many of the legislators lacked the taste—and the capacity—for brilliant political debate. 19. Unlike America, traveling abroad is a rare luxury in many foreign countries. 20. Few of my friends were preoccupied or even interested in making a living.

G 11 Parallel Structure

A sentence should be laid out with a regard for consistency.

Many sentences that work out grammatical relationships fully and accurately nevertheless suffer from inefficient construction. Like a road full of unexpected twists and turns, such sentences slow down and confuse the reader.

G 11a Faulty Parallelism. *Formal English requires consistency in the coordination of elements serving a similar function in a sentence.* Sentence elements joined by *and, or,* and *but* have to be **parallel**; they have to fit into the same grammatical category. If you put an *and* after *chicken,* the reader expects another noun: "a chicken and *a duck,*" "a chicken and *mashed potatoes.*" If you put an *and* after *swore,* he expects another verb: "swore and *affirmed,*" "swore and *raved.*" The same principle applies to other elements, including whole clauses:

INFINITIVES: Two things that a successful advertisement must accomplish are *to be noticed* and *to be remembered.*

PARTICIPLES: I can still see my aunt *striding* into the corral, *cornering* a cow against a fencepost, *balancing* herself on a one-legged milking stool, and *butting* her head into the cow's belly.

CLAUSES: The young people *who brood* in their rooms, *who forget* to come down to the dining hall, and *who burst out* in fits of irrationality are not worrying about who will win the great game.—Oscar Handlin, "Are the Colleges Killing Education?" *Atlantic*

Observe the following points in revising sentences for parallel structure:

(1) You can often make elements parallel by *shifting one of them to a different grammatical category.* For instance, "*ignorant* and *a miser*" is off balance because it joins an adjective and a noun. You could make *ignorant* into a noun (He was an *ignoramus* and a miser) or *miser* into an adjective (He was ignorant and *miserly*).

(2) Many ideas are not easily shifted from one grammatical category to another. You may have to consider several different ways of *shortening, expanding, or rewording a sentence* until you hit upon a satisfactory revision:

FAULTY: High school students want to be *popular* and *leaders.*
PARALLEL: High school students want to *be* popular and *become* leaders.

FAULTY: My grandfather liked *the country* and *to walk* in the fields.
PARALLEL: My grandfather liked *to live* in the country and *to walk* in the fields.

FAULTY: He told me *of his plans* and *that he was leaving.*
PARALLEL: He *informed* me of his plans and *told* me that he was leaving.

(3) Formal English often reinforces parallel structure by *retaining prepositions or connectives* that might be omitted in informal situations:

The high school teacher usually has little time *for helping* badly prepared students and (*for*) *performing* the many clerical tasks required of him.

NOTE: Lack of parallelism is especially obvious after **correlatives**: *either . . . or, neither . . . nor, not only . . . but also, whether . . . or.*

FAULTY: I used to find him either *on the porch* or *dozing* in the living room.
PARALLEL: I used to find him either *sitting* on the porch or *dozing* in the living room.

FAULTY: We wondered whether *to believe* him or *should we try* to verify his story.
PARALLEL: We wondered whether we should *believe* him or *try* to verify his story.

G 11b Faulty Series. *Faulty parallelism frequently occurs in a series of three or more elements.* Often a writer will lead his reader into what looks like a conventional series only to trip him up by making the last element snap out of the expected pattern: "Her new friend was polite, studious, and *an only child.*" "He liked to swim, relax, and *everything peaceful.*" In a revision, each element of the series would have to fit into the same grammatical category.

Sometimes the elements in a faulty series are parallel neither in form nor in meaning. A revision might then clarify meaning by breaking up the series altogether:

PARALLEL: Her new friend was *a gentleman, a scholar,* and *an only child.*

BROKEN UP: Her new friend, *an only child,* was a gentleman and a scholar.

PARALLEL: He liked *swimming, relaxation,* and *peaceful surroundings.*

BROKEN UP: He liked to swim and to relax and *preferred peaceful surroundings.*

EXERCISES

A. Check the following sentences for parallel structure. Label each sentence *S* (satisfactory), *FS* (unsatisfactory because of a faulty series), or *FP* (unsatisfactory because of other instances of faulty parallelism). If your instructor desires, rewrite unsatisfactory sentences.

1. The editorial called the governor's speech vague, insincere, and repetitious. 2. He seemed like the type of person who would brag about his income and be extravagant with his money. 3. What the children lacked was the feeling of really belonging and that someone really cared. 4. Barbara was waiting for a talent scout to discover her and who would take her to Hollywood. 5. Newspapers do not always provide a reliable record of what ordinary people are thinking, saying, and doing. 6. A girl learns a lot about children when she cares for younger brothers and sisters or as a baby sitter during high school days. 7. This country needs a President skilled in diplomacy and who knows foreign countries well. 8. A physician has to be good not only at diagnosing diseases but also at understanding his patients. 9. Advertisers should admit that a deodorant cannot make a woman beautiful and that a healthy complexion alone cannot make a person happy. 10. A successful businessman usually has a pleasant personality, poise, and is a good speaker. 11. We should not judge

a candidate's qualifications by whether he is a lawyer, farmer, or from some other occupation. 12. Maurice claimed to be Napoleon's great-grandson and that he was the rightful heir to the throne of France. 13. Apparently my friend's work consisted of sitting at a desk for eight hours a day and give orders. 14. Our Christmas dinner would consist of roast turkey with cranberry sauce, whipped potatoes, vegetables, and followed by mincemeat pie. 15. The mass media shy away from frank discussion of love but permitting the detailed treatment of crude violence. 16. Foreign exchange students often expect to see rugged, tanned cowboys roaming the prairies and pug-faced gangsters shooting people down in the streets. 17. My father thought that young girls should not go to dances, see young men only in the company of a chaperone, and many other old-fashioned prejudices. 18. In many gangster movies, the hero deceives the police, moves in the best society, and comes to a bad end only because his mother-in-law shoots him for having slapped her daughter. 19. To most readers, the word *home* suggests security and comfort as well as a place to live. 20. The success of a television program depends on how well the program has been advertised, the actors taking part, and is it comedy or serious drama.

B. Write or collect ten sentences illustrating parallel structure. Devote each sentence to a different type of word or construction.

G 12 Consistent Point of View

A writer should not confuse his readers by unmotivated shifts in tense, reference, or grammatical perspective.

The need for consistency makes a serious writer guard against confusing shifts in the perspective he adopts toward people and events.

G 12a Shifts in Tense. A writer should be consistent in his use of verb forms that indicate the relationship of events in time.

(1) *Avoid the shift from the past tense to the present tense when something remembered becomes so real that it seems to be happening in front of you.* Note the shift in time in the following sentences:

We *disembarked* at noon and fought our way through the jungle in the sultry afternoon heat. Suddenly, there *is* a tiger! I *aim* my rifle and *pull* the trigger! Nothing *happens*—the gun *wasn't* loaded. Luckily, one of my bearers *saved* me from the consequences of my carelessness.

If the writer wants the description to be especially vivid, he should tell the whole story as though it were happening now: "We *disembark* . . . *fight* our way . . . one of them *saves* me." Otherwise, he should describe everything in the past.

(2) *Avoid shifts in perspective when two events happen not at the same time or in simple chronological order but at different times or during different periods:* "When I *saw* the *F* on my report card, I *was* terribly disappointed, because I *studied* very hard." If studying hard was a matter of past history by the time the student received his grade, the **sequence of tenses** would be more accurate like this:

I was terribly disappointed, because I *had studied* very hard.

Formed with *have* or *has,* the **present perfect** indicates that something has happened recently, prior to events taking place now: "He *has finished* his supper and *is getting* up." Formed with *had,* the **past perfect** indicates that something happened in the relatively distant past, prior to *other* events in the past: "He *had finished* his supper and *was getting* up." A confusing shift often results when a writer makes the present perfect go with the simple past or the past perfect with the simple present:

SHIFT: Last March, the Secretary of the Air Force told the committee what *has happened* to air transport in this country.

CONSISTENT: Last March, the Secretary of the Air Force told the committee what *had happened* to air transport in this country.
(The secretary could not have told the committee what *has happened* since he testified and up to the present time.)

(3) *Avoid shifts resulting from failure to observe the distinction between direct and indirect quotation.* What the speaker felt or observed at the time he spoke would occur in the present tense in direct quotation: He said, "I *feel* fine." It would occur in the past tense in indirect quotation: He said that he *felt* fine. What the speaker felt *before* he spoke would occur in the past, or perhaps in the present perfect, when quoted directly: He said, "I *felt* fine." It would occur in the past perfect when quoted indirectly: He said that he *had felt* fine. Failure to adjust the tenses in indirect quotations can lead to sentences like the following:

Her husband admitted that he *was*—should be *"had been"*—a confirmed bachelor.
Mr. Chamberlain said that there *will be*—should be *"would be"*—peace in our time.

When *a statement made in the past formulates a general truth* many writers find the present tense plausible:

Galileo said that the earth *moves* and that the sun *is* fixed; the Inquisition said that the earth *is* fixed and the sun *moves;* and Newtonian astronomers, adopting an absolute theory of space, said that both the sun and the earth *move.*—A. N. Whitehead, *Science and the Modern World*

(4) *Avoid inconsistent combinations between forms that indicate differences in attitude toward possible events* (called differences in **mood**). In the following sentences, note the differences between factual reference to a possibility and the **conditional**, which makes the same possibility seem less probable, or contrary to fact. (See also G 4c.)

INCONSISTENT:	If he *comes* to this country, the army *would* draft him.
FACTUAL:	If he *comes* to this country, the army *will* draft him.
CONDITIONAL:	If he *came* to this country, the army *would* draft him.

G 12b Shifts in Reference. *No matter how a writer chooses to refer to himself and others, he should stick to his choice.* The least ambiguous pronoun he can use to refer to himself is of course *I, me,* or *my* (**first person singular**). When he does not want to focus attention on himself, he may use *we, us,* or *our* instead (**first person plural**). However, this "editorial" *we* sounds artificial in most student writing, especially in short themes. In reports, surveys, or formal arguments the author often keeps out all personal elements by using the **passive** ("it *has been found,*" "three experiments *were conducted,*" "it *must be concluded*").

Note the following special problems:

(1) When a writer wants to speak directly to his reader, he can of course call him *you* (**second person singular** and **plural**) and use *we* to refer both to the reader and himself:

You will agree that *we* must do everything in our power.
As *you* no doubt remember, *we* have witnessed several similar incidents during the past year.

On the other hand, *you* often appears as an informal equivalent of *one* or *a person,* referring not so much to the reader as to people in general:

FORMAL:	*One* cannot be too careful.
INFORMAL:	*You* can't be too careful.

Confusion results when a writer shifts to the indefinite, generalized *you* after he has already identified the person he has in mind in some other way: "I don't want to be a famous actress. *I* would rather lead my own life without people always knowing what *you* are doing." The easiest way to avoid this kind of shift is to use *you* only to mean "you, the reader."

(2) Similar in effect to shifts to *you* are shifts to the **imperative**, the request form of verbs: "*Come* in." "*Put* it down." "*Leave* him alone." Imperatives are most appropriate in directions and exhortations; they startle the reader when they suddenly break into ordinary expository prose:

SHIFT: High schools *should stop* educating all students at the same rate. *Give* aptitude tests for placement and then *separate* the students accordingly.

CONSISTENT: High schools *should stop* educating all students at the same rate. They *should give* aptitude tests for placement and then *separate* the students accordingly.

G 12c Shifts to the Passive. *Avoid shifting to the passive when the person in question is actually still the active element in the sentence.* Some sentences confuse the reader by shifting from an **active** construction ("*He built* the house") to a **passive** one ("*The house was built* by him"): [9]

INCONSISTENT: He returned to the office as soon as *his lunch had been eaten.* (This sounds as though his lunch might have been eaten by somebody else.)

CONSISTENT: He *returned* to the office as soon as he *had eaten* his lunch.

Unsatisfactory shifts to the passive are especially frequent after an impersonal *one* or *you:*

INCONSISTENT: As *you scan* the area of your backyard, a small patch of uninhabited earth *is located.*

[9] For a fuller discussion of the passive see S 2a.

CONSISTENT: As *you scan* your backyard, *you locate* a small patch of earth.

EXERCISES

A. Check the following passages for unnecessary or confusing shifts in perspective. Label each sentence *S* (satisfactory) or *U* (unsatisfactory). If your instructor desires, revise unsatisfactory sentences.

1. If one insists on telling the truth at all times, he is not likely to be very popular. 2. After I finished my pie, a cup of coffee was ordered and a cigarette lighted to top off a perfect meal. 3. In the next scene, Antonio, who has just arrived in Venice, tells his friends that he is going to elope with the beautiful Elvira. 4. If a war comes, many small nations would be at the mercy of those countries that have nuclear weapons. 5. Though Nietzsche is often mentioned, his books are infrequently read and seldom understood. 6. If you came early, you could join us for a walk along the shore. 7. Several witnesses testified that the crossing signal had failed to operate. 8. During the spring rains, the valley would have been flooded if it were not for the dams recently completed. 9. One doesn't gain anything by exercising to lose weight if afterward you are allowed to eat all you want. 10. The college catalogue says that all students would take a year of science and a year of mathematics. 11. Often when you have an unemployed father there may be friction in the home and the child may feel unwanted. 12. Our newspapers should stop wasting their time on trivialities. Leave the love life of the stars to the fan magazines and put the news back on the front page. 13. If we refuse poorly qualified students admission to college, we would solve the problem of overcrowding. 14. Having a friend that really cares for you is one of the best things that one can get out of life. 15. As the lights go out and the curtain rises, the principal was revealed trying to abate the clouds of smoke pouring from the witches' cauldron. 16. College should mean a place where one learns things to fit him for his chosen place in life. 17. If the club limited its membership, it would have to raise its dues. 18. Perhaps Marcia would have enjoyed the concert if her escort had stopped keep-

ing time with his foot. 19. Suddenly the sky darkens, a breeze springs up, and a premonitory rumble rolls across the lake. 20. The boat moved quietly down the river, the girls sang, and mandolins were played by some of the older boys.

B. (**Review**) Check the following passages for adequate sentence structure, including position of modifiers, parallelism, and consistency in point of view. Identify each sentence that needs revision.

1. (1) Marilyn was the only one of my classmates whom I thoroughly disliked. (2) She was one of those girls who talk to a person when they want something from him but completely ignore him at other times. (3) When she walked down the hall, she often pretends not to notice a fellow student getting ready to greet her. (4) She often walked into the classroom late, so that the boys could see her make a grand entrance.

2. (5) I recall an election in which two boys were running for student body president. (6) To outdo his fellow candidate, one of the boys invited the students to a steak dinner. (7) The second boy, unable to afford such an expensive meal, gave a hot-dog barbecue. (8) Unswayed by the bribe, the second boy was elected by a landslide.

3. (9) In a true gentleman, courtesy toward women would not be second but first nature. (10) He would always open doors, walk on the side toward the curb, and helping whenever needed. (11) Even when the lady did not actually need his assistance, he would, by his attentions, make her feel like a lady. (12) He would make her feel like something precious and fragile, something to be cared for and protected.

4. (13) My parents realized that each child has its own individuality and is different from any other child. (14) I was grateful to them because they were not always comparing my own achievements with my sister. (15) My sister had straight *A*'s in most of her high school subjects. (16) My parents, however, never asked me, "Why aren't your grades as good as hers?"

5. (17) The Mercedes is one of the finest and most expen-

sive cars sold in the United States. (18) The prices for the various models range from $4,000 to $14,000. (19) Considering the superior workmanship, these prices are not extravagant. (20) Being conservatively styled, many executives prefer it to other cars.

6. (21) In high school I had a friend who used to say, "I am too smart to have to study." (22) Even then I suspected that he studied more than he admitted. (23) But now that he is in college he definitely found that he must meet competition. (24) He no longer believes that knowledge is something with which a person is born.

2

DICTION

His first few weeks in college demonstrate to the student the need for paying close attention to vocabulary and **diction**; that is, word resources and word choice. In each major field he enters, he is confronted with terms for the objects and ideas discussed, the standards applied, and the procedures followed. In a literature class, he is confused by words like *monograph, didactic, elegiac,* and *allegory*. In a philosophy or humanities course, he has to learn the meaning of *metaphysics, asceticism, dogmatism,* or *anthropology*. In addition to new and unfamiliar words, he encounters familiar words used in unfamiliar ways. He is asked to write a critical paper and discovers too late that *critical* did not mean "fault-finding" but "objective," "thoughtful," or "analytical."

Still other words contain familiar elements which encourage the student to guess at their meanings. Often such guessing turns out to be misleading. *Apologist,* for instance, does not mean a person who apologizes for what he realizes is wrong. It means a person who defends what he claims is right. *Determinist* does not mean a person who believes that people determine their own actions by free choice. It means a person who believes that people's actions are determined by causes beyond their control.

D 1 College Dictionaries

A good dictionary is a comprehensive inventory of words, giving information on their history, meanings, and limitations.

A good dictionary is the result of scholarly teamwork. It records the way words have been used in the past and are being used at present, and tells how certain words are *not* used.

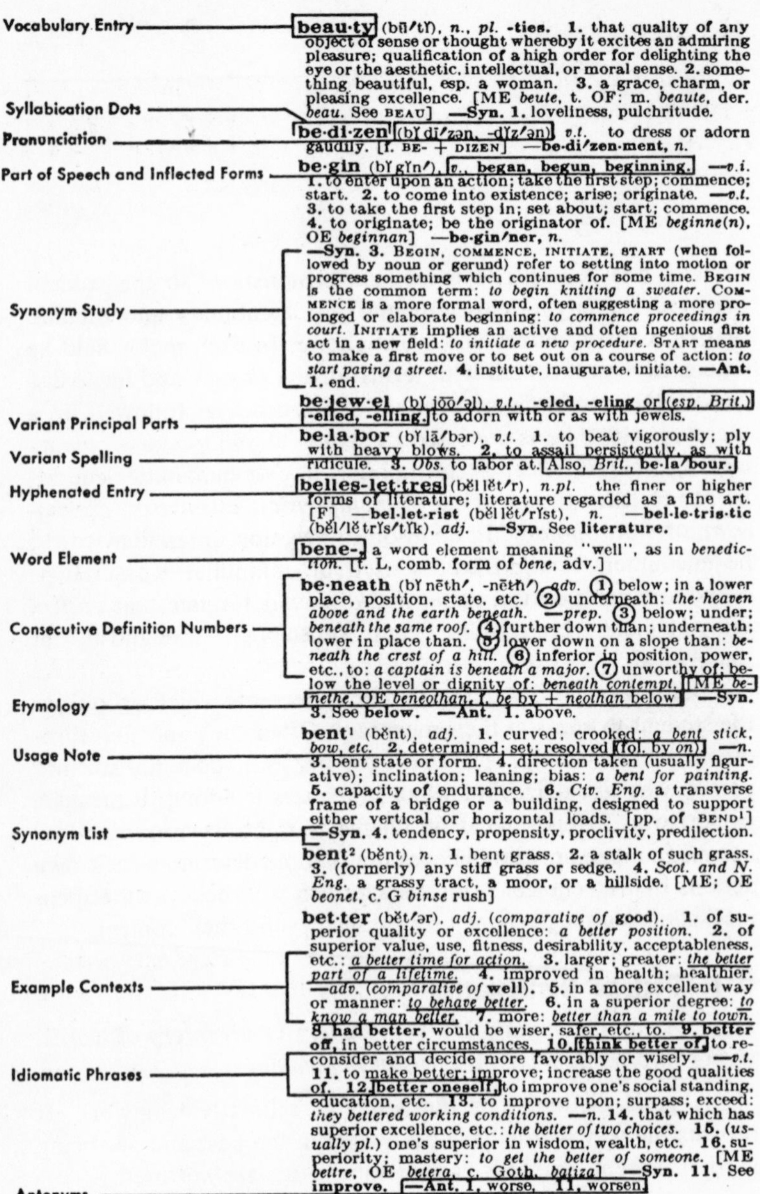

beau·ty (bū′tĭ), *n., pl.* **-ties.** **1.** that quality of any object of sense or thought whereby it excites an admiring pleasure; qualification of a high order for delighting the eye or the aesthetic, intellectual, or moral sense. **2.** something beautiful, esp. a woman. **3.** a grace, charm, or pleasing excellence. [ME *beute*, t. OF: m. *beaute*, der. *beau*. See BEAU] **—Syn. 1.** loveliness, pulchritude.

be·di·zen (bĭ dī′zən, -dĭz′ən), *v.t.* to dress or adorn gaudily. [f. BE- + DIZEN] **—be·di′zen·ment,** *n.*

be·gin (bĭ gĭn′), *v.,* **began, begun, beginning.** *—v.i.* **1.** to enter upon an action; take the first step; commence; start. **2.** to come into existence; arise; originate. *—v.t.* **3.** to take the first step in; set about; start; commence. **4.** to originate; be the originator of. [ME *beginne(n)*, OE *beginnan*] **—be·gin′ner,** *n.*
—Syn. 3. BEGIN, COMMENCE, INITIATE, START (when followed by noun or gerund) refer to setting into motion or progress something which continues for some time. BEGIN is the common term: *to begin knitting a sweater.* COMMENCE is a more formal word, often suggesting a more prolonged or elaborate beginning: *to commence proceedings in court.* INITIATE implies an active and often ingenious first act in a new field: *to initiate a new procedure.* START means to make a first move or to set out on a course of action: *to start paving a street.* **4.** institute, inaugurate, initiate. **—Ant. 1.** end.

be·jew·el (bĭ jōō′əl), *v.t.,* **-eled, -eling** or (*esp. Brit.*) **-elled, -elling.** to adorn with or as with jewels.

be·la·bor (bĭ lā′bər), *v.t.* **1.** to beat vigorously; ply with heavy blows. **2.** to assail persistently, as with ridicule. **3.** *Obs.* to labor at. Also, *Brit.,* **be·la′bour.**

belles-let·tres (bĕl lĕt′r), *n.pl.* the finer or higher forms of literature; literature regarded as a fine art. [F] **—bel·let·rist** (bĕl lĕt′rĭst), *n.* **—bel·le·tris·tic** (bĕl′lĕ trĭs′tĭk), *adj.* **—Syn.** See **literature.**

bene-, a word element meaning "well", as in *benediction.* [t. L, comb. form of *bene*, adv.]

be·neath (bĭ nēth′, -nēth′), *adv.* **1.** below; in a lower place, position, state, etc. **2.** underneath: *the heaven above and the earth beneath.* *—prep.* **3.** below; under; *beneath the same roof.* **4.** further down than; underneath; lower in place than. **5.** lower down on a slope than: *beneath the crest of a hill.* **6.** inferior in position, power, etc., to: *a captain is beneath a major.* **7.** unworthy of; below the level or dignity of: *beneath contempt.* [ME *benethe*, OE *beneothan*, f. *be* by + *neothan* below] **—Syn. 3.** See **below.** **—Ant. 1.** above.

bent[1] (bĕnt), *adj.* **1.** curved; crooked: *a bent stick, bow, etc.* **2.** determined; set; resolved (fol. by *on*). *—n.* **3.** bent state or form. **4.** direction taken (usually figurative); inclination; leaning; bias: *a bent for painting.* **5.** capacity of endurance. **6.** *Civ. Eng.* a transverse frame of a bridge or a building, designed to support either vertical or horizontal loads. [pp. of BEND[1]] **—Syn. 4.** tendency, propensity, proclivity, predilection.

bent[2] (bĕnt), *n.* **1.** bent grass. **2.** a stalk of such grass. **3.** (formerly) any stiff grass or sedge. **4.** *Scot. and N. Eng.* a grassy tract, a moor, or a hillside. [ME; OE *beonet*, c. G *binse* rush]

bet·ter (bĕt′ər), *adj.* (*comparative of* **good**). **1.** of superior quality or excellence: *a better position.* **2.** of superior value, use, fitness, desirability, acceptableness, etc.: *a better time for action.* **3.** larger; greater: *the better part of a lifetime.* **4.** improved in health; healthier. *—adv.* (*comparative of* **well**). **5.** in a more excellent way or manner: *to behave better.* **6.** in a superior degree: *to know a man better.* **7.** more: *better than a mile to town.* **8. had better,** would be wiser, safer, etc., to. **9. better off,** in better circumstances. **10. think better of,** to reconsider and decide more favorably or wisely. *—v.t.* **11.** to make better; improve; increase the good qualities of. **12. better oneself,** to improve one's social standing, education, etc. **13.** to improve upon; surpass; exceed: *they bettered working conditions.* *—n.* **14.** that which has superior excellence, etc.: *the better of two choices.* **15.** (*usually pl.*) one's superior in wisdom, wealth, etc. **16.** superiority; mastery: *to get the better of someone.* [ME *bettre*, OE *betera*, c. Goth. *batiza*] **—Syn. 11.** See **improve.** **—Ant. 1.** worse. **11.** worsen.

Explanation of Dictionary Entries, from *American College Dictionary.*

Webster's New World Dictionary (NWD), one of several widely used college dictionaries, makes a special effort to explain the meanings of a word in simple and clear language. It gives exceptionally full information on the history of a word and its current uses, including slang.

The American College Dictionary (ACD), like the NWD, strives for intelligibility, though it uses a greater number of technical and not-so-common words in its definitions. It thus offers an incentive to the user who likes to browse through an entry for related words. Unlike its two major competitors, the ACD usually places the most common meaning of a word first.

Webster's New Collegiate Dictionary (NCD), in its current seventh edition, is an abridgment of *Webster's Third New International Dictionary*. The latter, like the *Collegiate* published by the G. & C. Merriam Company, is the most authoritative and comprehensive unabridged dictionary of current American English. Like the parent work on which it is based, the NCD arranges different meanings in historical order. Thus the reader can easily survey the historical development of a word. Unlike the NWD and the ACD, the *New Collegiate* lists names of people and places in indexes at the end of the book.

The *Standard College Dictionary* (SCD) was first published in 1963. It presents the most common, rather than the earliest, meaning of a word first. Like the NWD, the *Standard College Dictionary* contains valuable introductory materials on the history of English and on modern approaches to the study of language.

In the wording of definitions, the major college dictionaries range from the everyday language of the NWD to the more technical and scholarly style of the NCD. Compare the first two meanings of *peach* in the following entries:

1. a small tree with lance-shaped leaves, pink flowers, and round, juicy, orange-yellow fruit, with a fuzzy skin and a single, rough pit. 2. its fruit.

From *Webster's New World Dictionary*

1. the subacid, juicy drupaceous fruit of a tree, *Prunus Persica*, of many varieties, widely cultivated in temperate climates. 2. the tree itself.

From *The American College Dictionary*

[1]peach \'pēch\ *n* [ME *peche*, fr. MF, fr. LL *persica*, fr. L, pl. of *persicum*, fr. neut. of *persicus* Persian, fr. *Persia*] **1 a :** a low spreading freely branching Chinese tree (*Prunus persica*) of the rose family that is cosmopolitan in cultivation in temperate areas and has lanceolate leaves, sessile usu. pink flowers borne on the naked twigs in early spring, and a fruit which is a single-seeded drupe with a hard endocarp, a pulpy white or yellow mesocarp, and a thin downy epicarp **b :** the edible fruit of the peach

From *Webster's Seventh New Collegiate Dictionary* [1]

D 1a Synonyms and Antonyms. *A good dictionary discriminates between the exact meanings of closely related terms.* Often, it indicates meaning by a **synonym**, a word that has nearly the same meaning as the word you are looking up. Thus, your dictionary may give "sad" or "mournful" as a synonym for *elegiac,* or "instructive" as a synonym for *didactic.* Often, your dictionary will explain a word by giving an **antonym**, a word of approximately opposite meaning. *Desultory,* for instance, is the opposite of "methodical"; *hackneyed* is the opposite of "fresh" or "original."

Synonyms are seldom simply interchangeable. Usually, they are only partially synonymous; their areas of meaning overlap, but at the same time there are subtle differences. *Burn, char, scorch, sear,* and *singe* all refer to the results of exposure to extreme heat, but whether a piece of meat is charred or merely seared makes a difference to the person who has it for dinner.

[1] By permission. Copyright, 1963 by G. & C. Merriam Co., Publishers of the Merriam-Webster Dictionaries.

Here is how a dictionary discriminates between the synonyms of *pay:*

> **syn** PAY, COMPENSATE, REMUNERATE, SATISFY, REIMBURSE, INDEMNIFY, REPAY, RECOMPENSE, REQUITE mean to give money or its equivalent in return for something. PAY implies the discharge of an obligation incurred; COMPENSATE implies a making up for services rendered or help given; REMUNERATE more clearly suggests paying for services rendered and may extend to payment that is generous or not contracted for; SATISFY implies paying a person what is demanded or required by law; REIMBURSE implies a return of money that has been expended for another's benefit; INDEMNIFY implies making good a loss suffered through accident, disaster, warfare: REPAY stresses paying back an equivalent in kind or amount; RECOMPENSE suggests due return in amends, friendly repayment, or reward

From *Webster's Seventh New Collegiate Dictionary* [2]

D 1b Denotation and Connotation. *A good dictionary pays attention to the associations of words and to the attitudes they imply.* Many words **denote**—that is, point out or refer to—very nearly the same objects or qualities. At the same time, they **connote**—that is, suggest or imply—different attitudes toward the objects or qualities they point out. *Cheap* and *inexpensive* both mean relatively low in price or cost. However, we may call an article "cheap" to suggest that we consider it shoddy or inferior; we may call it "inexpensive" to suggest that we consider it a good bargain, valuable in spite of its low price. *Unwise* and *foolish* both indicate a lack of wisdom. However, calling a proposal "unwise" suggests a certain amount of consideration or respect for the person who made it; "foolish" suggests ridicule and contempt. Similarly, we may call a boy of low intelligence a "slow learner" or a "dunce," a new history of the United States "ambitious" or "pretentious."

Here is how a dictionary discriminates between the connotations of synonyms of *plan:*

[2] By permission. Copyright, 1963 by G. & C. Merriam Co., Publishers of the Merriam-Webster Dictionaries.

SYN.—**plan** refers to any detailed method, formulated beforehand, for doing or making something (vacation *plans*); **design** stresses the final outcome of a plan and implies the use of skill or craft, sometimes in an unfavorable sense, in executing or arranging this (it was his *design* to separate us); **project** implies the use of enterprise or imagination in formulating an ambitious or extensive plan (they've begun work on the housing *project*); **scheme,** a less definite term than the preceding, often connotes either an impractical, visionary plan or an underhand intrigue (a *scheme* to embezzle the funds).

From *Webster's New World Dictionary*

D 1c Context. *Often a dictionary supplies phrases suggesting the kind of context where a given meaning is appropriate.* The **context** of a word may be another word ("square meal"), a whole sentence or paragraph ("Square your precepts with your practice"), a whole article or book (a treatment of squares in a book on plane geometry), or a situation (a policeman directing a pedestrian to a square).

Here is an entry showing a word used in different contexts:

bot·tle[1] (bŏt′əl), *n.*, *v.*, **-tled, -tling.** —*n.* **1.** a portable vessel with a neck or mouth, now commonly made of glass, used for holding liquids. **2.** the contents of a bottle; as much as a bottle contains: *a bottle of wine.* **3. the bottle,** intoxicating liquor. **4.** bottled milk for babies: *raised on the bottle.*

From *The American College Dictionary*

In an unfamiliar context, familiar words may have a new or different meaning. For instance, an author praising modesty and thrift may describe them as "homely virtues." Looking up the word, you will find that its original meaning, as you might expect, is "associated with the home." Favorable associations of domestic life account for such meanings as "simple," "unpretentious," "intimate"; unfavorable associations account for such meanings as "crude," "unpolished," "ugly." An eighteenth-century writer may talk about the "wit" of a person who does not seem at all "witty" in the sense of cleverly humorous or ironic. *Wit* in this context means general intellectual and imaginative capacity, as in phrases like "half-wit" and "at one's wit's end."

NOTE: Even when the denotation of a word remains fairly stable, its connotations may vary in different contexts. *Academic* basically means "associated with higher learning." "Academic standards," then, may mean standards of responsible and competent scholarship. An "academic argument," on the other hand, may mean an argument that is unrealistic or impractical because, like higher learning, it is removed from the hustle and bustle of economic and political reality.

D 1d Grammatical Labels. *A good dictionary gives reliable information about the functions a word can serve in a sentence.* For instance, *human* is usually labeled both as an **adjective** (adj.) and as a **noun** (n.), with some indication that the latter use ("a human" rather than "a human being") is not generally accepted as appropriate to written English. *Annoy* is labeled a **transitive verb** (v.t.); it is incomplete without an object. In other words, we usually annoy somebody or something; we don't just annoy. *Set* also is usually transitive ("*set* the bowl on the table"), but it is labeled **intransitive** (v.i.) when applied to one of the celestial bodies. In other words, the sun doesn't set anybody or anything; it just sets.

D 1e Idiom. *A good dictionary lists idiomatic phrases whose meanings may be more than the sum of their parts.* A word often combines with other words in an expression that is not modeled on common grammatical patterns but that nevertheless becomes the habitual way of conveying a certain idea. Such expressions are called **idioms**.

To write idiomatic English, you have to develop an ear for individual phrases and ways of saying things. For instance, we *do* a certain type of work, *hold* a job or position, *follow* a trade, *pursue* an occupation, and *engage* in a line of business. We *replace* an original *with* a copy, but we *substitute* a copy *for* the original. Here is an exceptionally full list of idiomatic phrases using the word *mind:*

bear in mind, to remember.
be in one's right mind, to be mentally well; be sane.
be of one mind, to have the same opinion; agree.
be of two minds, to be undecided or irresolute.
be out of one's mind, 1. to be mentally ill; be insane. 2. to be frantic (*with* worry, grief, etc.).
call to mind, 1. to remember. 2. to be a reminder of.
change one's mind, 1. to change one's opinion. 2. to change one's intention, purpose, or wish.
give a person a piece of one's mind, to tell a person plainly one's disapproval of him; rebuke; scold.
have a (good or great) mind to, to feel (strongly) inclined or disposed to.
have half a mind to, to be somewhat inclined or disposed to.
have in mind, 1. to remember. 2. to think of. 3. to intend; purpose.
keep in mind, to remember.
keep one's mind on, to pay attention to.
know one's mind, to know one's real thoughts, feelings, desires, or intentions.
make up one's mind, to form a definite opinion or decision; resolve.
meeting of minds, an agreement.
never mind, don't concern yourself; it doesn't matter.
on one's mind, 1. occupying one's thoughts. 2. worrying one.
pass out of mind, to be forgotten.
put in mind, to remind.
set one's mind on, to be determined on or determinedly desirous of.
speak one's mind, to say plainly what one thinks.
take one's mind off, to stop one from thinking about; turn one's attention from.
to one's mind, in one's opinion.

From *Webster's New World Dictionary*

A special problem for inexperienced writers is the idiomatic use of **prepositions**. The following list reviews idiomatic uses of some common prepositions:

abide *by* (a decision)
abstain *from* (voting)
accuse *of* (a crime)
acquiesce *in* (an injustice)
adhere *to* (a promise)
admit *of* (conflicting interpretations)
agree *with* (a person), *to* (a proposal), *on* (a course of action)
alarmed *at* (the news)
apologize *for* (a mistake)
aspire *to* (distinction)
assent *to* (a proposal)
attend *to* (one's business)
avail oneself *of* (an opportunity)
capable *of* (an action)
charge *with* (an offense)
collide *with* (a car)

compatible *with* (recognized standards)
comply *with* (a request)
concur *with* (someone), *in* (an opinion)
confide *in* or *to* (someone)
conform *to* (specifications)
deficient *in* (strength)
delight *in* (mischief)
deprive *of* (a privilege)
derived *from* (a source)
die *of* or *from* (a disease)
disappointed *in* (someone's performance)
dissent *from* (a majority opinion)
dissuade *from* (doing something foolish)
divest *of* (responsibility)
find fault *with* (a course)
identical *with* (something looked for)
ignorant *of* (a fact)
inconsistent *with* (sound procedure)
independent *of* (outside help)
indifferent *to* (praise or blame)
infer *from* (evidence)
inferior *to* (a rival product)
insist *on* (accuracy)
interfere *with* (a performance), *in* (someone else's affairs)
jealous *of* (others)
long *for* (recognition)
object *to* (a proposal)
oblivious *of* (warnings)
part *with* (possessions)
partial *to* (flattery)
participate *in* (activities)
persevere *in* (a task)
pertain *to* (a subject)
preferable *to* (an alternative)
prevail *on* (someone to do something)
prevent someone *from* (an action)
refrain *from* (wrongdoing)
rejoice *at* (good news)
required *of* (all members)
resolve *on* (a course of action)
rich *in* (resources)
short *of* (cash)
secede *from* (the Union)
succeed *in* (an attempt)
superior *to* (an alternative)
threaten *with* (legal action)
wait *for* (developments), *on* (a guest)

NOTE: College dictionaries vary in their coverage of idioms. Only an unabridged dictionary giving one or more sample quotations for each possible use of a word can come close to being a complete guide to idiomatic usage.

EXERCISES

A. Look up the following entries in your dictionary: *denouement, epigram, farce, flying buttress, hauberk, limerick, machete, solecism, symbiosis, syncopation.* What special fields of interest do they represent? How clear or adequate are the definitions?

B. Explain to what extent the synonyms in each of the following groups overlap and how they differ: *agreement—contract—covenant; amateur—dilettante—tyro; apology—excuse—pretext; bearing—behavior—conduct; betray—divulge—reveal; common—ordinary—familiar; correct—discipline—punish; decline—reject—spurn; democracy—representative government—republic; destiny—doom—lot; enterprise—project—venture; fad—fashion—vogue; fantastic—imaginary—visionary; flippant—glib—impertinent; mumble—murmur—mutter.*

C. Explain the differences in connotation between the words in each of the following pairs: *childish—childlike; clever—intelligent; famous—notorious; gaze—ogle; godsend—windfall; juvenile—youngster; lucre—wealth; obedient—obsequious; obstinate—persistent; petty—punctilious; populace—population; regret—remorse; revenge—retribution; revolt—revolution; slender—thin.*

D. How does your dictionary distinguish among the changing meanings of each of the following words? Show how context determines your choice of the meaning appropriate in each phrase.

> *Bay* leaves, at *bay, bayed* at the moon, *bay* window, bomb *bay,* a breeze from the *bay; head* of lettuce, *head* the procession, a *head* of steam, *heads* or tails, over the listeners' *heads,* went to his *head, heads* of government, *head* off complaints, not have a *head* for figures; *let* blood, without *let* or hindrance, *let* him be, *let* go, *let* me see it, *let* us ignore him, rooms to *let;* car of recent *make, make* the beds, *make* money, *make* excuses, *makes* my blood boil, *make* a speech, *makes* easy reading, *made* him a sergeant; *repair* a car, *repaired* to the meeting, in good *repair, repair* the damage; *straight* to the point, *straight* alcohol, *straight* party line, the comedian's *straight* man, *straight* hair, thinking *straight.*

E. Each of the italicized words in the following expressions is a familiar word used in an unfamiliar sense. Find the meaning that fits the context.

> To write an *abstract* of a speech; to write an *apostrophe* to the gods; a monster of fearful *aspect;* to give someone a *civil*

answer; an anti*clerical* political party; to give *countenance* to a crime; to wear a characteristic *habit;* to receive *intelligence;* to *justify* a line of type; to cultivate *polite* learning; a *process* server; to make a character stand out in full *relief;* to lie in *state;* to be *transported* with gratitude; the *virtue* of a medicine.

F. Check your answers to the following questions by consulting your dictionary: (1) Is *incompetent* used as a noun? (2) Which of the following words are used as verbs: *admonition, loan, lord, magistrate, minister, sacrilege, spirit, war?* (3) Is "superior than" idiomatic English? (4) Is *smooth* used as an adverb? (5) Is *entertain* used as an intransitive verb? (6) Is *very* used as an adjective? (7) What idiomatic preposition goes with *glory* used as a verb? (8) Do we always censure somebody or something, or can we just censure, period? (9) How many different grammatical categories can *ill* belong to? (10) Are "angry with," "angry at," and "angry about" interchangeable? (11) Is *animate* used as an adjective? (12) Is *predominate* used as an adjective?

G. Point out and correct unidiomatic use of prepositions:

1. To seek a good grade at someone else's expense would be a violation to our standards of conduct. 2. During the past fifty years, deaths caused by highway accidents have been more numerous than those incurred from two world wars and the war in Korea. 3. Plans for cost reduction have been put to action by different agencies of the federal government. 4. Several families volunteered to take care for the children of flood victims. 5. Only the prompt help of the neighbors prevented the fire of becoming a major disaster. 6. During the first years of marriage we had to deprive ourselves from many things that other people take for granted. 7. The arrival of the ship to its destination caused general rejoicing. 8. Though I support Mr. Finchley's candidacy, I take exception with some of his statements. 9. We Americans do not hesitate in waving our flag if the occasion arises. 10. The people of this country naturally shun at the thought of having any kind of censorship imposed upon their newspapers. 11. As an instrument of the popular will, the senate suffers from defects inherent to its constitution. 12. A businessman cannot succeed unless he takes heed to the preferences of his customers.

H. Study the general scheme, the introductory material, and several sample entries of *one* of the following specialized dictionaries. Report your findings.

Bartlett's Familiar Quotations; Lester V. Berrey and Melvin Van den Bark, *American Thesaurus of Slang;* Sir William A. Craigie and James R. Hulbert, *A Dictionary of American English on Historical Principles;* H. W. Fowler, *A Dictionary of Modern English Usage;* H. W. Horwill, *A Dictionary of Modern American Usage;* John S. Kenyon and Thomas A. Knott, *A Pronouncing Dictionary of American English;* Mitford M. Mathews, *A Dictionary of Americanisms;* Eric Partridge, *A Dictionary of Slang and Unconventional English;* Roget's *Thesaurus of English Words and Phrases.*

D 2 Word History

Knowledge of the history of a word helps a writer understand its uses, meanings, and associations.

After giving the spelling, pronunciation, and grammatical category of a word, college dictionaries often summarize its **etymology**; that is, they briefly trace its origin and history. The following sample entry relates the word *lock* to corresponding words in earlier English (ME. = Middle English; AS. = Anglo-Saxon or Old English), in other Germanic languages (G. = German; ON. = Old Norse or Early Scandinavian), and in the hypothetical common parent language of most European languages (IE. = Indo-European):

> **lock** (lok), ***n.*** [ME. *lokke;* AS. *loc,* a bolt, bar, enclosure, prison; akin to G. *loch,* a hole, ON. *lok,* a lid; prob. IE. base ***leug-,* to bend, seen also in AS. *lucan,* to close (cf. LEEK)],

From *Webster's New World Dictionary*

In addition to tracing words to other languages, the etymologist is concerned with **semantic change**—that is, gradual changes in meaning. The most complete record of such changes is the unabridged *New English Dictionary on Historical Principles,* reissued in 1933 as the *Oxford English Dictionary* (OED). This monumental reference work gives the earliest date a word occurs and then provides quotations tracing its development down through the centuries.

The most extensive changes in vocabulary come about through contacts between different cultures. Armed conquest, colonial expansion, international trade, and cultural influences all make possible the absorption of words from other languages. Roughly three-fourths of the words in your dictionary were absorbed into English from foreign sources. When the Anglo-Saxon tribes came to England from continental Europe during the period between 450 and 600 A.D., they spoke Germanic dialects, closely related in both grammar and vocabulary to the dialects from which modern Dutch and German are derived. The American tourist coming to Germany can still easily recognize the German equivalents of *arm, drink, father, fish, hand,* or *house.* However, the basic Germanic vocabulary of **Anglo-Saxon** or **Old English** was enriched and modified by an almost continuous absorption of words from other languages throughout early English history.

D 2a Latin and Greek Borrowings. *The most persistent influences on the English vocabulary were Latin and Greek, the languages of classical antiquity.* Latin had been the language of the Roman empire. It became the official language of the Roman Catholic Church, which established itself in England in the seventh century and remained the supreme spiritual authority until the sixteenth century. English early absorbed many Latin words related to the Scriptures and to the doctrines and ritual of the church, such as *altar, candle, chalice, mass, palm, pope, shrine, relic,* and *rule.* Other early borrowings were related to church administration, to the everyday life of monks and clergymen, and to the exclusively church-controlled and church-conducted medieval system of education. Many have long since lost all suggestion of foreignness: *beet, cap, circle, cook, fever, lobster, mat, pear, school, silk, sock,* or *turn.*

Greek was the language of the literature, philosophy, and scientific knowledge of ancient Hellenic culture, flourishing both in Greece proper and in other parts of the Mediterranean world. Either in the original Greek or in Latin translation, this body of knowledge exercised a continuous influence on Christianity and Western civilization during the Middle Ages and Renaissance. Modern philosophical, scientific, and technological terminology draws heavily on Latin and Greek roots. More generally, the language of educated people is saturated with words that are in one way or another derived from one of the classical languages. Examples of words absorbed either directly from Greek or from Greek through Latin are *anonymous, atmosphere, catastrophe, chaos, climax, crisis, enthusiasm,* and *skeleton.* Examples of words absorbed from Latin are *contempt, gesture, history, incredible, index, individual, intellect, legal, mechanical, picture,* and *rational.*

(1) *Latin and Greek Roots.* Knowledge of a common Latin or Greek root often provides the key to a puzzling word. For instance, the Greek root *phys-* usually refers to the body or to material things, whereas the Greek root *psych-* usually refers to the mind or the soul. This distinction explains *physician* (heals the body) and *psychiatrist* (heals the mind), *physiology* (study of bodily functions) and *psychology* (study of mental functions), *physical* (characteristic of material reality) and *psychic* (going beyond material reality).

Here is a brief list of common Latin and Greek roots. Explain how each root is used in the sample words given for it:

auto-	*self*	autocratic, automatic, automobile, autonomy
capit-	*head*	capital, decapitate, per capita
carn-	*flesh*	carnal, carnivorous, incarnation, carnival
chron-	*time*	anachronistic, chronometer, synchronize
culp-	*fault*	culpable, culprit, exculpate
doc-	*teach*	docile, doctor, doctrine, indoctrinate
graph-	*write*	autograph, graphic, geography, orthography
hydr-	*water*	dehydrate, hydrant, hydraulic, hydrogen
jur-	*swear*	conjure, juror, perjury
man-	*hand*	manacle, manicure, manual, manufacture
phon-	*sound*	euphony, phonetics, phonograph, symphony
terr-	*land*	inter, terrestrial, subterranean
urb-	*city*	suburb, urban, urbane
verb-	*word*	proverb, verbal, verbiage, verbose
vit-	*life*	vitality, vitamin
vol-	*wish*	volition, voluntary, volunteer

(2) *Common Prefixes and Suffixes.* Especially useful is a knowledge of the most common Latin and Greek **prefixes** and **suffixes**—that is, syllables attached at the beginning or at the end of a word to modify its meaning. A common prefix like sub-, meaning "below" or "beneath," helps to explain not only *substandard* and *subconscious* but *submarine* (below the sea), *sublunar* (below the moon—that is, on earth; characteristic of existence on this earth), *subterranean* (beneath the surface, underground). The suffix *-cide* means "killer" or "killing" in *homicide* (of a human being), *suicide* (of oneself), *fratricide* (of a brother), *parricide* (of a parent), and *insecticide* (of insects).

Here is a brief list of Latin and Greek prefixes:

bene-	*good*	benediction, benefactor, benefit, benevolent
bi-	*two*	bicycle, bilateral, bisect
contra-	*against*	contraband, contradict, contravene
ex-	*out, out of*	exclude, exhale, expel
extra-	*outside*	extraordinary, extravagant, extrovert
omni-	*all*	omnipotent, omnipresent, omniscient
per-	*through*	percolate, perforate, permeate

pre-	*before*	preamble, precedent, prefix
poly-	*many*	polygamy, polysyllabic, polytheistic
re-	*back*	recall, recede, revoke, retract
tele-	*distant*	telegraph, telepathy, telephone, television
trans-	*across, beyond*	transatlantic, transcend, transmit

D 2b French Borrowings. *Over the centuries, thousands of words were absorbed into English from French.* The historical event that most drastically influenced the development of the language was the conquest of England by the French-speaking Normans in the years following 1066. At the beginning of the so-called **Middle English** period, about 1150, the Norman conquerors owned most of the land and controlled the most important offices in state and church. The language of law, administration, and literature was French. When the native English of the conquered people gradually re-established itself as the language of political and social life, thousands of French words were retained. Many of these words were associated with the political and military role of the aristocratic Norman overlords: *castle, court, glory, mansion, noble, prince, prison, privilege, servant, treason, treasure, war.* But hundreds of other words absorbed into Middle English were everyday words like *avoid, branch, chair, demand, desire, disease, envy, praise, table, uncle.*

Many French words passed into English through the hands of English poets who found them in medieval French poetry and romance, both Norman and continental. Some of these words are still used primarily in imaginative literature and preserve a poetic and often old-fashioned flavor. Such words are *chevalier* for "knight," *damsel* for "girl," *fealty* for "loyalty," *paramour* for "sweetheart," *prowess* for "valor," *puissance* for "power" or "strength," *travail* for "toil."

D 2c Recently Borrowed Words. *A number of foreign languages have influenced the vocabulary of special fields of interest.* Since the consolidation of **Modern English** (about 1500), numerous words have come into English from French, Italian, Spanish, and various other sources. The leadership of seventeenth- and eighteenth-century France in elegant living, artistic style, and military organization is reflected in words like *apartment, ballet, battalion, cadet, caress, corps, façade, infantry, negligee, patrol.* Italy, which saw the origin of modern opera and symphonic music, provided terms like *cantata, concert, falsetto, sonata, solo, soprano, violin.* From Spain, which pioneered in the discovery and exploitation of new continents, came words like *alligator, banana, cannibal, cocoa, mosquito, Negro, potato, tobacco, tomato,* some of them absorbed into Spanish from New World sources.

Modern English has a number of foreign words in different stages of assimilation. If they are still felt to be foreign rather than English, your dictionary puts a special symbol in front of them or labels them "French," "Italian," or whatever is appropriate. A writer may use an occasional foreign word because it sums up the particular flavor of a thing or of an idea more aptly than any possible native equivalent. For instance, the French word *esprit* describes a kind of irreverent and brilliant wit for which it is hard to find an English name. Do not use such foreign phrases merely in order to impress your reader.

EXERCISES

A. Investigate the history of the following words: *bedlam, bowdlerize, bowie knife, carnival, credit, curfew, dollar, emperor, fellow, gerrymander, glamour, gossip, hallmark, Halloween, jeep, kerchief, lynch, picayune, propaganda, thug.*

B. Select one of the following words. Report fully on the contrast in nature and extent of its treatment in your own dictionary and in the *Oxford English Dictionary: boor, cattle, fee, husband, hussy, knave, lewd, meat, villain, virtue.*

C. Explain the meaning of the common element in each of the following groups of words: *anarchy—monarchy—oligarchy; anthropology—misanthrope—philanthropy; antibiotic—biography—biology; audio-visual—audition—inaudible; biennial—centennial—perennial; centipede—century—per cent; cosmic—cosmopolitan—microcosm; credence—incredulous; describe—prescribe—proscribe; eugenics—eulogy—euphonious; heterogeneous—homogeneous; insect—intersection—section; magnify—magnificent—magnitude; portable—portage—transport; precedent—procedure—secede.*

D. Indicate the basic meaning of each Latin and Greek prefix used in the following words: *anesthetic, ambivalent, antedate, antipathy, circumvent, concord, disunity, hypersensitive, international, introvert, malpractice, multimillionaire, neofascist, postgraduate, prelude, pseudo-scientific, retroactive, semitropical, synchronize, ultramodern, unilateral.*

E. Find out from which languages the following words were derived: *bandana, boomerang, brunette, caviar, chocolate, crescendo, cynic, focus, hurricane, Mumbo Jumbo, pretzel, pundit, skin, snoop, vaudeville.*

F. What are the meanings of the following expressions? How many of them does your dictionary consider foreign rather than English? *Ad hoc, ad nauseam, aficionado, à la carte, auto-da-fé, alma mater, blitz, corpus delicti, coup de grâce, cum laude, de jure, enfant terrible, ersatz, eureka, fait accompli, femme fatale, hara-kiri, hoi polloi, laissez faire, non sequitur, pax Romana, quod erat demonstrandum, touché, tour de force, Zeitgeist.*

D 3 Usage Labels

Some words are appropriate only to certain situations or limited to specific uses.

No matter what dictionary you buy, you should study the

introductory notes and find out the significance of the various symbols and abbreviations used. The most important abbreviations are the so-called **restrictive labels**. They indicate that a word is used only under certain circumstances and that it can be out of place when used without attention to its limitations. In the following dictionary entry, six of the nine principal meanings of *brass* are preceded by restrictive labels:

brass (brăs, bräs), *n.* **1.** a durable, malleable, and ductile yellow alloy, consisting essentially of copper and zinc. **2.** a utensil, ornament, or other article made of brass. **3.** *Mach.* a bearing, bush, or the like. **4.** *Music.* **a.** a musical instrument of the trumpet or horn families. **b.** such instruments collectively in a band or orchestra. **5.** *Brit.* a memorial tablet incised with an effigy, coat of arms or the like. **6.** metallic yellow; lemon, amber, or reddish yellow. **7.** *U.S. Slang.* **a.** high-ranking military officers. **b.** any important officials. **8.** *Colloq.* excessive assurance; impudence; effrontery. **9.** *Brit. Slang.* money. —*adj.* **10.** of brass. **11.** using musical instruments made of brass. [ME *bras*, OE *bræs*] —**brass′-like′**, *adj.*

Subject Label

Geographic Label

Usage Label

From *The American College Dictionary*

D 3a Nonstandard Words. *Some words suggest nonstandard speech rather than educated usage.* Many words are appropriate to almost any occasion. A hand can be appropriately called a "hand" at any time and at any place. Other words are limited in their usefulness because of the associations they suggest. For instance, words like *anywheres, nohow,* and *irregardless* are either not listed in your dictionary at all or labeled illiterate, **nonstandard**, or vulgate. Like nonstandard grammatical patterns, they are often associated with low social standing or a lack of formal education. (See G 1a.)

D 3b Colloquial Words. *Some words suggest relaxed conversation rather than systematic exposition or argument.* Many dictionaries label such words **colloquial**. The word does *not* mean "local" but "characteristic of informal speech." People use colloquial language when at ease and with their friends; as a result, it tends to sound relaxed and folksy. However, the man who is most comfortable in a robe and slippers puts on a tie and a business suit when going to the office on Monday morning. Similarly, a writer has to be able to use formal language in formal situations. In particular, he has to guard against sudden shifts from the tone of the lecture hall to that of the snack bar around the corner.

COLLOQUIAL	FORMAL	COLLOQUIAL	FORMAL
boss	superior	kid	child
brainy	intelligent	knock off	stop working
buddy	friend	mean	ill-natured
faze	disconcert	skimpy	meager
flunk	fail	sloppy	untidy
folks	relatives	snoop	pry
hunch	premonition	snooze	nap
job	position	stump	baffle

Other familiar words are generally acceptable in one sense but colloquial in another. Colloquial are *alibi* in the sense of "excuse," *aggravate* in the sense of "annoy," *funny* in the sense of "queer," and *mad* in the sense of "angry."

Colloquial language uses qualifiers like *kind of, sort of, a lot, lots;* abbreviated forms like *ad, bike, exam, gym, phone.* It uses many **phrasal verbs**, verbs that combine a short basic verb with one or more prepositions: *check up on, chip in, come up with, cut out* (noise), *get across* (a point), *take in* (a show), *take up with* (a person). Colloquial English usually contains a liberal sprinkling of catch-all words like *nice, cute, awful, wonderful,* or *terrible.* It is fond of **figurative expressions** like *play ball, polish the apple, have a brainstorm.*

Used with discretion, colloquial expressions can set a casual, leisurely tone:

There was a broad streak of mischief in Mencken. He was forever *cooking up* imaginary organizations, having *fake* handbills printed, inventing exercises in pure nonsense. I remember a fake business card that he *got* some job printer to execute for him and that gave him great joy.—Philip M. Wagner, "Mencken Remembered," *The American Scholar*

On the other hand, colloquialisms can easily suggest a put-on folksiness, the public-relations heartiness of some advertisers and some political candidates (Uncle Sam from a billboard: "My folks mostly drive Ford V-8's"). Many college teachers require the student to keep expository writing free from a colloquial tinge.

D 3c Slang. *Slang is appropriate only in the most informal kinds of writing or when deliberately used for special effects.* **Slang** has some characteristically adolescent qualities: a disregard for convention, a lack of restraint, a tendency to regard people and accepted social attitudes with condescension or contempt. One unmistakable characteristic of slang is its faddishness. New slang expressions are born overnight, repeated over and over, and then forgotten. Different high schools, colleges, and professions develop their own special varieties of slang, which change from year to year. As a result, much slang is unintelligible to outsiders.

Slang often has a vigor missing in more cautious and pedestrian diction. The figurative expressions it substitutes for less imaginative formal terms are often apt: *highbrow* for "sophisticate" or "intellectual," *rubberneck* for "tourist," *sawbones* for "surgeon" or "physician," and *whirlybird* for "helicopter." Often a striking slang expression has no very satisfactory formal equivalent: *eager beaver, eyewash, runaround, stuffed shirt.* Many slang terms appeal to our sense of the incongruous: *blow one's top, chew the fat, fly off the handle, hit the ceiling, kick the bucket, lay an egg.*

Slang is the major resource of many a humorous writer:

> Despite that great wellspring of love and pity I have for the afflicted and the misbegotten, and those who have been *just plain took,* I find it hard to get worked up over the plight of those *gaffers* who play golf on the city's links. Little boys lurk in the brush, and when one of the superbly conditioned athletes knocks a *nifty* their way, they keep the ball. Then, if things haven't changed since my day, they sell the balls to other superbly conditioned athletes, who then *scream like banshees* when the golf-ball connoisseurs *steal 'em* again. Since grabbing the little thieves by the scruff of their necks and *beating the bejabbers out of them* would obviously be in violation of their civil rights, we must look elsewhere for a solution.

On the other hand, the humor in slang tends to be crude. Calling a person "fatso" or "skinny" or "bonehead" may be funny, but it also suggests a lack of tact or respect. The extravagant and contemptuous elements in slang make many readers interpret all slang expressions as signs of bad taste and bad manners.

D 3d Fancy Words. *When writing formal English, avoid words that are pompous, affected, or stilted.* Students whose writing has been criticized as slangy or excessively colloquial sometimes have difficulty finding middle ground. Trying to avoid excessive informality, they may go to the opposite extreme. Do not imitate writers who habitually prefer the fancy word to the plain word, the elegant flourish to the blunt phrase.

Dictionaries do not usually distinguish between plain and fancy words. Some of the latter may carry the label *poetic* or *literary,* indicating that they are most appropriate in poetry, in fiction, in imaginative description. Here is a brief list of words that can make your writing seem affected:

FANCY	PLAIN	FANCY	PLAIN
adumbrate	hint	betrothal	engagement
ameliorate	improve	commence	begin
asseverate	assert	concomitant	result
astound	amaze	demise	death

FANCY	PLAIN	FANCY	PLAIN
diurnal	daily	presage	predict
emolument	pay, reward	pulchritude	beauty
eschew	avoid	purchase	buy
gelid	cold	quaff	drink
nuptials	wedding	residence	home
obsequies	funeral	tome	volume
pachyderm	elephant	vernal	springlike
potentate	ruler	vista	view

NOTE: Whether a word sounds natural or affected depends on its use. A word appropriate in a stylized social note may sound artificial in a personal letter. Contemporary expository prose, on the whole, avoids both "fine writing" and the strained joviality of a deliberately colloquial style in favor of simple, unpretentious language.

EXERCISES

A. Which of the following expressions would you expect to carry restrictive labels? Check your answers with the help of your dictionary. *Bookworm, Chinaman, go Dutch, grease monkey, guttersnipe, guzzle, hubbub, highfalutin, jalopy, mob, moniker, mooch, moonshiner, persnickety, rake-off, ritzy, schoolmarm, shyster, victuals, walkie-talkie, windbag, wallop, Yankee.*

B. Check the standing of the following abbreviations. Which does your dictionary list without a restrictive label? *Ad-lib, auto, bus* (for "omnibus"), *doc, econ, IQ, lab, math, photo, plane* (for "airplane"), *prof, snafu, TV, ump* (for "umpire"), *VIP.*

C. Observe the language used by your fellow students, friends, or acquaintances to find ten current slang expressions not listed in your dictionary. Define them, explain their use, and indicate what, if anything, they reveal about the speaker's attitude.

D. Study the writing of a columnist who makes frequent use of colloquialisms or of slang. Examine and describe his attitude toward his material and toward his readers.

E. Point out colloquialisms and slang expressions and comment on their appropriateness. If your instructor desires, rewrite the sentences, avoiding all expressions that are not appropriate to formal written English.

1. Uncle Amos was a spendthrift in his youth, but he changed after he married a penny-wise wife. 2. My family was on the move all through my early childhood, but we finally located in the state of New York. 3. Psychologists have discovered that many young people get a kick out of cutting up in front of a group. 4. Our unlimited material resources will avail us nothing unless we keep alive the gumption that comes down to us from colonial farmers. 5. When the refugees were told that the train was going to leave in ten minutes, there was a mad rush to the station. 6. Parents only confuse a child by bawling him out every time he commits a minor mistake. 7. I prefer being blown to pieces by an atomic bomb to being brained with a club. 8. Sent to size up our new allies, he found most of them in good shape. 9. The concert was scheduled to start at eight o'clock, but unfortunately the soloist did not show up. 10. Guests who crash a party must not be surprised if the host gives them a cold shoulder. 11. In view of the late hour, we decided we better shove off and get some shuteye. 12. My education was rather lopsided; it never came to grips with the problems that really interested me. 13. It is too bad that we should run out of gas only a couple of miles from home. 14. When Lovelace fails to suggest a definite date for the wedding, Clarissa begins to suspect that he is only pulling her leg. 15. Modern medicine has found ways of licking many dread diseases.

D 4 Geographic Labels

Some words have only regional or local currency; dictionaries indicate their status by geographic labels.

D 4a American and British English. *In the different English-speaking countries variations in vocabulary have developed.* The British reader of an American magazine may occasionally stumble over **Americanisms**. The Canadian reader of an Australian newspaper will be puzzled by words that only a dictionary specializing in the regional variations of English could explain.

The regional variants that you are most likely to encounter in your own reading are words common in **British English**. Reading a novel about life in Liverpool or Manchester, you will discover that a "tram" is a streetcar, a "lorry" a truck, a "lift" an elevator, a "torch" a flashlight, a "wireless" a radio, or a "fortnight" two weeks. Most college dictionaries indicate words occurring primarily either in Britain or in the United States by restrictive labels.

D 4b Dialects. *Through the centuries, most European languages, including British English, have developed a great number of local varieties.* The American tourist exploring Europe soon finds that there are language differences not only from country to country but also from province to province, from county to county, and sometimes from village to village. These regional varieties, or **dialects**, often differ greatly in pronunciation, grammar, and vocabulary from the standard language used in the schools, on stage and radio, or in books, magazines, and newspapers.

Students of English literature usually encounter some dialect writing. For instance, a poet to whom a pretty girl is a "bonny lass," a church a "kirk," and a landowner a "laird" is using one of the dialects of Scotland and Northern England rather than standard British English. In the United States, various circumstances have prevented the development of dialect differences comparable to those of British English, German, or French. The migrations of large numbers of people have led to a continual intermingling of settlers from various parts of the country, with a resulting leveling of language differences. Today, the mass media of communication promote national norms of taste, fashion, and language.

Such dialect differences as have developed in the United States are primarily a matter of pronunciation rather than of grammar and vocabulary. Linguists are now in the process of tracing a number of **American dialects**. The results of their work are being recorded in linguistic atlases mapping out differences in speech from region to region. However, few areas have a regional identity distinct enough to make possible the preservation of differences easily caught by the untrained ear of the layman. A Yankee may recognize a Southerner by his use of *you all* instead of "both of you" or "all of you," *reckon* instead of "guess" or "suppose," *poke* instead of "bag," or *tote* instead of "carry." A student from the Middle West may recognize something like an Eastern or New England accent that in some ways comes close to standard British English.

Dialect differences are exploited by comedians and comic-strip writers for comic effects. Serious dramatists and novelists reproduce dialectal differences to give a realistic, down-to-earth quality to the conversation of their characters. You yourself may at times experiment with dialect expressions when striving for local color or a quaint, folksy touch.

EXERCISES

A. Investigate the regional or dialect uses of the following words. Where necessary, consult an unabridged dictionary: *bannocks, bloke, bonnet, boot, cant* (*vb.*), *complected, coulee, cove, dogie, goober, petrol, power, pram, quid, rant, trolley, tube.*

B. Collect and discuss five expressions that you associate with a particular region or locality.

D 5 Temporal Labels

Some words are no longer in general use or not yet generally established.

When you see a play by a contemporary of Shakespeare or read a sermon preached to the Pilgrim Fathers, you will find words that have since gone out of use or changed in meaning. A complete record of such words can be found in the *Oxford English Dictionary*. Your own dictionary, though less complete, records most of the words you are likely to find in the works of early English and American historians, philosophers, playwrights, and novelists.

D 5a Obsolete Words. *Some words, or meanings of words, have gone out of use altogether.* Such words and meanings are called **obsolete**. Examples of obsolete meanings are the use of *coy* in the sense of "quiet," *curious* in the sense of "careful," *nice* in the sense of "foolish." Explanations of obsolete words and meanings account for most of the bulky footnotes in student editions of early English classics.

D 5b Archaic Words. *Some words or meanings are no longer in common use but still occur in special situations.* Such words are called **archaic**. The King James version of the Bible and the vocabulary of religious devotion preserve many archaisms that were in common use in seventeenth-century England. *Thou* and *thee* for "you," *brethren* for "brothers," and *kine* for "cattle" are familiar examples.

Here are some archaisms familiar to readers of poetry and historical fiction:

anon	(at once)	*fere*	(companion)
brand	(sword)	*forsooth*	(truly)
childe	(aristocratic youth)	*methinks*	(it seems)
erst	(formerly)	*rood*	(cross)
fain	(glad or gladly)	*sprite*	(ghost)

Some words have an old-fashioned flavor even though they may not be labeled archaic in your dictionary. *Albeit* (though), *lief* (gladly), and *threescore* (sixty) would sound quaint in a paper written by a college student.

D 5c Neologisms. *A writer should use new words with caution and restraint.* Newly coined words are called **neologisms**. Occasionally a writer coins an apt and useful word that finds general acceptance. Technological and scientific advances create a constant need for new words, from *typewriter* and *refrigerator* to *cybernetics* and *semantics*.

On the other hand, inexperienced writers sometimes coin new words inadvertently by extending common words analogously to other familiar forms: *vanishment* (analogous to "banishment"); *neglectfulness* (analogous to "bashfulness"). Much awkward, inexact prose suffers from improvisations like *cowardness* (cowardice) and *unpainful* (painless). In addition, journalists and advertisers are constantly inventing terms designed to dazzle their customers. The most popular type is the combination of two familiar words, as in *beautility* (beautiful utility) or *modelovely* (lovely model). Some of these are entertaining, like *Time's phenomoppet* (phenomenal moppet), but many are neither humorous nor ingenious. Words like the following are likely to offend conservative readers:

escapee	outdoorsman
finalize	paperamics
jumboize	personalize
moisturize	usership

EXERCISES

A. Which of the following words (or which of their uses) are archaic? Which are obsolete? *Bower, cark, costermonger, favor, gentle, goodman, hackney, perpend* (vb.), *thorpe, yestreen, ywis.*

B. Read a scene from a play by Shakespeare or by one of his contemporaries. Compile a list of ten words or meanings that have become obsolete, archaic, or old-fashioned. Check in an unabridged dictionary words not listed in your own.

C. Compile a list of ten current advertising terms that you consider neologisms. Indicate those that you think may eventually become standard English and explain why.

D 6 Subject Labels

A term, or one of its several meanings, may be used mainly by specialists and may not be familiar to laymen.

Labels like *Law*, *Naut.* (nautical), or *Mach.* (machinery) are called subject labels. The **technical terminology** or, on a less formal level, the **shoptalk** of a trade or profession makes possible precise and rapid communication among its members but requires careful definition or explanation in writing addressed to the general reader.

NOTE: Some words associated with a specific field have acquired unfavorable associations. *Contact* for "get in touch with," *deal* for "transaction," *feature* for "exhibit" or "offer for sale," and *proposition* for "proposal" are words used primarily by salesmen. Even when used in a noncommercial context, they may carry overtones of the hard sell. *Personnel, domicile,* and *dependents* are used primarily by public officials and administrators. When used in a nonofficial situation, such words suggest impersonality and red tape.

EXERCISES

A. What special fields of interest do the following technical terms represent? Which of the terms would you expect the average high school graduate to know? *A priori, barbican, bend sinister, brochure, calorie, camshaft, crochet, de facto, denouement, epistemology, graupel, hole in one, lien, plinth, solstice, sonata, sprit, symbiosis, tachistoscope, thyroid, transubstantiation, umlaut, valence, venireman, ventricle.*

B. Compile a brief list of important technical terms that you would have to use in describing the characteristic features of one of the following: this year's women's fashions, a complicated mechanism (the engine of a foreign sports car, an electronic brain), one of the traditional styles of architecture (classic, Romanesque, Gothic, baroque), a recent scientific or philosophical theory (theory of relativity, existentialism). Define and explain each of the terms for the interested layman.

D 7 Accurate Words

An effective writer uses accurate words, employs exact shades of meaning.

Effective diction is a matter not only of learning new words but also of making discriminating use of old ones.

D 7a Hit-or-Miss Diction. *Inaccuracy in the use of words often results from lack of time.* Hastily written words may express the intended meaning almost but not quite. Thus, an editorial may start like this: "Only by widespread voting will the desires of the nation be executed on the administrative and legislative levels of our government." There are several inexact expressions here: Orders are "executed," but desires are "realized," "fulfilled," or "complied with." They would be fulfilled not *by* voting but perhaps as a result of it. The main divisions of the United States government are not really "levels" of which one could be more elevated than another, but collateral branches, each with more or less clearly defined and independent authority.

Similar instances of hit-or-miss diction are common in student papers that are merely a hasty first draft rather than a carefully revised final version:

HASTY: *The news* about widespread corruption was first *exposed* by the local press.

REVISED: The news about widespread corruption first *appeared* in the local press. (Evildoers or shortcomings are "exposed," but news about evildoers is "printed," "presented," or "reported.")

Often, inaccurate diction results from a writer's being insensitive to overtones and associations:

HASTY: Life in the suburbs *subjects* a family to the beauties of nature.

REVISED: Life in the suburbs *brings* a family *closer* to the beauties of nature. (The connotations of *subject* are unfavorable; it implies that we are exposed to something unwillingly.)

D 7b Imprecise Connectives. *The relationship between ideas may be obscured by vague all-purpose connectives.* Avoid overusing *and, as,* and *so:*

As—better "because"—we had no money, we gave him a check.
He was growing sideburns *so*—better "so that"—he would look like Valentino.

While is less precise than *whereas* in sentences that point out a contrast:

The administration occupies an ultra-modern building, *while*—better "whereas"—the faculty offices are located in temporary wooden structures.

EXERCISES

A. Make sure you can distinguish between the confusing words in the following pairs: *antic—antique; biography—bibliography; clique—cliché; connive—conspire; difference—deference; ethical—ethnic; feudalism—fatalism; gentle—genteel; literal—literary—literate; manners—mannerisms; sensible—sensitive; specie—species; unfaithful—infidel; venal—venial.*

B. Select the appropriate word.

1. Soldiers and government workers lined the streets; the former in colorful uniforms, the *(1)later/(2)latter* in drab civilian clothes. 2. An important problem facing all of us is the *(3)amount/(4)number* of traffic accidents that occur each day of the week. 3. The March of Dimes was organized to help those *(5)afflicted/(6)inflicted* with infantile paralysis. 4. The chairman *(7)attributed/(8)contributed* the low attendance figures to inadequate publicity. 5. Although he has not yet resigned, his remarks *(9)implied/(10)inferred* that the would shortly do so. 6. One of the things my teachers never *(11) learned/(12)taught* me was how to improve my diction. 7. His fiancée used to tell him that she was too *(13)impracticable/ (14)impractical* to make a good housewife. 8. According to one of the students, the *(15)moral/(16)morale* of Ibsen's play was that a girl should not marry a college professor. 9. The voters can hardly be *(17)credible/(18)credulous* enough to believe some of the things they are told. 10. Arvin had accumulated a small fortune through *(19)judicial/(20)judicious* buying and selling of stocks.

C. Point out and correct examples of inaccurate or unidiomatic diction.

1. He felt that a hands-off policy was the best one for the government to play. 2. A teacher has to be able to handle emotionally disturbed children without bias or ill-favored feelings. 3. Few people accomplish the asset of ignoring gossip circulated about them by thoughtless persons. 4. The United States lost much of the prestige that other countries used to have for her. 5. The support we received from our parent organization has aided greatly to our success. 6. The situation has become drastic and requires immediate action. 7. Nations armed with nuclear weapons will be a constant fear to their less powerful neighbors. 8. In his speech, the mayor suggested several ways of helping the traffic problem. 9. The administration, in exposing the apathy of Congress, has done a great deed to the country. 10. If we accept your theory, our whole concept of democracy will have to make a drastic change. 11. If the new city hall is to serve the whole community, it should be centralized in the city. 12. In an

emergency, some drivers become a panic and freeze to the wheel. 13. Most of our objections to the behavior of other people fall under the generalization of prejudice. 14. Competence alone should be the judge whether a teacher should be allowed to teach or not. 15. In high school many of us never realized the importance that grammar would portray in later life.

D 8 Economy

Effective writing is clear and concise.

An effective writer gets to the point without being weighed down by mere verbiage. He avoids unnecessary repetition. As a rule, a finished paper is the better for some vigorous pruning.

D 8a Redundancy. *Many sentences become redundant through mere careless repetition.* The most easily spotted kind of wordiness is **redundancy**, or unnecessary duplication. The phrase *basic fundamentals* is redundant because *basis* and *foundation* mean very nearly the same thing. *Important essentials* is redundant because something could not be essential and unimportant at the same time.

In the following sentences one or the other way of expressing the same idea should be omitted:

We left *in the morning* at about six o'clock *a.m.*
As a rule, the weather was *usually* warm.
There is more to it than *seems apparent.*
I was given the *choice* of *choosing* whether I wanted to go.
Physically, he has not grown much in *height.*
In my opinion, I think you are right.

NOTE: Colloquial English uses many phrases that show a weakening of etymological meanings. *Continue* means "go on," *refer* means "point back," *eliminate* means "take out." *Continue on, refer back,* and *eliminate out* would be considered redundant in formal situations.

D 8b Padding. *Some words come easily because they say nothing specific.* Look at the word *situation* in the following sentence: "When I first came to Smith College, *there was a situation where* some students lived in better houses than others." This sentence would say the same if shortened to read: "When I first came to Smith College, some students lived in better houses than others." **All-purpose nouns** like *situation, angle, factor, aspect, line,* or *element* are often mere senseless padding:

PADDED: Another *aspect* of the *situation* that needs to be considered is the consumer relations *angle.*
CONCISE: We should also consider consumer relations.

D 8c Economical Transition. *A common cause of wordiness is lack of simple and direct transition from one sentence or one paragraph to another.* Suppose you have said: "Many students feel that liberal-arts courses are impractical." Perhaps you want to continue with an example. Don't say: "*An example of this is the fact that* only five per cent of our freshmen take English literature." Say: "*For example,* only five per cent of our freshmen take English literature."

WORDY: *In considering this situation we must also take into account the fact that* other students do not feel this way.
ECONOMICAL: Others, *however,* do not feel this way.

WORDY: *Taking these factors into consideration, we must conclude that* your request is unjustified.
ECONOMICAL: *Therefore,* your request seems to us unjustified.

EXERCISES

A. Point out and correct examples of wordiness.

1. The reason that married students have high grades academically is that they have a definite goal in the future to come.

2. At the present time, some of today's popular music seems to revert back to music popular thirty years ago. However, in due time a new fad will eventually replace this current craze.

3. The fact that the college forces one to pay for membership in a student organization seems to me a coercion of the student's funds.

4. As far as weather conditions are concerned, the climate of the country is very much like that of my native state.

5. Though many steps toward equal opportunities were taken in the early days of our government's reign, for various reasons the reaching of this goal has been impeded.

6. In the modern world of this day and age, economical operation has become an indispensable condition for business success. The modern businessman knows that he cannot cut expenses by continually adding on new employees to the payroll.

7. As a traveler who has made several trips to Europe of varying lengths of stay, I venture to say that I have reasonable background to discuss the merits of the various different types of transportation now available for travel to Europe.

8. To be right at home in this modern age of today, one should choose a hobby like flying, which is right up to date with the times.

9. The majority of the time the literature of the nineteenth century was didactic in nature.

10. One important factor in the accident situation is the consumption of alcohol by the drinking driver.

B. From your themes, select a paragraph that is wordy. Rewrite it, using more economical and precise diction. Hand in both versions.

D 9 Directness

A writer must know how to be blunt and direct.

At times, a writer will be deliberately indirect for tactical reasons. More common is the kind of careless or self-indulgent indirectness that for no good reason slows down the reader.

D 9a Euphemisms. *Much roundabout diction results from the desire to be elegant.* Refined or impressive names for unpleasant or trivial things are known as **euphemisms**. The most familiar euphemisms are those for elementary facts of human existence:

(birth)	*blessed event; new arrival*
(pregnancy)	*to be expecting; to be in a family way*
(spinsterhood)	*bachelor girl; career woman*
(age)	*senior citizens; the elderly*
(death)	*pass on, expire; the deceased; mortal remains*

Often euphemisms are required by politeness or tact. When referring to people you respect, you will prefer *stout* to *fat*, *intoxicated* to *drunk*, *indolent* to *lazy*, and *remains* to *corpse*. More often, however, euphemisms mislead, or even deliberately deceive. Waitresses become "hostesses," plumbers "sanitary engineers," file clerks "research consultants," undertakers "funeral directors," door-to-door salesmen "customer-contact personnel," and fortune tellers "clairvoyant readers." In much public-relations prose and political propaganda, euphemisms cover up facts that the reader is entitled to know: *straitened financial circumstances* for "bankruptcy"; *planned withdrawal* for "disorganized retreat"; *resettlement* for "forcible expatriation."

NOTE: The use of euphemisms to avoid the repetition of more unpretentious words is called **elegant variation**. A writer describing the habits of the swordfish will rightly feel that repeating the name of the fish in every second sentence would be monotonous. However, his writing will sound strained if he starts using circumlocutions like "scaled creature," "aquatic marauder," "denizen of the deep," and "knight of the brine."

D 9b Jargon. *Much inflated diction results from a writer's using two highbrow words where one lowbrow word would do.* **Jargon**, like the use of euphemisms, reflects the desire to make the trivial seem important. It cultivates an impressive pseudo-scientific air by using indirect, impersonal constructions; by blowing up simple ideas through abstract or roundabout diction; and by seeking out heavy, technical-sounding Latin and Greek terms.

The jargon addict says "Reference was made" rather than "I mentioned"; "the hypothesis suggests itself" rather than "I think." He prefers *effectuate* to "bring about," *hypothesize* to "assume," *magnitude* to "size," *methodology* to "methods," *interrelationship* to "relation." He uses terms like *essential, primary,* and *individual* where no distinction between essential and nonessential, primary and secondary, or individual and society is implied or important. He discusses simple everyday happenings in terms of "factors," "phases," "aspects," "situations," "criteria," "data," "problems," "facets," "phenomena," "structures," "levels," and "strata."

JARGON: Procedures were instituted with a view toward the implementation of the conclusions reached.

PLAIN ENGLISH: We started to put our ideas into practice.

JARGON: Careful consideration of relevant data is imperative before the procedure most conducive toward a realization of the desired outcomes can be determined.

PLAIN ENGLISH: Look before you leap.

D 9c Flowery and Extravagant Diction. *Flowery and extravagant diction interferes with a writer's doing justice to his subject.* Some writers cannot resist the temptation to call a policeman a "minion of the law," an Irishman a "native of the Emerald Isle," a colonist who served in the War of Independence a "gallant warrior defending our infant republic."

FLOWERY: The respite from study was devoted to a sojourn at the ancestral mansion.

PLAIN ENGLISH: I spent the vacation at the house of my grandparents.

FLOWERY: The visitor proved a harbinger of glad tidings.

PLAIN ENGLISH: The visitor brought good news.

In the more showy kinds of journalism, the flowery phrase is supplemented by the journalist's tendency toward exaggeration for dramatic effect. "Crises" are constantly "racing toward a climax," "tragedies" are "stunning" peaceful communities, "daring" new detergents are overjoying housewives by bleaching clothes to a "dazzling" white. Basketball teams "clobber," "bludgeon," and "exterminate" each other; a 250-pound fullback "gambols," "capers," or "romps" to a touchdown; a boxer "slaughters" his opponent. Such **journalese** would sound breathless or juvenile in serious discussion.

EXERCISES

A. Collect five expressions that you consider euphemisms. Explain how they are used and discuss their effect and appropriateness.

B. Translate the following specimens of jargon into plain English.

1. To answer this question without clarification of my rationalizing would be senseless, since there are a great number of determinants that can be expressed pro and con.

2. Being in a profession marks a tangible asset usable as a means of support throughout life, including advancing years.

3. The individual's mental attitude is the factor that seems to make time spent in one geographical location more enjoyable than time spent in another.

4. Finding genuine leadership is a deciding factor in the possibility of the existence of good government.

5. As far as the status of women is concerned, I feel the strong tendency toward domestication in our society will never change, only modify. The physical aspect plays an important part, it being the role of a woman to reproduce the offspring.

6. If an observation of the streets in various cities were to be made, it would reveal a considerable number of situations where traffic is delayed because of congested conditions.

7. Aid along the lines of scholastic achievement and integration into the social group is accorded the younger members of a fraternity by their older brothers.

8. The student commencing matriculation in the institution of his choice should not be subjugated to general education requirements above and beyond the prerequisites stipulated in his major field.

9. The existence or nonexistence of sufficient socio-economic incentives can be presumed to be a major factor in determining the availability of instructional personnel requisite to the successful functioning of the nation's educational establishment.

10. A regular percentage of the remuneration I received was applied toward the purchase of phonograph records.

C. From one of your past or present textbooks, select a passage that you consider jargon. Explain which features of jargon it illustrates.

D. Study the language used by your favorite sports writer, fashion analyst, or society editor. Write a brief report, providing samples of characteristic diction.

D 10 Expressive Language

A writer who has something fresh to say should say it in fresh and expressive language.

Careful word choice can make the difference between vague or colorless language and language that is fresh, graphic, and concrete.

D 10a Specific Words. *A conscientious writer searches for specific and informative words.* Instead of using the colorless, generally applicable term *building,* he will use a more expressive word like *barn, mansion, warehouse, bungalow, shack, workshop,* or *cabin.* Instead of *gadget* or *contraption,* he uses *lid, lever, valve, coil, tube,* or whatever is appropriate.

ALL-PURPOSE: talk

EXPRESSIVE: chat, mumble, coo, whisper, shout, rant, quip, orate, jeer, scold, brag, proclaim, argue, bluster, assert, drone, stammer, blurt

D 10b Figurative Language. *Figurative expressions make writing graphic and colorful by exploiting similarities between different things.* A compressed but explicit comparison, introduced by *as* or *like,* is called a **simile**. An implied comparison that uses one thing or quality as the equivalent of another is called a **metaphor**. Literally, *monkey* refers to a small, long-tailed animal. Metaphorically, it may mean a person who, like a monkey, is agile, mischievous, imitative, or playful.

(1) To be effective, a metaphor *must be apt and unforced.* Avoid figurative expressions that are labored or extravagant:

EXTRAVAGANT: When the average overmothered college student is removed from parental control, the severance of the umbilical cord causes him to bleed to death, psychologically speaking.

(2) When you use more than one figurative expression at a time, the pictures they evoke *should blend in a more or less harmonious whole.* Too often, a writer jumps from picture to picture so rapidly that the reader has trouble keeping up with him. The result is known as the **mixed metaphor**:

MIXED: America's colleges are the key to national survival, and the future of the country lies in their hands.
(The second part of the statement is illogical, because keys do not have hands.)

MIXED: Enriched programs give the good student a chance to dig deeper into the large sea of knowledge.
(Most people do their digging on solid ground rather than at sea.)

D 10c Triteness. *Many phrases that may originally have been vigorous or striking have become trite through overuse.* Such trite phrases are called **clichés**. To the cliché expert, ignorance is always "abysmal," fortitude always "intestinal," necessity always "dire." Daylight is always "broad," silence always "ominous," and old age always "ripe." People make a "clean break" and engage in "honest toil" till the "bitter end." When they make something clear, they make it "crystal clear"; when they wait, they wait "with bated breath"; when they work, they work "by the sweat of their brow"; when they marry, they marry a "blushing bride."

Here are some of the clichés that tend to appear in student writing:

(ex.)

believe it or not
better late than never
beyond the shadow of a doubt
bolt out of the blue
burn the midnight oil
crying shame
easier said than done
the facts of life
few and far between
the finer things
first and foremost
free and easy
get in there and fight
good time was had by all
green with envy
in one fell swoop
in the last analysis
it goes without saying
it stands to reason
last but not least
the last straw
let's face it
malice aforethought
nature's glory
off the beaten track
pride and joy
proud owner (father, mother)
rear its ugly head
rude awakening
a shot in the arm
sink or swim
sneaking suspicion
something tells me
straight and narrow
strike while the iron is hot
to all intents and purposes
truer words were never spoken
truth is stranger than fiction

EXERCISES

A. Comment on the use of figurative language in the following sentences:

1. The student council elections were a fascinating spectacle from the first kick-off to the final curtain.

2. The television audience is becoming more aware of the pitfalls used by advertisers.

3. Descriptions of the average American which are based on statistical evidence tend to be portraits of a statistical meatball, with the lean and the fat all ground together to produce the average man.

4. The man who merely "plays back" what he has heard or read without any understanding of it is not truly educated.

5. Today our industrial giant, streamlined in accordance with the needs of the atomic age, stands on the threshold of a horizon of unlimited prosperity.

6. In this poem, the poet seems to be coming out of a dream-world and stepping into the face of reality.

7. Many American writers now famous made their way in part by feeding the grist of the weekly magazines.

8. The railroads, once a powerful force in the nation's economy, have been rapidly losing headway in recent decades.

9. Americans revere their constitution, because the birth of their country was founded from its pages.

10. Coming at a point when our country faces a serious re-appraisal of our policy toward Latin America, this timely book fills a much-needed void.

11. Neither of the major characters in the play turned out to be a pillar of moral fiber.

12. Scientific progress is a stream that owes its strength to many tributaries.

13. Africa is on the brink of television, and in one fantastic giant step the Dark Continent will be hurtled from the tom-tom to the television screen.

B. Compile a list of ten clichés widely used in news reporting, in campaign oratory, or in advertising. What explains their popularity?

C. (**Review**) Examine and evaluate the diction of each of the following passages. Point out features that limit their effectiveness or appropriateness.

1. For some people the cartoons shown at the theaters are the high spot of the program. The majority of these people is the children. The slapstick comedy affords loads of laughs to the younger folks. However, the cartoons have more than a little effect on the older people too. Sometimes this effect is negative, and sometimes it is positive. The main criticism against the cartoons is that they are so completely abstract and ridiculous. For those people who enjoy the cartoons, the abstractness is the backbone of their favoritism.

2. Alpha Tau Omega's hopes for the local basketball championship were put to what the chemistry kids call the acid test

last night. A tall gang of Pi Alpha Kappa cagers staged a tremendous second half point-scoring spree to wallop the ATO underlings and win the intramural basketball crown. ATO's glaring lack of rebounding strength told the tale in the second half, as the champs made a farce of it by canning 43 points while holding the small hustling ATO's to but 18 counters. After ATO held a razor-thin halftime lead, PAK's Glen Abel, who until recently was in drydock with a pulled leg muscle, led the offensive surge and the PAK's were off to the races.

3. Tax money is just a great big beautiful hunk of coin toward which few persons in government feel the slightest moral responsibility. It means a bigger and faster gravy train, a better pork barrel, and more pie in the sky, and not by-and-by. It means further funds to be whacked up among the ever more powerful blocs that scratch each other's respective backs and operate in and around government. Everyone is in there getting his, and never mind that poor faceless slob, the taxpayer, with the achin' back.

4. We think of our audio-visual program as a method or medium, not as an end in itself. For example, a curriculum committee at its inception does not necessarily include a visual-aids representative. However, following the formulation of general philosophy and basic content, visual aids become an active and integral part of curriculum organization. The materials available then serve in many ways to orient and implement the program. The individual teacher is responsible for enriching the individual learning situation through the preplanned utilization of visual materials that vitalize interest. The principal must provide for physical and monetary aspects. But perhaps the greatest contributing factor to the success of the program is provision for continuous growth. Our concentration of effort is on individual evaluations of materials immediately following their use. This is further implemented by periodic evaluations by groups, on the vertical and horizontal grade-level basis.

5. Whistling Dick waited as long as his judgment advised, and then slid swiftly to the ground. Assuming as far as possible the air of an honest laborer who seeks his daily toil, he moved across the network of railway lines, with the intention of

making his way by quiet Girod Street to a certain bench in Lafayette Square, where, according to appointment, he hoped to rejoin a pal known as "Slick," this adventurous pilgrim having preceded him by one day in a cattle-car into which a loose slat had enticed him.—O. Henry, "Whistling Dick's Christmas Stocking"

3

SENTENCE STYLE

A paper may be tiring to read even if it contains no obvious deviations from standard usage. It may suffer from awkwardness, indirectness, misplaced emphasis, and monotony. To cure these defects, the writer has to be able to recognize grammatical patterns. The defects themselves, however, are not so much a matter of grammar as of **style**. Attention to style makes the difference between writing that is easy to grasp and easy to remember, and writing that is easy on the writer but hard on the reader.

Generalizations about effective style are necessarily tentative and inconclusive. You will have to rely primarily on a kind of sixth sense that comes from careful reading. You will have to become aware of variations in sentence length, of different ways in which clauses combine to form sentences, of the ways in which sentence patterns vary and repeat themselves.

S 1 Word Order

A writer should learn to exploit the resources of English word order for variety and emphasis.

Word order can become monotonous when repeated in sentence after sentence without change; it can become awkward when changed without good reason.

S 1a Varied Word Order. *Variations from normal word order can keep sentences from being tiresomely alike.* Though the great majority of your sentences will follow the subject-verb sequence, there will usually be enough variety in the remaining sentence elements to prevent tiresome repetition. Monotony is most likely to result when a number of sentences start with the same subject, especially a pronoun like *I* or *he:*

MONOTONOUS: He reversed the direction of the canoe. . . . He stopped paddling. . . . He made the canoe drift close to the bank. . . . He grabbed one of the overhanging branches. . . . He tied a piece of rope around one of the trunks. . . . He picked up his jacket. . . . He leaped ashore.

(1) One way to break up a monotonous sequence is to *make a modifier that usually occurs later in the sentence precede the subject.* Like all stylistic effects, the **introductory modifier** can become an annoying mannerism if overused. Used sparingly, it becomes a reliable way of introducing variety into a group of plodding sentences:

VARIED: He reversed the direction of the canoe. *After a few seconds* he stopped paddling. *Slowly* he made the canoe drift to the bank. *When within a yard of the shore,* he grabbed one of the overhanging branches.

VARIED: The Trans World Terminal stems from the work of contemporary architects like Corbusier of France and Nervi of Italy, masters of the curve in concrete. *Like a true eagle,* this building is all curves and muscle, no right angles. *Built of reinforced concrete,* the whole structure swoops and turns and rises.—Ken Macrorie, "Arriving and Departing," *The Reporter*

(2) A less frequent variation from normal word order is to *make a verb precede its subject.* The subject-verb sequence is usually reversed only in questions, where all or part of the verb characteristically precedes the subject: "*Are* you ready?" "*Will* he *be* back?" "Why *did* your wife *leave* the car?" Writers aiming at poetic or dramatic effects occasionally use **inversion** even in ordinary declarative sentences:

Slowly *climbs* the summer moon.
Everywhere *was* silence.

S 1b Emphatic Word Order. *Variations from normal word order can direct attention to the word or phrase occurring in an unusual position.*

(1) To gain emphasis, a writer may *shift a complement to a more emphatic initial position.* The **introductory complement** is normal in exclamations beginning with *what* or *how:* "*What stories* that man told!" "*What a liar* you are!" "*How true* that is!" In other situations, the introductory complement is effective especially when it takes up something mentioned earlier:

EFFECTIVE: The committee has asked me to resign. *That* I will never do.

EFFECTIVE: Mr. Schlumpf fried two small pieces of fish. *One of these* he fed to his cat. *The other* he ate himself.

EFFECTIVE: We really should not resent being called paupers. *Paupers* we are, and *paupers* we shall remain.

NOTE: Like other attention-getting devices, the introductory complement sometimes attracts attention to the speaker rather than to what he is saying. Sometimes the construction smacks of old-fashioned oratory:

More patient wife a husband never had.
Gone are the days of my youth.
Such deeds of glory we shall see no more.

(2) Often a sentence becomes clearer after you *shift the predicate of the main clause toward the end* and work some of the modifiers into the sentence as interrupters. Such treatment may strengthen a sentence especially if a **final modifier** is a belated qualification or concession:

WEAK: We shall never dismiss a teacher because of the political beliefs of his associates without careful investigation. (*Without careful investigation* is a lame reversal of what starts out as a strong statement in support of teachers with controversial associations.)

IMPROVED: We shall never, *without careful investigation,* dismiss a teacher because of the political beliefs of his associates.

WEAK: Richard Wagner became one of the most successful composers of all time in spite of the jeers of his contemporaries. (This version may make your readers remember the jeers rather than the man's success.)

IMPROVED: Richard Wagner, *though jeered at by his contemporaries,* became one of the most successful composers of all time.

NOTE: Sentences that make the ending of the sentence coincide with the ending of the main clause are known as **periodic** sentences. Sentences that complete the main statement first and then add various secondary elements are known as **loose** sentences:

PERIODIC: Having lost the position he had held for twenty-five years, *Harry became unbearably depressed.*

LOOSE: *Harry became unbearably depressed* after he lost the position he had held for twenty-five years.

Long periodic sentences often seem formal and deliberate; they look as though they were carefully planned. Long loose sentences often seem natural and relaxed; they look as if they just grew:

LOOSE: Bird-watchers were once figures of fun and they are still good for a laugh in *New Yorker* cartoons but they are so numerous and often so highly placed that they might protest against "offensive stereotypes" as effectively as the other large minorities—racial, national, and religious

—so vociferously do.—Joseph Wood Krutch, "If You Don't Mind My Saying So . . . ," *The American Scholar*

S 1c Awkward Word Order. *Unintentional variations from normal word order may result in awkward sentences.* Many students compose their sentences a phrase at a time. The result often sounds awkward and synthetic:

AWKWARD: The committee was to meet him *in the morning* at the station.
IMPROVED: The committee was to meet him at the station *in the morning.*

Here awkwardness resulted from a violation of the general tendency in English sentences to make place modifiers precede time modifiers. Usually, however, the reasons for awkward word order are difficult to schematize. You will often have to rely on the kind of sentence sense that a competent writer develops through careful listening and reading.

S 2 Awkward Construction

A writer should avoid constructions that make for an indirect, awkward, wooden style.

A special problem in student writing is the overuse of constructions that change the relationships existing within the normal subject-verb-complement pattern.

S 2a Awkward Passive. Students often make their writing awkward and indirect by overusing the **passive**, which looks at an action from the point of view not of the actor or agent but of the target or recipient.

(1) *The passive can serve to pull an object into an emphatic initial position.* Compare the changes in emphasis in the following sentences:

ACTIVE: The general gave many an actress a sports car.
PASSIVE: *Many an actress* was given a sports car by the general.
PASSIVE: *Many a sports car* was given to actresses by the general.

As a result, the passive is often the most appropriate construction when the *recipient or target of an action seems more important than the performer:*

The unpretentious monarchs of Scandinavia and the Low Countries are respectfully accepted by their sober subjects.—Kingsley Martin, "Strange Interlude," *Atlantic*

When no special emphasis is intended, the passive is most appropriate when the *originator or the performer of an action is unimportant, irrelevant,* or *hard to identify:*

Some of John's brain cells *were damaged* when he was a small child.
In World War II, millions of people *were driven* from their homes.

(2) *Reversing the actor-action-target perspective when the actor is important may create an upside-down effect.* It often makes necessary a kind of mental translation:

AWKWARD: Preparations *are being made* by the freshman class for a picnic at Wallflower Lake.
IMPROVED: The freshman class *is planning* a picnic at Wallflower Lake.

(3) *Since it shifts attention away from the agent or performer, the passive tends to be indirect.* The reader may find it hard to determine the person responsible for a statement or an idea:

EVASIVE: A plan for popular election of Supreme Court justices *is* now *being advanced.*

Advanced by whom? The passive spreads a protective cloak of anonymity around the authors of the proposal.

NOTE: Students sometimes use the chopped-off passive from false modesty. "Here *are presented* some of the underlying fundamentals of football" usually means "I am going to explain football."

S 2b Impersonal Constructions. The impersonal *one,* the *it* without antecedent, and *there-is* or *there-are* constructions are most appropriate when the identity of persons or forces initiating an action is of secondary importance. We naturally say "it rains" or "it snows" when we are interested in the process and its results rather than in its causes.

(1) *Impersonal constructions are annoying when they unnecessarily obscure the identity of the forces at work.* The **impersonal one** is often a tiresome substitute for fuller identification of the persons concerned, especially if their identity is indirectly revealed by modifiers:

TIRESOME: *When teaching, one* should be patient.
IMPROVED: *Teachers* should be patient.

TIRESOME: *As a father, one* should not spoil his children.
IMPROVED: *Fathers* should not spoil their children.

TIRESOME: *If one is a citizen of a democracy, he* should exercise his voting rights.
IMPROVED: *A citizen of a democracy* should vote.

(2) *In "it-is" and "there-is" sentences, the first two words are mere structural props, which can make the sentences sound lame and indecisive.* Sometimes the subject of a sentence receives needed emphasis if it is introduced by *it is* or *there is* and has its predicate changed into a modifying clause:

EMPHATIC: It is *his competence* that we question—not his honesty.

However, more often the rearrangement of sentence elements made necessary by *it is* or *there is* causes awkwardness:

AWKWARD: In 1958, *there was* a strike participated in by five thousand union members.
IMPROVED: In 1958, five thousand union members went on strike.

S 2c Excessive Use of Nouns. *A characteristic feature of much contemporary jargon is overuse of nouns.*

(1) If *actions, events, and activities frequently appear as nouns* rather than verbs, writing becomes static and opaque:

STATIC: *Violent arguments* frequently took place.
IMPROVED: We often *argued violently*.

STATIC: A certain *element of confusion* was present.
IMPROVED: He *confused* me.

STATIC: A *criticism* which is prevalent against modern poetry is that its *appeal* is to the super-sophisticated.
IMPROVED: Many critics *charge* that modern poetry *appeals* only to the super-sophisticated.

STATIC: The *solution* to the problem was the result of a careful *examination* of available records.
IMPROVED: We *solved* the problem by carefully *examining* available records.

(2) Much bureaucratic writing owes its lumpy quality to its frequent use of *nouns as modifiers preceding another noun.* Often an adjective or a prepositional phrase would make for more natural or more fluent English:

AWKWARD: The report cards record the child's *school* and *activities* achievement.
IMPROVED: The report cards record the child's *academic* and *social* performance.

AWKWARD: At Kilby College the *student-teacher* relationship was exceptionally cordial.

IMPROVED: At Kilby College the relationship *between students and teachers* was exceptionally cordial.

EXERCISES

A. Write three sentences showing normal word order. Then rewrite each sentence showing several possible variations in emphasis or perspective.

EXAMPLE: An old man taught the boy chess on a hot afternoon.

(introd. modifier)	*On a hot afternoon,* an old man taught the boy chess.
(introd. complement)	*Chess* an old man taught the boy on a hot afternoon.
(*there-is*)	*There was* an old man *teaching* the boy chess on a hot afternoon.
(first passive)	*The boy was taught* chess by an old man on a hot afternoon.
(second passive)	*Chess was taught* to the boy by an old man on a hot afternoon.

B. Revise the following sentences to eliminate excessive or awkward use of nouns.

1. A conscientious teacher's satisfaction is incomplete unless he reaches a full realization of his goals. 2. The public schools must serve personal and society needs as they evolve. 3. My high school teachers never analyzed my essays from the structural and content point of view. 4. A plan for safe driving is of no use if the cooperation of the individual driver is not present. 5. The accumulation of pressures to conform is so great that the student is in constant awareness of their presence. 6. The new dean will need a few days to acquaint himself with the school's administration procedures. 7. The conclusion is inevitable that there has been a considerable impairment of our country's military strength. 8. There were repeated interruptions of the deliberations of the committee.

S 3 Sentence Building

A writer should make effective use of variations in sentence length and exploit the resources of coordination and subordination.

Word order and grammatical perspective have a bearing on the effectiveness even of simple sentences consisting of only one clause. Other problems of style become important when several clauses combine to form more complicated sentences.

S 3a Sentence Length. *A skillful writer maintains at least some variety in the length of his sentences.*

(1) Excessive use of *short, isolated clauses* can make your writing sound immature. The more you develop your capacity for sustained thinking, the more you will get away from clauses like the following:

CHOPPY: Many teachers can give students information. Very few can inspire students to learn. Information is of little use to the student. Soon he will leave college. Then he will forget what he has memorized. He must be inspired to learn on his own.

IMPROVED: Many teachers can give students information, but few can inspire them to learn. When a student leaves college, the information he has memorized will be of little use and will soon be forgotten. What he needs most is the ability to learn on his own.

NOTE: Sentence length in itself does not guarantee maturity of thought. If a steady succession of short sentences can seem breathless and childish, a steady succession of long sentences can seem rambling and undisciplined.

(2) A complex, elaborate sentence is often appropriate for

detailed explanation or argument. A short, incisive sentence is often appropriate for a *summary of key ideas:*

ELABORATE: Though the tobacco industry has been understandably reluctant to admit it, all the evidence now available points to the conclusion that smoking may be a major threat to the health of our people.

INCISIVE: Smoking is a threat to health.

Your writing will gain in clarity and emphasis if you occasionally make your reader stop at a *concise, memorable statement of an important point.* Notice the emphatic short sentences in the following passages:

With the great growth in leisure-time activities, millions of Americans are turning to water sports: fishing, swimming, water skiing, and skin diving. *Clean water exhilarates and relaxes.*—Vance Packard, "America the Beautiful—and Its Desecraters," *Atlantic*

Bennett was always facing the wonder of the actualities of living. It was wonderful to him that we live as we do, that time will pass and change us, that we will die and perhaps die painfully, that life is what it is. *He never decorates or embroiders. He is wholly materialistic. Common sense is the salt of his plate.* We are never swept away, but we are curiously won over, and we, too, are filled with wonder at the slow unspinning of life.—John Van Druten, "My Debt to Arnold Bennett," *Saturday Review*

(3) A short sentence can be especially effective if it sets off an important conclusion or a *key observation at the end of a passage composed of longer sentences:*

They have a constitutional right, of course, to tell us what we must do to be saved; as they have always done. Twenty years ago they were telling us the direct opposite of what they tell us now; but they were just as sure then as now that they had the sole and sufficient key to salvation, and that those who did not accept it were forever damned. *One becomes bored.*—Elmer Davis, "History in Doublethink, *Saturday Review*

S 3b Effective Coordination. *Coordination is most appropriate when related ideas are about equally important.* In sentences like the following, both clauses are about equally relevant to the general trend of the report, narrative, or argument:

We tried to locate the files, *but* we were unsuccessful.

We shall have to build several new classrooms, *for* we expect a large increase in the school-age population.

Our press is essentially provincial in this country, *and* except for a few syndicated columnists the reputation of our newspapermen is mainly local.

(1) *Excessive use of coordination* suggests a failure to examine the relative importance of ideas. *And,* for instance, merely adds without indicating any specific relationship; it does not prepare the reader for what is coming:

RAMBLING: A member of the Reserve has to participate in weekly drills, *and* it may be called up in emergencies, which came as an unpleasant surprise to me during the Korean war, *and* so you would do better to stay away from it.

(2) If you doubt the appropriateness of a coordinating connective like *and* or *but,* test the sentence by inserting a parenthetical "equally important":

EFFECTIVE: Each member of the group received a monthly living allowance, *and* (equally important) his four-year college course was paid for in full by the Navy.

EFFECTIVE: Under one of the plans, a reservist spends only six months on active duty, *but* (equally important) he remains in the Ready Reserve for seven and one-half years.

S 3c Effective Subordination. *Subordination is most appropriate when details, reasons, or qualifications accompany a main point.* Subordinating connectives (*when, while, since, because, if, though*) and relative pronouns (*who, which,* and *that*) can make the material they subordinate seem of secondary importance.

(1) Effective subordination *clarifies relationships in a sentence.* Merely placed next to each other, the following two statements may seem disjointed: "Kroger organized a counterfeiting ring. He had studied printing in Germany." When one is subordinated to the other, the connection between them becomes clearer:

EFFECTIVE: Kroger, *who had studied printing in Germany,* organized a counterfeiting ring.

Coordinated by *but,* the following *two* statements leave the relationship between fishing and strong wind vague: "We spent the days fishing, but sometimes there was a strong wind." The subordinating connective *unless* leaves no doubt about the relationship:

EFFECTIVE: We spent the days fishing *unless there was a strong wind.*

(2) Unskillful subordination *blurs emphasis.* "*I was ten* when we moved to Alaska" focuses the reader's attention on you and your age. "When I was ten, *we moved to Alaska*" focuses the reader's attention on Alaska. **Upside-down subordination** results when the wrong item seems to stand out. When

tucked away in a subordinate part of a sentence, important information may catch the reader unaware and, as a result, have an ironic effect:

UPSIDE-DOWN: The salary was considered good by local standards, *though* it was not enough to feed and clothe my family.

IMPROVED: *Though* considered good by local standards, my salary was not enough to feed and clothe my family.

UPSIDE-DOWN: He had a completely accident-free record up to the last day of his employment, *when* he stepped on a power line and almost lost his life.

IMPROVED: On the last day of his employment, *after* ten years without a single accident, he stepped on a power line and almost lost his life.

S 3d Effective Modifiers. *Part of the secret of effective prose is skillful use of modifying words and phrases where an inexperienced writer might use coordinated and subordinated clauses.* Observe the tightening of relationships and the gain in continuity in the following pairs:

ROUTINE: She had shiny eyes, an upturned nose, and a lively mouth, and her face never seemed to be at rest.

EFFECTIVE: Her face, *with its ever-shining eyes, its up-turned nose, and mobile mouth,* was never in repose.—John Mason Brown, "Blithe Spirit," *Saturday Review*

ROUTINE: We caught two bass. We hauled them in briskly, as though they were mackerel. After we pulled them over the side of the boat, we stunned them with a blow on the back of the head.

EFFECTIVE: We caught two bass, *hauling them in briskly* as though they were mackerel, *pulling them over the side of the boat* in a businesslike manner without any landing net, and *stunning them with a blow on the back of the head.*—E. B. White. *One Man's Meat*

EXERCISE

Write three pairs of related clauses. Then combine each pair in different ways, illustrating different possibilities of coordination and subordination.

EXAMPLE: The spring rains were heavy. The weeds grew at a furious rate.
The spring rains were heavy, *and* the weeds grew at a furious rate.
The weeds grew at a furious rate, *for* the spring rains were heavy.
Because the spring rains were heavy, the weeds grew at a furious rate.
The spring rains being heavy, the weeds grew at a furious rate.
The weeds, *with the spring rains heavy,* grew at a furious rate.

S 4 Sentence Overloads

Sentence overloads result when a writer becomes entangled in cumbersome grammatical machinery.

Effective sentences may be long and complicated, as long as the words and structural relationships convey meaning clearly and directly. On the other hand, the grammatical equipment even in relatively short sentences may become so heavy that it interferes with effective communication.

S 4a Deadwood. *Often a sentence proceeds more smoothly after it has been pruned of deadwood.* Avoid unnecessary *there are*'s and *who were*'s:

AWKWARD: *There are* many farmers in the area *who* are planning to attend the meeting *which is* scheduled for next Friday.

IMPROVED: Many farmers in the area are planning to attend the meeting scheduled for next Friday.

Other sentences can be cleared of deadwood by effective use of pronouns:

AWKWARD: A child of pre-school age often shows a desire to read, but *the child's* parents often ignore this *desire*.
IMPROVED: Often a child of pre-school age shows a desire to read —*which his* parents ignore.

Some connectives, prepositions, and pronouns are unnecessary or unnecessarily heavy:

AWKWARD: I wrote little, *because of the fact that* my childhood had been *an* uneventful *one*.
IMPROVED: I wrote little, because my childhood had been uneventful.

S 4b Excessive Subordination. *Excessive subordination causes various types of overburdened sentences.*

(1) One common type *dovetails several dependent clauses into each other,* thus making a subordinating connective follow another subordinating connective or a relative pronoun. The resulting ***that-if, if-because, which-when*** **constructions** need not be awkward, but they almost always are when used by inexperienced writers:

AWKWARD: I think *that if* there were less emphasis on conformity in high school, college students would be better prepared for independent thinking.
IMPROVED: In my opinion, college students would be better prepared for independent thinking *if* there were less emphasis on conformity in high school.

AWKWARD: I am against football scholarships *because if* football players are given preferential treatment, who will want to participate in other college sports?

IMPROVED: I am against football scholarships. *If* football players are given preferential treatment, who will want to participate in other college sports?

(2) Another type of excessive subordination results in **"house-that-Jack-built" sentences**. Several dependent clauses of the same type follow each other, making the sentence trail off into *a confusing succession of modifiers:*

AWKWARD: When I was in Mexico City, I visited Jean, *who* was living with a Mexican girl *who* posed for the local artists, *who* are usually too poor to pay their rent, let alone the model's fee.

IMPROVED: When I was in Mexico City, I visited Jean. She was living with a Mexican girl *who* posed for the local artists but seldom received any money for her work. Most Mexican artists are too poor to pay their rent, let alone the model's fee.

AWKWARD: We had to rely on home-brewed beverages *because* the well had run dry *because* it was a very hot summer.

IMPROVED: We had to rely on home-brewed beverages *because* it was a very hot summer and the well had run dry.

Sometimes too many dependent clauses of the same type delay the main clause:

AWKWARD: *When* a child is constantly watched *when* he is born and *while* he is a baby, the reason is that his mother wants to see whether he is developing as her books say he should.

IMPROVED: Some mothers constantly watch young children to see whether they are developing as the books say they should.

(3) Unskillful subordination sometimes causes sentences with a teeter-totter effect. Such **seesaw sentences** start with a dependent clause, proceed to the main clause, and then add a

second dependent clause that in a confusing way qualifies the meaning of the first:

CONFUSING: *If you are a good boy,* I'll buy you an ice-cream cone *if I can spare the money.*

CLEARER: *If you are a good boy,* I might buy you an ice-cream cone. *However,* I'm not sure I can spare the money.

CONFUSING: *Because many teen-agers marry hastily,* their marriages end in divorce, *because they are too immature to face adult responsibilities.*

CLEARER: Many teen-agers are too immature to face adult responsibilities. They marry hastily, and often their marriages end in divorce.

S 4c Awkward Modifiers. *Awkwardness results when disproportionately heavy modifiers break up the pattern of a clause.* Lengthy appositives, complicated verbal phrases, or clumsy dependent clauses sometimes separate elements that belong together:

AWKWARD: The pilot told his friends that he had flown Clinton Morris, *a resident of New York City sought by the government for income tax evasion,* out of the United States.

AWKWARD: The club treasurer, *being* the son of a father constantly *stressing* the importance of *maintaining* a proper sense of the value of money, refused to pay our expenses.

AWKWARD: In 1943, Independence Hall, *which had been the first building built on the campus and which had housed the administration of the college for many decades,* was torn down.

NOTE: The exact line between just enough and too much is hard to draw. Successful authors sometimes use sentences that would trip up a writer with a less sure touch:

The boys in his books got ahead by outwitting thieves and sharpers—yet he himself, a mild and generous little man who gave freely of his earnings to newsboys and bootblacks on the New York streets (the sort of boys who were his favorite heores), was an easy mark for impostors.—Frederick Lewis Allen, "Horatio Alger, Jr.," *Saturday Review*

S 5 Repetition

A writer must learn to make effective use of repetition and parallelism.

Unintentional, haphazard repetition can make a passage sound clumsy. Deliberate repetition, on the other hand, can emphasize important points and give continuity to a sentence or a paragraph.

S 5a Awkward Repetition. *Unintentional repetition of sounds, syllables, words, or phrases violates the requirements of* **euphony**. A passage should sound pleasing, or at least inoffensive, when read aloud. Carelessly repeated sounds grate on the reader's ears:

AWKWARD: Congress *str*engthened the laws re*str*icting the right to *str*ike.
IMPROVED: Congress bolstered the laws qualifying the right to strike.

AWKWARD: Commercials seldom make for entertain*ing* and relax*ing* listen*ing*.
IMPROVED: Commercials seldom entertain and relax the listener.

AWKWARD: Close examin*ation* of the results of the investig*ation* led to a reorganiz*ation* of the department.
IMPROVED: Close study of the results of the inquiry led to a reorganization of the department.

AWKWARD: We listened to an account *of* the customs *of* the inhabitants *of* the village.
IMPROVED: We listened to an account of the villagers' customs.

Unintentional repetition is especially annoying when the similarity in sound covers up a *shift in meaning or relationship:*

My father lost his savings during the depression because he had *banked* on—better "relied on"—the well-established reputation of our hometown *bank.*

S 5b Emphatic Repetition. *Intentional repetition makes for clarity and continuity.* A writer may repeat important words and phrases for emphasis:

EMPHATIC: When I returned to State, *I studied* as I have never studied since. *I studied* before classes. *I studied* after classes. *I studied* till English, history, and zoology merged into one blurry mass of incoherent erudition.

EMPHATIC: In my mother's world, *no one ever* shrugged his shoulders; *no one* was *ever* bored and lazy; *no one* was *ever* cynical; *no one ever laughed.*—Alfred Kazin, "The Bitter 30's," *Atlantic*

More often, a writer will make use of parallel structure, *drawing together related elements by repeating characteristic grammatical patterns.* The following passage makes effective use of **parallelism**:

The air *must be* pure *if we are to* breathe; the soil *must be* arable *if we are to* eat; the water *must be* clean *if we are to* drink.

In prose of exposition and argument, repetition and parallel structure are used for some of the following purposes:

(1) Parallel structure helps to *line up related ideas in a sentence;* it *draws together related ideas in a paragraph:*

When the world wars came, the people of the liberal democracies could not be aroused to the exertions and the sacrifices of the struggle until they *had been frightened by* the opening disasters, *had been incited to* passionate hatred, and *had become intoxicated with* unlimited hope.

The people wanted to be told that when this particular enemy had been forced to unconditional surrender, they would re-enter the golden age. *This* unique *war would end* all wars. *This* last *war would make* the world safe for democracy. *This crusade would make* the whole world a democracy.—Walter Lippmann, *The Public Philosophy*

(2) Often, parallel structure helps to *line up dissimilar ideas for comparison or contrast:*

His remarks provoked much comment, *self-righteous from his enemies, apologetic from his friends.*

Whereas *it is desirable that* the old *should treat with respect* the wishes of the young, *it is not desirable that* the young *should treat with respect* the wishes of the old.

The European democracies *chose to rely* on unarmed appeasement, and the American democracy *chose to rely on* unarmed isolation.

(3) Parallel structure enables a writer to *make a series of parallel sentences build up to a* **climax**. Notice how the author of the following passage starts with fairly innocuous generalities and leads up to a specific point dear to his heart:

The future *is not for little* men with little minds. It *is not for* men without vision who fear progress. It *is not for* timid men who early were frightened by the story of Frankenstein. And it *is not for* those arch reactionaries who seek to shatter big enterprise and to force American industry back into the puny production patterns of its nineteenth-century infancy.

S 5c Rhythm and Balance. *Frequent use of parallel constructions makes for regularity and balance, especially when the parallel elements are of approximately equal* *length.* Parallelism produces rhythmical patterns that are more distinctly felt than the highly variable rhythms of ordinary speech.

(1) A writer with an ear for rhythm makes use of the *variations* in sentence structure that prevent regularity from becoming predictable. In the following sentence the *which*-clause separating the subject and verb of the main clause makes for variety, while the prepositional phrases (*with remarkable vistas . . . , with weeping birches . . .*) make for balance:

> Seattle, *which sits like Rome on seven hills,* was endowed by nature *with remarkable vistas* of water and mountains, *with weeping birches and monkey trees and dogwoods* big as maples.—Russell Lynes, "Seattle Will Never Be the Same," *Harper's*

Notice the role of variety and balance in the following passage:

> India *is a poetic nation, yet it demands* new electrical plants. It *is a mystical nation, yet it wants* new roads. It *is* traditionally *a peaceful nation, yet it could,* if misled, *inflame* Asia.—James A. Michener, "Portaits for the Future," *Saturday Review*

There is just enough variation to keep the repetition of the pattern from becoming monotonous: "poetic—mystical—traditionally peaceful"; "demands—wants—could, if misled, inflame."

(2) The prose of a writer with a strong sense of rhythm often has a *musical quality.* Here is a passage whose rhythm is exceptionally stately and elaborate:

> *That* Man is the product of causes which had no prevision of the end they were achieving; *that* his *origin,* his *growth,* his *hopes and fears,* his *loves and* his *beliefs,* are but the outcome of accidental collocations of atoms; *that* no *fire,* no *heroism,* no *intensity of thought and feeling,* can preserve an individual life beyond the grave; *that* all *the labours* of the ages, all *the devotion,* all *the inspiration,* all *the noonday brightness* of human genius, are destined to extinction in the vast death of the solar system, and *that* the

whole temple of Man's achievement must inevitably be buried beneath the débris of a universe in ruins—all these things, if *not quite beyond dispute,* are *yet so nearly certain,* that no philosophy which rejects them can hope to stand. *Only within the scaffolding of* these truths, *only on the firm foundation of* unyielding depair, can the soul's habitation henceforth be safely built.—Bertrand Russell, *Mysticism and Logic*

The long series of noun clauses making up most of the first sentence, and the multiple subjects in most of them, are the most obvious instances of parallelism. Toward the end of the passage there are several pairs of neatly balanced phrases (*if not quite beyond dispute—yet so nearly certain; only within the scaffolding of these truths—only on the firm foundation of unyielding despair*).

NOTE: Like other stylistic devices, patterns that make for euphony and balance are most effective when the reader responds to them without becoming consciously aware of them. Today, workaday expository prose avoids elaborate parallelism and obtrusive rhythm.

EXERCISES

A. (**Review**) Which of the following sentences suffer from obvious stylistic defects? If your instructor desires, rewrite weak sentences to make them clearer, more coherent, more direct, or more emphatic.

> 1. My father came from a wealthy family, and my mother came from a very poor home, and it was strange that she held the purse strings in the family. 2. The magazine that is chosen by the reader is one that contains articles that the reader enjoys. 3. The contribution of the alumni to the growth of the college will be in proportion to their information about its educational situation. 4. The natural environment of the college, atop beautiful rolling hills, is the kind that a benevolent Providence must have created to induce men to quiet reflection. 5. A child's first impressions of peo-

ple and places shape the course of his future life, frequently. 6. One incident which I remember vividly is the time when all three of us children had committed the same offense but my younger sister, who was very sensitive to disapproval, criticism, and pain suffered by others, was spared a spanking because after watching my brother and me being punished besides being scolded first was crying so hard and had learned her lesson so well that it wasn't necessary. 7. Knowing the right answers is sometimes less important than asking the right questions. 8. As we left the city, we approached a range of hills which seemed like giant waves which were about to break. 9. Having brothers and sisters to argue with and to adjust to was a useful experience because it helped me understand other people, because I don't always meet people sharing all my opinions. 10. John Milton was the first English writer who clearly and convincingly stated the idea that incompatibility is grounds for divorce, if I am not mistaken. 11. His grandfather had left Haiti because of the constant threat of revolution, the abnormally high disease rate, and the mosquitoes. 12. If a student wants a gay social life and a sense of belonging, he should try to join a Greek organization if he feels confident that he will be accepted. 13. There are many ways in which a student who is interested in meeting a foreign student may come to know one. 14. Is the child who after he has spent the afternoon at the movies spends the evening watching television and goes to bed late at night (this is the daily routine of many children I know) leading a healthier life than the boy who would climb up into a tree to read *Robinson Crusoe?* 15. Warren believed in applauding politely to reward effort, generously to reward competence, and frenetically to reward genius.

B. Examine the following paragraphs for sentence style. Point out weaknesses or strengths. Suggest improvements where necessary.

1. The monkey family is large. It includes monkeys, baboons, lemurs, and apes. The animals in the monkey family are closely related to man. They are imitative. They can be trained to perform simple tasks. However, their intelligence is low.

2. We go to our libraries in order to read and take advantage of the experiences of others. I think we all realize that not every written word in a library is entirely true. Many different authors have here written what they think, what they have experienced, what they believe is true, and sometimes what they wish were true. Some are wrong, a few are right, and many are neither entirely wrong nor entirely right.

3. Many high school teachers follow a textbook word for word, and they go over each page until everyone understands it. In college, many teachers just tell the student to read the textbook, and then they start giving lectures on the material covered in the text, but they don't follow it word for word.

4. A good example of a topic drawn from personal experience is a bus accident I once had. I wrote a paper about this experience of mine. I remembered the events which took place during the accident. I could describe them well. After all, I had experienced them. It was a shocking experience. I will never forget it. The facts stand out in my memory because it was so shocking.

5. In high school, the student finds that his teachers act like parents toward him—always nagging. One moment it's "You're growing up now; you should know better." The next moment it's "I'm sorry, but you know perfectly well you aren't old enough." What is the teen-ager supposed to do?

C. Examine the following passages for sentence style. Comment on such features as length, complexity, variety, emphasis, and parallelism. Point out any special or unusual effects.

1. This is not a Utopian tract. Some of those who complain about the quality of our national life seem to be dreaming of a world in which everyone without exception has talent, taste, judgment and an unswerving allegiance to excellence. Such dreams are pleasant but unprofitable. The problem is to achieve some measure of excellence *in this society,* with all its beloved and exasperating clutter, with all its exciting and debilitating confusion of standards, with all the stubborn problems that won't be solved and the equally stubborn ones that might be. —John W. Gardner, *Excellence*

2. If canned baby-food were free no doubt some people would eat nothing but canned baby-food day in and day out. But not many. Not for long. The most miserly person, after working his way through a certain number of cans, would break down and buy something more tempting to the adult palate. No doubt baby-food is nourishing, aseptic, reinforced with abundant vitamins; no doubt it would sustain life indefinitely if there were nothing else obtainable, but you don't want it and I don't. You don't want the first bland bite probably, to say nothing of long, increasingly boring years on the stuff.

Yet the case of baby-food, if it were free, would be the same as the case for the television and radio fare provided for humans throughout the United States. That fare is made up out of the cheapest available nutrients, put together with the intent of offending no taste, of remaining so innocent and innocuous that no sect, no religion, no race, no school of thought, no philosophy, no frame of mind, no possible audience can find it objectionable. This severely limits the flavors and contents of the cans. The networks have been searching for years for the lowest common denominator. Sometimes they think they have found it. Sometimes I think they have found it. However, writers, actors, directors and producers are human and unpredictable. They sometimes give a little meaning to a program. When this happens there is a rush of feet and a strangled cry.—Maxwell Anderson, "It Comes with the Set," *New York Herald Tribune*

3. Twenty-five years ago, when Calvin Coolidge and George V reigned over the English-speaking peoples, when H. L. Mencken was tearing the booboisie to shreds, when Lytton Strachey was demolishing one reputation after another, and when the monthly discovery of a radical new masterpiece by each of several book clubs still carried conviction, one department of literature was being thoroughly purged, revolutionized, and set in its place. This was biography. It had been attacked by various columns of shock-troopers. Groups who had read "Eminent Victorians" with savage glee; groups who had gone like a cyclone through Freud (or a manual on Freud); groups intoxicated with the satiric mockery of Shaw and the mordant irony of Henry Adams; groups of second-sight psychologists who at a moment's notice could describe

the ideas which surged through Cromwell's mind the night before Naseby, and report the precise words of an unrecorded conversation of Emerson and Thoreau—all these were lustily creating a "new biography."—Allan Nevins, "How Shall One Write of a Man's Life?" *New York Times Book Review*

4. For the production of a work of art is not the result of a miracle. It requires preparation. The soil, be it ever so rich, must be fed. By taking thought, by deliberate effort, the artist must enlarge, deepen and diversify his personality. Then the soil must lie fallow. Like the bride of Christ, the artist waits for the illumination that shall bring forth a new spiritual life. He goes about his ordinary avocations with patience; the subconscious does its mysterious business; and then, suddenly springing, you might think from nowhere, the idea is produced. But like the corn that was sown on stony ground it may easily wither away; it must be tended with anxious care. All the power of the artist's mind must be set to work on it, all his technical skill, all his experience, and whatever he has in him of character and individuality, so that with infinite pains he may present it with the completeness that is fitting to it.—W. Somerset Maugham, *The Summing Up*

4

THE PARAGRAPH

In some kinds of writing, paragraph division is arbitrary, in others conventional. In many newspapers, a paragraph break occurs after every long sentence and after every group of two or three short ones. In much informal writing, the writer starts a paragraph as nonchalantly as a speaker pauses momentarily in cultivated conversation. In dialogue, a paragraph break conventionally signals each change from one speaker to another.

In an expository essay, some paragraphs are primarily helps to continuity: programmatic paragraphs stating the author's intention, transitional paragraphs helping the reader see the connection between ideas, summarizing paragraphs recapitulating important points. Some are primarily helps to effectiveness: introductory paragraphs catching the reader's attention, one-sentence paragraphs setting off a statement for emphasis. However, the meat of an essay is likely to be contained in a different kind of unit: the expository paragraph that presents and develops an important idea or an important step in an argument.

O 1 Structural Devices

In serious expository prose, the paragraph tends to be a logical, rather than a typographical, unit.

In studying paragraphs written by professional writers, and in strengthening paragraphs in your own papers, you should look for clues to their logical coherence. You should look for devices that reveal structure and guide the reader.

O 1a Topic Sentences. *By formulating topic sentences for key paragraphs, a writer can greatly improve the clarity and continuity of his discussion.* A **topic sentence** contains the central idea of a paragraph. Some paragraphs revolve around a central idea without containing an explicit, concise statement of it. Others range over a number of closely related ideas. In many a typical paragraph, however, a topic sentence serves as the key to the rest of the paragraph. Formulating topic sentences for major paragraphs helps the writer to weed out irrelevancies and digressions.

Typical topic sentences might look like this:

Many animals are capable of emitting meaningful sounds.

Most of us are less tolerant than we think.

The African students I know are unanimous in demanding complete political independence.

"Impulse buying" plays as much of a role in the buying of a car as in other purchases.

Many campus buildings show the influence of imitation Gothic.

Notice how systematically the material in the following paragraph follows up the key idea stated in the topic sentence:

Latin American culture has been and is a dynamic element in the development of our own. It has, for example, furnished more than 2000 place names to the United States postal directory. Its languages have influenced American English, as such simple examples as "rodeo" and "vamoose" indicate. Its customs are part of our "Westerns" on television. Its housing, its music, its dances, its scenery, its ruins and its romance have been imitated and admired in the United States. One third of the continental area of this republic was for a long period, as modern history goes, under the governance of Spanish viceroys or of Mexico. The largest single Christian church in the United States is identical with the dominant church in Latin America.—Howard Mumford Jones, "Goals for Americans," *Saturday Evening Post*

NOTE: The topic sentence does not have a fixed place in a paragraph. Often, in fact, it appears at the end of an introductory or transitional paragraph rather than in the paragraph that actually develops it. Usually, however, it is most helpful immediately before or after the material to which it is related.

O 1b Transitional Phrases. *Transitional phrases help the reader see a paragraph as a well-ordered whole.* A well-written paragraph does not need elaborate directional signals. When used economically and unobtrusively, however, **transitional phrases** help the reader proceed smoothly from sentence to sentence.[1] Notice their use in the following paragraphs:

Many animals are capable of emitting meaningful sounds. Hens, *for instance,* warn their chicks of impending danger. *Similarly,* dogs growl at strangers to express distrust or hostility. Most of man's pets, *in fact,* have a "vocabulary" of differentiated sounds to express hunger, pain, or satisfaction.

Most of us are less tolerant than we think. *It is true that* we tend to be tolerant of things sufficiently remote, such as Buddhism or impressionist painting. *But* we lose our tempers quickly when confronted with minor irritations. My friends, *at any rate,* will rage at drivers who block their way, at acquaintances who are late for appointments, or at manufacturers of mechanisms that break down.

Notice how unobtrusive and yet how effective the transitions are in the following excerpt:

. . . What must be *even more surprising* is the thinness of coverage right here at home in the center of our national news, Washington. Washington has a very large press corps. The roster of the National Press Club is substantial, *and* the State Department auditorium is easily filled by a glamour press conference. *The trouble* is that most of the Washington press corps runs as a herd, concentrating on the "big" story of the day to the neglect of much else. The news services

[1] On the problem of economical transition, see D 8c.

have large staffs, *and* a few papers priding themselves on their national news maintain bureaus ranging from a half-dozen full-time correspondents to three times that number. *But* most of the so-called bureaus in Washington are one-man affairs. Except for an hour of gossip at the Press Club or at one of the other informal meeting places, and for what a lonesome man picks up from his home Congressional delegation, and the steady stream of inspired handouts, the average Washington reporter never gets beneath the surface of the day's one obvious story.—Philip M. Wagner, "What Makes a Really Good Newspaper," *Harper's*

O 1c Recurrent Terms. *A unified paragraph is often marked by the repetition or paraphrase of important words and phrases.* Such **recurrent terms** reflect continuity of thought and subject matter. Similar in effect is the recurrence of "pointers" like *he, it, they, this, these,* and *those*. Notice in the following excerpt how the idea of change recurs in each successive sentence:

It is an ominous fact that in the long chain of evolution the latest link, man, has suddenly acquired alchemic powers to *alter* whatever he touches. No other species before has been able to *change* more than a tiny fraction of his habitat. Now there is but a tiny fraction that he has *left unchanged*. A bulldozer *undoes* in an hour the work of a million years.—Paul Brooks, "Canyonlands," *Atlantic*

Notice how the following paragraph on the relation of the "ends" and "means" in politics keeps playing off these two terms, and their synonyms or related terms, against each other:

The *technical* man isolates one particular field or activity, in order to concentrate upon the *procedure* within it. In order for his work to proceed, he must assume the worth of the *end* to which his work is addressed; in order to get on to his own question, *"How?,"* he must assume that the *end* he is serving has an assured place in a hierarchy of *values* that he does not himself examine. As a cobbler cannot continually be asking himself whether shoes as such are a *good,* so an economist cannot continually ask himself whether "productivity" or "satisfaction" or—now apparently—"economic growth" is a *good;* he must take that for granted and get on with his job. Where the *end* is simple and noncontroversial, such a *technical approach* raises no problems. But in social policy the *ends* to be served admit of no such description: it is of the essence of politics that their meanings shift, that *values* conflict, and that men differ about them. The *ends* of politics, moreover, are not neatly separable from the *"means"* the *technical man* thinks he deals with exclusively; usually he bootlegs in some assumptions about *ends* in his work on the *means*. One might argue that political leadership, which must interpret the situation and fit together these several and conflicting *ends,* is pre-eminently the activity that cannot properly be reduced to sheer *technique.*—William Lee Miller, "Some Academic Questions About a New Yale Man," *The Reporter*

NOTE: In the sample paragraphs reprinted in the rest of this section, words and phrases that make for unity or continuity are italicized.

O 2 Paragraph Development

By paying serious attention to paragraph development, you can learn to do justice to one thing at a time.

By developing your paragraphs fully and systematically, you can make your papers seem like a sequence of solid, well-placed steps. The substantial, well-ordered paragraph is both the basic unit of, and a model for, the substantial, well-ordered theme.

O 2a Filling in Detail. *In descriptive writing, in technical exposition, or in narrative, a paragraph often corresponds to a major unit in the material treated.* Such a paragraph may take up one limited aspect of a scene, outline a step in a process, recount an episode. Often the sequence of details is inherent in the subject matter. Thus, a paragraph may trace structural or geographical relationships (**spatial order**), follow the order of events in time (**chronological order**), or proceed from causes to effects (**order of causation**).

Study the selection and the order of details in the following sample paragraphs:

The jockey *came to the doorway of the dining room, then after a moment stepped to one side* and stood motionless, with *his back to the wall. The room* was crowded, as this was the third day of the season and all the hotels in the town were full. *In the dining room* bouquets of August roses scattered their petals on the white table linen and from the *adjoining bar* came a warm, drunken wash of voices. The jockey *waited with his back to the wall* and *scrutinized the room* with pinched, crêpy eyes. He *examined the room until at last* his eyes reached a table in *a corner diagonally across from him,* at which three men were sitting. *As he watched,* the jockey raised his chin and tilted his head back to one side, his dwarfed body grew rigid, and his hands stiffened so that the fingers curled inward like gray claws. Tense *against the wall of the dining room, he watched* and waited in this way.—Carson McCullers, "The Jockey"

The *greeting ceremony* when one bird of the pair, after having been away at the feeding grounds, rejoins its mate *is also beautiful. Some little time before* the human watcher notes the other's approach, the waiting bird rises on its branch, arches and spreads its wings, lifts its aigrettes into a fan and its head-plumes into a crown, bristles up the feathers of its neck, and emits again and again a hoarse cry. The other approaches, settles in the branches near by, puts itself into a similar position, and advances towards its mate; and *after a short excited space* they settle down close together. *This type of greeting* is repeated *every day until* the young leave the nest; for after the eggs are laid both sexes brood, and there is a nest-relief four times in every twenty-four hours. *Each time* the same attitudes, the same cries, the same excitement; only now at the end of it all, one steps off the nest, the other on. One might suppose that this closed the performance. But no: the bird that has been relieved is still apparently animated by stores of unexpended emotion; it searches about for a twig, breaks it off or picks it up, and returns with it in beak to present to the other. *During the presentation* the *greeting ceremony* is again gone through; *after each relief* the *whole business of presentation and greeting* may be repeated two, or four, or up even to ten or eleven times before the free bird flies away.—Julian Huxley, *Essays of a Biologist*

Most of New England is glacial country and is, geologically speaking, a rocky *shambles* made by an ice-sheet that ground its massive way eastwards, ripped off the tops of hills and scattered a *hailstorm of stones and boulders* in all the lowlands. It *also* smeared some places with layers of good soil. *But* the only crop you can absolutely depend on anywhere through New England and along the North Atlantic coastal plain is a *crop of stones. So,* although New England is God's garden to a native (unless he happens to be a farmer), to an Englishman it is *pretty rough ground.* I remember one Briton who lived here moodily for years until he found the source of his homesickness: "There isn't a *field you can lie down in,*" he said. *This* may sound very fussy but when you consider that the *grass-pack* of the pasture regions of Iowa and Minnesota is the pride of the United States, and that it is still only about one third as tight and luscious as the grass-pack of southern England, it is easy to see why southern Englishmen can seem so snooty when real-estate men confront them with a *"rural paradise"* in Connecticut. —Alistair Cooke, *One Man's America*

NOTE: These sample paragraphs show the amount of **specific detail** the professional writer uses to give substance to one limited point. Apart from fluency and effectiveness of expression, a superior command of detail is often the most noticeable qualification of the successful writer.

O 2b Explanation and Illustration. *In many expository paragraphs, developing a key idea is a matter of explanation and illustration.* A topic sentence is often intentionally terse and emphatic. It may be developed by material that amplifies it, spells out its implications, clarifies a key term (**definition**). It may be developed by two or three representative examples, or by one example that is exceptionally detailed (**illustration**).

Notice how the following sample paragraphs vary the basic pattern of *statement—explanation—illustration:*

key idea / detailed restatement / first example / second example / third example

The deep sea has its *stars,* and perhaps here and there an eerie and transient equivalent of *moonlight,* for the mysterious *phenomenon of luminescence* is displayed by perhaps half of all the fishes that live in dimly lit or darkened waters, and by many of the lower forms as well. Many fishes carry *luminous torches* that can be turned on or off at will, presumably helping them find or pursue their prey. Others have *rows of lights* over their bodies, in patterns that vary from species to species and may be a sort of recognition mark or badge by which the bearer can be known as friend or enemy. The deep-sea squid ejects a spurt of fluid that becomes a *luminous cloud,* the counterpart of the 'ink' of his shallow-water relative.—Rachel Carson, *The Sea around Us*

key question / key idea / first set of examples / second set of examples / restatement of key idea

Where do the terms of businesese come from? Most, *of course,* are hand-me-downs from former generations of businessmen, *but* many are the fruit of cross-fertilization with other jargons. A businessman who castigates government bureaucrats, *for example,* is at the same time apt to be activating, expediting, implementing, effectuating, optimizing, minimizing, and maximizing—and at all levels and echelons within the framework of broad policy areas. *Similarly,* though he is amused by the long-hairs and the social scientists, he is beginning to speak knowingly of projective techniques, social dynamics, depth interviewing, *and* sometime soon, if he keeps up at this rate, he will probably appropriate that hallmark of the sound sociological paper, "insightful." Businesese, *in fact,* has very nearly become the great common meeting ground of the jargons.—William H. Whyte, "The Language of Business," *Fortune*

introductory anecdote

When Paul Garrett arrived in Detroit twenty-five years ago to begin General Motors' public relations program, the first question fired at him was: "How do you make a billion dollars look small?" Garrett said damned if he knew, and furthermore damned if he thought that was his job. Public relations, he argued, was not an "act," but a continuing effort on the part of management to win the confidence of the people with whom it came into contact. *Hence* you will find General Motors engaged in a host of activities in which altruism and self-interest come together in a creamy blend. Plant City and Field Relations, *for example,* stimulates local GM participation in the community affairs of the sixty-eight cities where it has factories, thereby helping both the community and itself. Educational Relations works with the schools, providing them with such useful education material as films on safe driving, and providing itself with a flow of applicants for jobs. The Speakers Bureau is glad to send a company-sponsored lecturer to your club or association to edify it with an inspirational talk—or to educate it with a "sound" economic one. Institutional Advertising tells the story of GM's role in supporting some twenty thousand suppliers, and leaves you with the pleasant impression that what's good for General Motors is good for small business, too. The billion dollars may not look any smaller as a *result of these efforts. But* it looks much, much nicer.—Robert L. Heilbroner, "Public Relations—The Invisible Sell," *Harper's*

key idea; first example; second example; third example; fourth example; restatement of key idea, alluding to initial anecdote

key idea

Not the least remarkable thing about Huck's feeling for people is that his tenderness goes along with the *assumption that his fellow men are likely to be dangerous and wicked.* He

first example

travels incognito, never telling the truth about himself and never twice telling the same lie, for he *trusts no one* and the lie comforts him even

second example

when it is not necessary. He *instinctively knows* that the best way to keep a party of men away from Jim on the raft is to beg them to come aboard to help his family stricken with small-

further support for key idea

pox. And if he had not already had the *knowledge of human weakness and stupidity* and cowardice, he would soon have acquired it, for all his encounters forcibly teach it to him—the insensate feud of the Graingerfords and Shepherdsons, the invasion of the raft by the Duke and the King, the murder of Boggs, the lynching party, and the speech of Colonel

restatement of key idea

Sherburn. Yet his *profound and bitter knowledge of human depravity* never prevents him from being a friend to man.—Lionel Trilling, *The Liberal Imagination*

key idea

Perhaps the most wearing thing about television is that most of the time it talks in a language so bare, so elementary, and so lacking in overtones that it can only be called baby

narrowed to limited area

talk. *Certainly* the commercials are baby talk, complete with coo and wheedle; and some of them even press the toddlers into service to do

specific examples

the selling for them. *I am thinking of* the little girls who wash their dolls' clothes in Ivory and of the one little girl who, holding up a roll of paper, says "Hudson tissues tear so stwaight!"—Marya Mannes, "Channels," *The Reporter*

NOTE: Observe in these paragraphs the satisfying and self-evident **relevance** of explanations and examples to the central idea. Not only is the illustrative material ample, but its appropriateness is immediately clear.

O 2c Logical Patterns. *Many expository paragraphs, instead of presenting one key idea, weigh several closely related points or work out a conclusion in a series of closely related steps.* Such a paragraph may follow a number of different logical patterns:

(1) *Comparison and contrast.*

key idea (linked to preceding step in discussion)

first subtopic (situation in Alger's books)

second subtopic (contrasting situation today)

Just as Alger's view of money as something to be made and kept no longer generally operates, [neither] does his view of how it should be given away. There is a great deal of "charity" in Alger, but *it is always man-to-man, even palm-to-palm.* It is a gesture in the tradition of the New Testament, a retail transaction between two individuals, spiritual in essence, monetary in form. The adjective that comes first to mind when we think of it is "Christian." *The adjective that comes first to mind when we think of charity today is "organized."* Via drives, community chests, red feathers, we can give more away more quickly. At the same time the primitive-Christian heart of the process, man-to-man giving, is weakened. Warmheartedness is communized.—Clifton Fadiman, "Party of One," *Holiday*

(2) *Examination of causes and effects.*

key idea

cause (with specific examples)

Europeans with time-honored experience in the technique of painlessly extracting cash from foreigners' pockets have correctly gauged that Americans like to travel abroad provided they don't really have to leave home. *They've seen* the U.S. armed forces and U.S. oil companies spend millions to give their personnel the illusion of living in a European or African suburbia filled with shopping centers, post exchanges, movie houses, ice-cream parlors, juke boxes,

effect (with specific examples)

and American-style parking lots. *Smart promoters now give* the American abroad exactly what he wants. Hotel rooms are furnished to please him, meal hours drastically advanced to suit the American habit of eating dinner at 6 p.m., arrangements made to satisfy the Americans' affection for crowds, action, and noise.—Joseph Wechsberg, "The American Abroad," *Atlantic*

(3) *Drawing logical conclusions from evidence* (**inductive order**).

detailed report of experiment

Psychologists studying race prejudice have many times made an interesting experiment. They seat a few people in a row, show a picture to the first in line, and ask him to whisper a description of it in a few words to a second who will whisper the information to the third, and so on. The picture is of a policeman and a badly dressed, uncouth Negro. The policeman is holding a knife in his hand; the Negro is unarmed. Almost never is the description transmitted to more than two or three individuals in succession, before the knife has passed from the hand of the policeman and is now being held in a threatening manner, by the Negro! *In other words,* the picture is transformed until it fits the preexisting concept in the mind, which is that an open knife is far more likely to be held by a Negro than a policeman. *This sort of unconscious alteration* of what is percieved, to make it accord with what is already believed, is universal and is one of the most important of all the facts with which communication has to deal.—Bruce Bliven, *Preview for Tomorrow*

interpretation of experiment

general application of findings

(4) *Drawing logical conclusions from accepted premises* (**deductive order**).

first observation — In the history books of the future this age of ours may come to be known as the Age of Statistics. In the biological and physical as well as the sociological sciences, statistics have become, as they never were before, the most important tool of investigation. second observation — *But* as every philosophical scientist knows, the conclusions drawn by a science depend to a considerable extent upon the tools used. third observation (specific application of point 2) — *And* it is in the nature of statistics not only that they deal with quantity but that they emphasize the significance of averages and medians. What usually exists or usually happens establishes The Law, and The Law is soon thought of as identical with The Truth. fourth (contrasting) observation — In all the arts, *nevertheless,* it is the exceptional and the unpredictable which really count. It is the excellent, not the average, which is really important. logical conclusion — And there is, *therefore,* one aspect of the cultural condition of a civilization to which statistical study is curiously inappropriate.—Joseph Wood Krutch, *Is the Common Man Too Common?*

(5) *Choosing among alternatives.*

History shows that wars between cities, states, and geographic regions cease once the originally independent units have amalgamated under the leadership of a single government with the power of making and enforcing laws that are binding upon individuals. first alternative examined and rejected — *One might reason on this basis that* if all of the industrialized and semi-industrialized regions of the world were to federate under a common government, the probability of another war would be greatly decreased. It seems likely that this conclusion would be valid if the resultant federation were as complete as was the federation formed by the original thirteen colonies

second alternative presented and supported

in America. *On the other hand,* it is extremely unlikely that such a highly centralized federation could come into existence at the present time; nationalistic feelings of individual men and groups of men, and conflicts of economic interests, are too strong to permit rapid transition. *Also,* those nations which have high per capita reserves of resources and high per capita production would be most reluctant to delegate their sovereignties to higher authority and to abandon the economic barriers that now exist. —Harrison Brown, *The Challenge of Man's Future*

What matters about such a paragraph is not whether it fits into a familiar logical scheme but whether it is written with a sense of purpose and direction. The writer needs to focus clearly on the point that he wants his readers to reach. He can then proceed to help them bridge the gap from thought to thought.

O 3 Paragraph Revision

A major aim in your revision of a paper should be to strengthen paragraphs that are underdeveloped or out of focus.

In revising the first draft of a paper, you will do well to look for common sources of weak paragraph development. Generally, both a sequence of one- or two-sentence paragraphs and a typed page without any paragraph breaks at all are signals of inadequate paragraphing.

O 3a Lack of Focus. Some paragraphs show that the writer has not proceeded beyond the first jotting down of possibly significant details and observations.

(1) *Give focus to a blurred paragraph by eliminating material not bearing on the central point.* A paragraph in a paper

describing a magazine might contain a comment on a striking cover, information about the price, and a brief summary of an interesting article. However, once the eye-catching qualities of the magazine are mentioned, describing and illustrating them adequately will take at least one full paragraph. Observations and comments not **relevant** to eye appeal will have to make room for more unified material.

(2) *Give unity to a rambling paragraph by selecting and rearranging details in order to bring out a logical connection previously missed or ignored.* Study the revision of the following paragraph for greater **coherence**:

POOR: San Francisco is a city of beautiful parks and public buildings. Golden Gate Park, with its spacious lawns and graceful ponds, enjoys international fame. The city's Bohemian section has become the national headquarters for jazz-age poetry and philosophy. Every tourist must visit Fisherman's Wharf and Coit Tower. The city is famed for its cultural events and conventions.

REVISED: It is not surprising that tourists and convention managers are attracted to San Francisco. Miles of varied waterfront, spacious parks, and impressive public buildings contribute to the city's unique appearance and cosmopolitan atmosphere. Fisherman's Wharf, with its seafood smells and colorful shops, attracts sightseeing crowds. Coit Tower affords a spectacular view of bay and city. Golden Gate Park, with its spacious lawns and graceful ponds, enjoys international fame.

O 3b Undeveloped Generalizations. Some paragraphs consist of nothing more than a statement of a general point, often in a single sentence. Such one-sentence paragraphs make for stringy writing unless the author deliberately uses them to emphasize an idea elaborated in what precedes or what follows.

(1) *Avoid paragraphs that merely reiterate a single point*

already sufficiently clear. Strengthen your paragraphs by removing weak repetition and providing **specific detail**:

POOR: My roommate is very considerate. I have always found him helpful and eager to be of service. He has really taught me something about the role of kindness in everyday living.

REVISED: My roommate is very considerate. He makes a point of not disturbing me when I study. He is always glad to let me use his typewriter or lend me a small sum. When I have visitors, he helps to make them feel at home. His example is teaching me something about the role of kindness in everyday living.

(2) *Avoid paragraphs that are merely a series of undeveloped general observations,* each a possible topic sentence for a separate paragraph:

POOR: The poems I liked best were those by A. E. Housman. *His poems were easy to comprehend without being overly simple.* With most other poems I need the assistance of an expert who can "translate" them for me. *The thoughts and attitudes expressed in Housman's poems represent the wisdom of an experienced, educated man. His poems are short and to the point,* a great help to enjoyment. *They are written in such a manner that the reader does not feel the author is preaching to him.*

Unless intended for forecast or summary, such a paragraph suggests inadequate **restriction of the subject** or excessive confidence in the reader's willingness to accept the writer's mere say-so.

(3) *Avoid weakening otherwise well-developed paragraphs by undeveloped afterthoughts.* Suppose a paragraph illustrates in some detail the thoughtful critical attitude a voter should have toward political leaders. The last sentence adds: "Of course, a

respectful attitude is also deserved." Obviously, the question of respect needs separate explanation and illustration.

EXERCISES

A. Describe in detail the methods of development used in each of the following student-written paragraphs. Point out topic sentences, transitional phrases, and other clues to continuity and relevance. Comment on the general effectiveness or adequacy of each paragraph.

> 1. My own pet feature of the magazine are the advertisements. Well I know that their sole purpose is to induce the reader, including me, to spend as many dollars as possible for the product pictured. Knowing this in no way detracts from my enjoyment of the color and pictorial values of what I see. Fully aware as I am of the appeals being made to my baser instincts (snobbishness and greed, to name just two) by the artful devices of the advertising fraternity, I still enjoy looking at the pictures. The allure of an ordinary metal cooking utensil pictured in a setting more fit for a precious gem can spur me, a representative reader, on to the kitchen with grim determination to substitute for my own quite adequate pots just *such* pots, with or without daisies. Utilized more sensibly, the power of such an imaginative appeal can bring about many small changes in the average home simply by giving a new slant on an old topic.

> 2. Although I never attended a class there, the abandoned main building that crowned the top of the hill was a favorite monument of mine. It was weathered by salt air, wind, and fog; its surface was scarred by dozens of holes where engineers and inspectors had bored into the plaster for samples; many of the windows were broken or missing, and they stared out at the rest of the campus like the huge, vacant eye-sockets of a skull. In spite of these mutilations, the old building radiated an atmosphere of dignity and benevolence. Its massive stone steps extended outward from the barricaded door like the arms of the Lincoln monument, inviting students to gather there.

3. When I attended my first class meeting in World History, I was disappointed to learn that during the year we were not to study and discuss the reasons why an event occurred; we were apparently expected to spend most of our time memorizing dates and names. At least, I thought, when a test came up I would have to think back to remember what happened in 1492, for instance. But when the students sat down for the final examination, the question was not "What important event occurred in 1492, and how did it affect world history?" No! It was as follows: "In 1492, Columbus sailed to the New World—true or false?" or "What year did Columbus sail to the New World? (a) 1942; (b) 1812; (c) 1912; (d) 1492." What kind of thought is provoked by tests such as these?

4. Detective stories tend to glorify crime. Murderers, gangsters, and crooks of all kinds are described as tough, cunning, and courageous individuals who know how to take care of themselves and who know how to get what they want. In James M. Cain's *The Postman Always Rings Twice,* for instance, the villain is a much more impressive character than his victim. He is casual, brave, smart, and successful with women. It is true that he finally gets caught. But he is punished for a crime that he did not commit, so that his conviction is hardly a triumph of justice. Besides, looking back over the exciting life of the criminal, the reader might conclude that it was worth the risk.

5. One obvious result of modern technology has been the increasing dependence of one workman upon another. We have "geared the machines and locked all together into interdependence." In Detroit's factories, thousands of workers are specialized; each performs a specific task. On the assembly line, an automobile is mass produced in a matter of hours. One worker installs wires, a second fastens lining in the interior, a third installs the windshield. Further down the line, groups of specialized personnel have assembled the dashboard and the seats. The finished body is lowered onto a chassis that has come down a similar line, operating on the same principle of each man doing a particular job. In a short time, the test driver drives the finished car through the factory gates. This is division of labor. This is specialization.

B. Discuss in detail the principles of paragraph development illustrated in the following examples. Pay special attention to the features that give each paragraph focus and direction.

1. Nobody has succeeded in explaining the connection between the private sources and the public functions of art. But art does have its public functions, though we often lose sight of them. In primitive agricultural societies, and even in Western Europe until the Renaissance, the functions were more clearly defined. It was the duty of the artist to celebrate the community in its present oneness, in its divine past, and in its glorious future. Thus he invented dances and rituals for the group, he retold the stories of its gods and heroes, he fashioned their images, and he persuaded the "people"—his own tribe that is, the only genuine persons—that they were reenacting the lives of the gods, who would some day return and reinstitute the golden age. Thus the artist played a recognized part in the daily life of the people.—Malcolm Cowley, "Artists, Conscience, and Censors," *Saturday Review*

2. Primarily, the brain is an organ of survival. It was built by nature to search for food, shelter, and the like, to gain advantage—before addressing itself to the pursuit of truth. Hence most human brains are unable to distinguish between truth and advantage, and accept as truth that which is only advantage. We use our brain mainly for finding ways to reach what we want. Simultaneously, we produce the thoughts and arguments which justify our feelings and dealings. I suspect that if I were in the business of selling shelters, my brain would tend to dwell rather steadily on the probability of nuclear war. If I were in politics, I might find my brain devoting itself less to the next generation than to the next election.—Albert Szent-Gyorgyi, "The Persistence of the Caveman," *Saturday Review*

3. The real Baltimorean is convinced that the real Baltimore vanished long ago. That damnable contraption, the horseless carriage, put it on the skids, and Kaiser Wilhelm II finished it. It was during the incivilities exchanged with the Kaiser that Baltimore, a drowsy but delectable city of half a million people, was dragooned into becoming a great port by reason of the Allies' insatiable demand for steel, coal, and foodstuffs, especially grain. The wharves of Baltimore lie ninety miles

nearer the wheat fields of the Middle West than those of any other saltwater port. Speed was of the essence in the task of feeding J. J. Pershing's personally conducted party then touring Europe, so Baltimore was hustled into the twentieth century willy-nilly, and in the process lost its identity.—Gerald W. Johnson, "Baltimore: The City Nobody Knows," *Atlantic*

4. Reading is a habit. Once you've got the habit you never lose it. But you must somehow be exposed to reading early enough in life to have it become a part of your daily routine, like washing your face or breathing. Many an unfortunate grade-school child in our highly seasoned, electronic, picture-conscious age has never been exposed to the reading habit and cannot, therefore, read without effort. Some modern children seldom if ever read for fun. Like muscles that are almost never used, their concentration and interest give way quickly. They long for the automatic, pictorial sensation of TV (which can be highly instructive and entertaining at times) rather than the tedium of moving the eyes from left to right, from left to right, from left to right on line after line after line of unillustrated print. There's a certain sadness in realizing that a whopping segment of the exploding new teen-age generation never *really* reads anything, unless forced to do so.—Richard L. Tobin, "Reading Is a Habit," *Saturday Review*

5. When films first broke on the world, let's say with the full-length, full-scale achievement of D. W. Griffith, *The Birth of a Nation,* one of its most persuasive and hitherto unexperienced powers lay in the absolute reality of the moving image. The camera is a scientific instrument, not a paintbrush: its special virtues are accuracy and actuality. Thus, when Griffith organized a pan-shot which began with a mother and child huddled in terror on a mountain and then moved slowly to a raging battle on the plain beneath, we were left breathless by a juxtaposition in scale—from the individual to the group, from the passive to the active—that was, quite literally, taking place before our eyes. Our belief in the medium had begun with actual railroad trains roaring down actual tracks right at us, with actual ocean waves breaking somewhere near our feet. Griffith moved from simple documentation to high

imagination, from fact to fiction, from present to past; and he took us with him because he used his camera as a faithful recorder of something that was really and truly going on: he did not abandon his camera's ability to state visual facts.—Walter Kerr, "What Good Is Television?" *Horizon*

C. Examine the material in the following paragraphs for relevance and continuity. Write a topic sentence summing up the general idea that the paragraph implies.

1. I am sure that the Romans, whose lives were lived under stately porticoes and amid the pomp of great temples, found in that background an ever present dignity which must have followed them even into the poverty and confusions of the crowded, many-storied *insulae*. The wide forums and the glittering *thermae* did not arise merely from the vanity of emperors and the corruption of the people. These were the songs in which the Roman soul made itself known above the cries of the circus and the clash of civil swords. The Gothic cathedrals were, in part at least, prayers of thanksgiving for a joy discovered in the revival of cities, and the *piazze* into which Venice poured her compressed splendor are jubilant with that new enfranchisement. These are not each an ornament added to a city but summations of a city's spirit to which houses and streets, walls, canals, and the domes of public buildings are the harmonious counterparts. Florence, Padua, Cordoba; the Paris of Richelieu, the Philadelphia of Franklin: each of these might have been the work of a single architect so consistent is the ordinance and expression of their streets and structures.—Joseph Hudnut, *Architecture and the Spirit of Man*

2. During my month of vigil and research, I heard an able physiologist who has a radio program say, quite simply, "We do not use up all the food we take in." He wasn't allowed to get away with that piece of clarity, however. "Ah," cut in his announcer, for the benefit of those no longer able to understand simplicity, "the utilization factor!" I turned from this station to a droning psychologist, just in time to hear him say, "The female is sometimes the sexual aggressor." Here a familiar noun of mental illness and military invasion was

clumsily at work beating in the skull of love with a verbal bung-starter. The sweetheart now often wears the fustian of the sick man and the Caesar. In the evening, I tuned in on one of the space-patrol programs that gleefully exude the great big blockyisms. "Your astrogation bank will tell you!" cried the captain of a space ship to another interplanetary pilot, meaning his navigational instruments. In a fairy tale, an astrogation bank would be a "star panel," but the quality of fairy tale is nowhere to be found in these dime novels of the constellations.—James Thurber, "The Psychosemanticist Will See You Now, Mr. Thurber," *The New Yorker*

D. Write a one-paragraph theme describing a face, a dress, the façade of a building, an abstract painting, or a tree. Work out a plausible sequence of details and try to achieve a unified general impression.

E. Write a one-paragraph theme describing a memorable moment. Avoid anticlimactic or confusing sequence of details.

F. Write a one-paragraph theme describing and illustrating a character trait of someone you know fairly well.

G. Select a key sentence from your current writing or reading. Use it as a topic sentence in three different paragraphs. Follow a different pattern of development each time, using different material as far as possible.

H. Study paragraph division and sequence of material in half a dozen news reports selected from a local newspaper. What is the relation between paragraphing and over-all organization? What effect does the paper's system of paragraphing have on its presentation of news? Report your findings.

I. Study paragraph division and paragraph development in an essay by a nineteenth-century writer like Thomas Babington Macaulay, Robert Louis Stevenson, or John Henry Newman. Report distinctive features.

5

THE WHOLE THEME

The first step in writing an expository paper is to assemble the raw materials. Here the generally observant and well-informed writer necessarily has an advantage over his less receptive colleague. Your own success as a writer will depend partly on your collecting the material for assignments yet undreamed of—by extensive reading, by careful scrutiny of other people, by looking at the world through open eyes.

Assuming that a writer can draw on adequate material, he faces the problem of organizing it. He has to sort things out in his own mind, so that he can present his ideas systematically, with **clarity** and vigor. His writing must have **coherence**; his readers must feel that they know where they are going, and that their effort will have been well spent when they get there. The writer has to attend to the problem of **transition**, helping his readers proceed from step to step.

The more substantial a project, the greater usually the need for systematic planning. Such planning is not the result of following a pat formula or a set of simple rules. If a writer forces his material into the straitjacket of a tried-and-true scheme, he may keep himself from doing justice to his subject and from discussing it with conviction. On the other hand, there are general principles of organization that can help a writer find his bearings. There are conventional devices for checking and strengthening the structure of a paper or of a paragraph.

O 4 The Need for Focus

A writer must concentrate on one point at a time.

Many papers begin with a vague interest in a general subject area. The instructor assigning a topic does part of the job of narrowing down the general area to something manageable. The writer has to do the rest.

O 4a Limiting the Subject. *The shorter the paper, the greater the danger that an inadequately restricted subject will get only thin, superficial treatment.* No one could write a paper on a vast general subject like "Education in America." A writer interested in American education may restrict this field according to area: a state, a town, the nation's capital, Indian reservations in Arizona. He may limit himself to a particular level: kindergarten, grade school, high school, college. He may limit his discussion to a certain type of student: gifted, retarded, emotionally disturbed. A manageable topic might look like this:

Science education for gifted students at Washington High
Home economics for boys at San Lorenzo Junior College
Released-time religious instruction in local grade schools

Usually, the writer limiting his subject sets out to restrict a less general area. Here are some typical ways in which such a less comprehensive area might be narrowed down:

GENERAL AREA: City Life

TOPICS:
Keeping up with the Joneses in Suburbia
"Redeveloped" vs. "grown" neighborhoods
An alternative to teenage gangs
A new trend in city architecture
One major cause of urban blight
Developing a sense of community

O 4b Stating the Thesis. *In a short paper, try to limit yourself to one major point that can be fully explained, illustrated, and supported in the space available.* Writing gains in clarity and focus when the writer clearly formulates this major point in his own mind. When it appears in the final paper, this statement of the central idea is called the **thesis sentence**:

TOPIC: Urban Redevelopment
THESIS: "Redeveloped" neighborhoods lack the varied life of the "grown" neighborhoods they replace.

TOPIC: Life in Suburbia
THESIS: Living in the suburbs does not prevent people from developing a sense of community.

NOTE: The thesis should be a true statement, an assertion of a limited point. It cannot be a question, though one excellent way of formulating the thesis is to sum up in one sentence the answer to a question like "What is missing in the typical redeveloped neighborhood?" Nor should the thesis sentence merely map out the general territory:

TOO VAGUE: A modern suburb is an exciting place to live.
MORE CLEARLY FOCUSED: Modern suburbs have kept alive the American tradition of being a good neighbor.

TOO VAGUE: Today's children are spoiled.
MORE CLEARLY FOCUSED: Grade school teachers lack the means of disciplining their students.

O 5 Patterns of Organization

A writer must learn to present his material in a clear and consistent sequence.

Adequate restriction of the subject area sets the outside limits of a theme. In its internal organization, the theme is likely to follow one, or a combination, of a number of common patterns.

O 5a Space and Time. *Much descriptive writing, technical exposition, and autobiographical narrative follows a sequence inherent in the writer's material.* Often such material fits naturally into a **spatial** or **chronological order**. An account of a vacation trip may trace a trail up into mountainous country. An article on radio transmitting may follow the voice of the soprano through microphone and transmitter to the receiving set and the listener's ear. An autobiographical paper may follow a "before-and-after" pattern: family life before and after the loss of a parent; a boy's attitude toward military service before and after induction.

To strengthen a paper of this kind, observe the following cautions:

(1) *Make the progression in space or in time clear and consistent.* The professional may attain special effects by flashbacks and by calculated shifts of perspective. The amateur, however, especially when writing a short paper, usually does well to follow a consistent pattern: from the foothills to the wind-swept peak, from childhood to adolescence.

(2) *Break up the whole sequence into major divisions or emphasize the most significant steps.* Suppose a paper follows the assembly line in an automobile factory: the basic parts of the body are welded together; the doors are hung; the body shells are dipped into a chemical solution; they are spray-painted; they are dried in ovens; electrical wiring is laid; door locks and other mechanisms are installed; glass is installed; interior lining is installed; and so on. To protect the reader against a monotonous "and-then" sequence, the writer will probably break up the body's progress into three major stages:

I. Building the body shell
II. Painting the body
III. Outfitting the painted shell

O 5b Classification and Analysis. *Many papers dealing with people, problems, and issues require a writer to sort out or break up his material so as to group together related points.* A writer may have to sort out miscellaneous material into several major categories (**classification**). He may have to break up a sprawling, formless subject into three or four plausible parts (**analysis**). He may merely arrange several major points of equal importance in the most convenient sequence (**enumeration**). **Order of division** is the general term sometimes applied to the kind of organization that these methods yield.

Here is a typical preliminary collection of material for a paper about a person:

SUBJECT: Last semester's psychology teacher
(1) had a loud, clear voice
(2) told some interesting stories about students helped by psychology
(3) came to class late several times
(4) explained difficult words
(5) wasn't sarcastic toward students
(6) wore colorful neckties
(7) walked with a limp
(8) had been an exchange teacher in France
(9) outlined subject clearly
(10) spaced assignments well
(11) talked over test I did poorly on

On studying this list, the writer will conclude that some of his observations are more closely related than others. He might establish three or four major categories:

I. Teaching methods: (2) relevant anecdotes, (4) explanation of terms, (9) clear outline, (10) spacing of assignments, and perhaps (1) effective speech habits
II. Attitude toward students: (5) absence of sarcasm, (11) assistance after class

III. Personal habits: (6) sporty clothes, (7) limp, (3) lack of punctuality
VI. Miscellaneous: (8) teaching experience abroad

If the writer is a student concerned about his academic progress, he may conclude that categories I and II are the most significant. A second look at III may suggest a convenient overall scheme: an introduction re-creating an unpromising first impression, belied by the teacher's effectiveness. A rough outline of the final paper might look like this:

I. Unpromising external characteristics
II. Effectiveness as a teacher
    A. Presentation of subject
    B. Dealing with students
III. Lesson learned ("Don't judge a teacher by his ties.")

Here are possible major divisions for two other typical papers:

CENTRAL IDEA: President Swenson has several qualifications that a college president needs.

I. Wide and varied experience
II. Selection of a varied and well-qualified faculty
III. Authoritative yet friendly attitude toward students
IV. Firm grasp of administrative and financial problems

CENTRAL IDEA: Joining a fraternity has many advantages.

I. Belonging to a group he is proud of gives the student the incentive to do well.
II. The active social life of the fraternity provides many opportunities for meeting people.
III. The many group projects carried on by the fraternity provide training in cooperation.

In working out the major divisions of such a paper, a writer has to solve various problems of logic, relevance, and proportion.

(1) *The categories should be appropriate to the purpose of the paper.* A paper on campus social life might divide students into Greeks, Co-op dwellers, and Independents. A study of the role of the humanities in a vocational curriculum might divide students into nursing majors, engineering majors, police majors, and so on.

(2) *The major categories should not suffer from illogical overlapping or from a confusing mixture of criteria.* A reader is bound to be bewildered if the writer divides students into graduates of local high schools, children from low-income homes, and Catholics. Suppose a paper investigating student opinion on teen-age marriage sets up the following categories: A. Boys. B. Girls. C. Married Students. This arrangement makes it seem as though the married students were neither boys nor girls. A scheme like this would be more plausible:

I. Single students
  A. Unmarried boys
  B. Unmarried girls

II. Married students
  A. Husbands
  B. Wives

(3) *Thoroughness of treatment should not vary unreasonably from one major category to the other.* Some papers seem unbalanced because the writer has tried to analyze the subject exhaustively instead of fully developing perhaps three major categories. A paper on teen-age marriage might proceed like this:

CENTRAL IDEA: Teen-age marriages are not always the result of mature affection.

I. One possible motive is the desire for independence from parental control. (Several case histories are discussed.)
II. Another motive may be the sense of satisfaction derived from

marrying a popular boy or a popular girl. (No details or examples are given.)

III. A person may marry "on the rebound," marrying one person to spite an other. (A sketchy and inconclusive case history is provided.)

IV. A couple may mistake physical attraction for love. (Several cases are discussed; similar cases in fiction and drama are cited.)

V. A boy about to be drafted may marry a girl for fear of losing her. (A case in point is discussed at length.)

The paper is likely to be unconvincing, because the author is stretching himself too thin. In a long paper, he might successfully tackle I, IV, and V. In a short paper, he might do well to limit himself to either I or IV.

(4) *If the major divisions of the paper vary in importance, familiarity or plausibility, their presentation should follow a consistent pattern.* Many effective papers move from the less important to the more important. This order produces a **climactic effect** and leaves the most important point firmly embedded in the reader's memory. The paper on teen-age marriage, for instance, might start with motives related to external circumstances (I, V) and end with the problem that is probably the most important and the hardest to discuss (IV).

O 5c Comparison and Contrast. *Often a paper works out significant similarities between apparently dissimilar things, points out important differences between similar ones, or shows why the writer prefers one of several alternatives.* Why drive a Volkswagen rather than a Ford? Why attend a small private college rather than a state university? Answering such questions calls for systematic **comparison and contrast**.

(1) In many papers of this kind, the writer has collected the necessary material but failed to work out the parallels or the dissimilarities. For instance, a paper might break apart in the middle because it is divided between a discussion of the

Volkswagen and a separate discussion of the Ford. One way of unifying the paper would be to set up a *point-by-point comparison:*

I. Economy
  A. Initial cost (data for both cars)
  B. Cost of operation (data for both cars)
  C. Resale value (data for both cars)
II. Comfort and convenience
  A. Space for passengers and luggage (data for both cars)
  B. Maneuverability (data for both cars)
III. Performance
  A. Acceleration and speed (data for both cars)
  B. Durability (data for both cars)

(2) Sometimes a comparison will be more meaningful or effective if two things are described separately. The writer then has to make a special effort to *keep the two descriptions parallel,* taking up important criteria in the same order and, if necessary, working out similarities or contrasts in a summarizing third section.

O 5d Logical Argument. *Many papers dealing with issues and ideas follow the order of a logical argument.* Several patterns of such argument are especially worth noting:

(1) The logical coherence of the paper may derive from *cause-and-effect relationships*. The following outline might represent an essay by a teacher concerned about his students' lack of interest in poetry:

I. *First step:* The author states his central concern, bringing out its interesting, startling, or paradoxical aspects:

> Children like poetry; they make up jingles and keep chanting them to each other; they listen avidly to poems about little pigs and clever cats. Most college freshmen, on the other hand, are either indifferent or hostile toward poetry, both traditional and modern.

II. *Second step:* The author asks and answers the obvious question: Why?

Poetry is often presented to students as something special and solemn; memorizing and reciting make many students regard it as drudgery; prose paraphrase necessarily emphasizes the most prosaic aspect of poetry.

III. *Third step:* The author suggests remedies at least partly implied in the diagnosis:

Teachers of poetry should emphasize oral reading; they should cater to their students' interest in song and story by including ballads and narrative poetry; they should encourage discussion and writing rather than make poetry the subject of objective tests.

(2) A second logical pattern leads to the desired conclusion through *qualification of* or *attack upon a familiar idea:*

I. *First step:* A familiar idea is confirmed:
It is true that many required courses do not help to prepare the student for his professional career (detailed illustrations).

II. *Second step:* A qualification or objection is stated:
But a responsible citizen must be able to recognize competence and quackery in fields other than his own (detailed illustrations).

III. *Third step:* A balanced conclusion is drawn:
Therefore, a student needs required courses that give him a basic understanding of some important disciplines outside his own field.

The same scheme is applicable to more general or more demanding subjects:

I. *Thesis:* It is true that modern industrial society makes for unprecedented interdependence among its citizens.

II. *Antithesis:* But such interdependence is an essential condition of mass production and mass consumption.

III. *Synthesis:* Interdependence is the price modern society pays for a high standard of living.

(3) A third logical pattern is modeled on the **inductive argument**, which *presents examples, case histories, or evidence and then draws a general conclusion.* Inductive order is especially effective when a writer has to overcome prejudice or distrust:

I. *First step:* Data are presented:
Carlotta Brink, heroine of *Vengeance Is Mine,*
  A. is rude to her servants (examples)
  B. insults tradesmen (examples)
  C. attempts to put other people in the wrong (examples)
  D. is unconcerned about her husband's business problems (examples)
  E. scolds her children without provocation (examples)

II. *Second step:* The conclusion is drawn:
Carlotta is inconsiderate and unkind.

(4) The inexperienced writer often does well to *state a general conclusion first and then present the material that supports it.* This way, he can keep out irrelevant material by checking details against the statement of his main idea. At the same time, he escapes the censure of the reader impatient with a paper that "beats around the bush." Here is a tentative outline for a paper putting the central idea first:

I. *First step:* The general conclusion is stated:
A part-time job can supplement a student's academic training.

II. *Second step:* The reasons for the conclusion are enumerated:
  A. Part-time work can provide a valuable practical education (training for do-it-yourself projects; knowledge useful to future housewife, car owner).
  B. It can provide field work related to the student's major field of study (hospital work for future nurses, tutoring for future teachers, playing in a commercial band for music students).
  C. It can provide valuable psychological training (association with people from different backgrounds, taking orders from superiors).

(5) In many papers an inductive paragraph becomes one link in a logical chain. Sustained logical reasoning makes unusual demands both on writer and reader. It is necessarily rare in popular or informal exposition and most common in scholarly controversy. Here is a rough outline of a **deductive argument**, which *draws conclusions from premises previously established* or *applies generalizations to specific instances:*

I. A college should develop in its students a sense for spiritual values (elaboration and support).
II. Architecture gives tangible expression to such values as dignity and permanence (elaboration and support).
III. The buildings facing the traditional Inner Quad of the college exhibit several of these qualities (elaboration and support).
IV. Of the modern classroom buildings on this campus, few suggest a sense of tradition, a sense of style, a feeling of dignity (elaboration and support).
V. Therefore, the buildings surrounding the Inner Quad should not be torn down to make room for additional "cell block" structures.

O 5e Imaginative Unity. *A writer may rely on imaginative rather than logical unity.* Writing with a strong imaginative touch often owes its coherence to its consistency of mood or to a unifying **symbol**. For instance, a foreign visitor may unify his impressions of California by choosing as his central subject a California highway, stretching for hundreds of miles with one built-up area merging into another. As he describes the cars, the supermarkets, the jerry-built roadside stores, the highway becomes a unifying symbol for the mobility of the population, the rapid and uncoordinated growth of the state, the lack of focus and tradition in sprawling towns and cities.

NOTE: The more substantial an essay or an article becomes, the less likely it is to fit into any one simple organizational scheme. A chapter in a book may follow a chronological order in its main outline, with different sections illustrating various kinds of analytic, inductive, and deductive order. Such devices as repeated references to a symbolic incident or repetition of a key quotation can help the writer keep the discussion focused on his basic concerns.

EXERCISES

A. Sort out the suggestions in each of the following lists into major categories. Arrange both your major categories and their subdivisions in the most plausible or the most logical order.

(a) STUDY HINTS

1. Make study time as regular as possible.
2. Work out an understanding with friends and roommates concerning unnecessary interruptions.
3. Avoid dim or glaring light.
4. Get an understanding of the purposes and organization of a course from course outlines, introductory materials in a textbook, or chats with the instructor.
5. If you can, work at an uncluttered desk.
6. Ask yourself practice questions about what you study.
7. Make a point of not protracting lunch hours and coffee breaks indefinitely.
8. If you can, find a congenial corner in a library or study hall.
9. Start studying the first week of each term.
10. Take two or three *short* breaks during each two- or three-hour period of study.
11. In studying a textbook, try to relate what you read to the instructor's lectures or to class discussion.
12. If a subject does not seem immediately practical or interesting, treat it as a challenge to your resourcefulness, agility, and perseverance.
13. Break up the material to be studied into convenient chunks.

14. Reserve the cramming session before final examinations for review and for attention to special difficulties.

15. Summarize, review, and think about one major section before going on to another.

(b) TAKING ESSAY EXAMINATIONS

1. Take up those questions first that you feel best qualified to answer.

2. Check the questions for important qualifying words like *only, always, for the first time, major, most important.*

3. Bolster general points with specific detail.

4. Budget your time carefully.

5. If a question calls for a comparison, trace differences and similarities instead of giving two separate, unrelated accounts.

6. If you gain five points by treating one question at great length, and then lose twenty-five points by slighting the next two questions, you are twenty points behind.

7. Allow time for rereading and revision.

8. Pay attention to the exact wording of the questions.

9. Use preliminary jottings or a scratch outline to organize answers running to more than paragraph length.

10. If you are asked to select "three reasons" or "four qualities," don't list more than are asked for.

11. Think about the questions before you answer them, but don't brood over them.

12. Get a general picture of the examination before you start writing.

13. Be prepared to depart from the order of material in your textbook or in your lecture notes. (Many essay questions call for correlation of material from different parts of a course.)

14. Do not pad weak answers with irrelevant material.

15. Once you have started writing on one of several alternative questions, try to make the best of it rather than shift to an "easier" question in midstream.

16. If a question asks you to "evaluate," a mere recapitulation of facts is not enough.

17. Whenever possible, bolster your answers with specific references to the reading you have done for the course.

(c) WRITING A LETTER OF APPLICATION

1. Be courteous without being elaborately or excessively polite.

2. Stress previous practical experience, especially if relevant to the position for which you apply.

3. Be factual in describing your qualifications, while at the same time presenting them to advantage.

4. Ordinarily, avoid references to such personal reasons for wanting the position as financial need, family pressure, desire for a change of scenery, or lack of more promising prospects.

5. Avoid gimmicks.

6. Proofread your letter carefully for typing errors.

7. Describe your previous training, stressing courses or reading relevant to the employment you seek.

8. Avoid self-praise.

9. Include a list of references.

10. Avoid erasures.

11. Avoid offensive or gross flattery.

12. Make a special effort to secure neat, pleasing appearance of the finished letter.

13. If possible, be specific about the position for which you apply.

14. If possible, obtain prior permission from those whose names you use.

15. Introduce the letter by mentioning the advertisement or the person that informed you of the vacancy (but do not mention leads that smack of the "grapevine").

16. Ask for an interview, suggesting (but not setting) a possible time for it.

17. If the account of your qualifications is extensive, put it on a separate "data sheet."

B. Find three current magazine articles that are clearly or plausibly organized. Choose articles from different magazines and of varying degrees of difficulty. Write a well-developed paragraph on each, describing its organization or the general strategy adopted by the author in presenting his material.

O 6 Beginnings and Endings

A writer must learn how to enlist the reader's attention and how to leave him with a strong final impression.

Many writers spend too much time wondering how to begin and how to conclude. Often, the best advice to such a writer is to begin in the middle and to stop when he has finished what he has to say. Nevertheless, once a writer has worked out the body of his essay, he should think seriously about how to approach his readers and how to shape their final reaction to the paper as a whole.

O 6a Titles. *A good title is specific enough to stake out a limited area, honest enough to prevent later disappointment, and striking enough to compete successfully with other claims on the reader's time.* Conversely, bad titles tend to be vague, colorless, sprawling, or, if colorful, deceptive. Here are some weak titles followed by a choice of suggested alternatives:

BEFORE: BUSINESS SUCCESS
AFTER: SELLING HOME ENCYCLOPEDIAS
WHERE THE CUSTOMER IS KING

BEFORE: QUALITIES OF A FUTURE HUSBAND
AFTER: WHAT MAKES ELIGIBLE MEN ELIGIBLE
BREADWINNER OR PRINCE CHARMING?

BEFORE: JUVENILE DELINQUENCY
AFTER: MY STAY AT JUVENILE HALL
WHAT JUDGE GOODWIN DID ABOUT JUVENILE GANGS

BEFORE: THE NEUTRALITY OF POLITICAL SCIENCE TEACHERS
AFTER: IMPARTIALITY IN THE CLASSROOM
TEACHERS, TOO, HAVE OPINIONS

O 6b Introductions. *An effective introduction may sketch out the territory to be covered, establish a common basis for discussion, lead up to a central idea.* Like the title, a good introduction helps to set the tone, whether formal or informal, objective or emotional, serious or facetious. Here are some typical ways of introducing a paper, ranging from the relatively formal to the informal or flippant:

(1) The writer may attract the reader's attention by relating his subject to a *topical event or a current controversy:*

RUSSIAN, ANYONE?

On August 12 . . . the Soviet government announced the launching of Russia's first . . . Though Russian scientific journals had published detailed accounts of . . . , the lack of qualified translators had kept American scientists unaware of the Russians' rapid progress in this field. . . .

(2) The writer may start with a statement that makes the reader take a *new look at a familiar situation:*

THE LIFE OF STRESS

A lot of sympathy is being wasted on executives for leading lives so full of stress and strain that it impairs their health. Actually, their subordinates suffer more from high blood pressure and artery disease. These surprising findings . . .—*Time*

(3) The introduction may limit the subject by *proceeding from a general situation to a specific instance:*

THE WASTELANDS REVISITED

School people have to put up with a lot, not only from the kids, who must be bad enough, but also from the grown-ups, who probably are worse. Pummeled, pressured, and advised from every side, still bearing the wounds inflicted by super-patriots, super-religionists, super-taxpayers, and super-superintendents, the educators now have to deal with yet another attack from Arthur E. Bestor, Jr.—William Lee Miller, *The Reporter*

(4) An *initial quotation* may serve as the keynote for the rest of the paper:

NO SOCIAL SECURITY FOR COACHES

"Coach Jones Resigns After Second Bad Season." Who has not seen headlines like this one after the annual football or baseball craze has run its course? No matter what his past record, the coach of every prominent team . . .

(5) *Striking facts or statistics* may dramatize the issue to be discussed:

MONOLINGUALISM IS OBSOLETE

Last year, only one out of ten American high school graduates had studied a foreign language. In spite of the publicity recently given to the teaching of foreign languages in primary and secondary schools. . . .

(6) A *striking contrast* may heighten the point to be made:

AMERICAN CHILDREN ARE SPOILED

Not too many decades ago, young children were early taught the difference between what they were, and were not, allowed to do.

Today, many American parents treat their children as if they could do no wrong. The most obvious manifestation of this change . . .

(7) An *initial definition* may clarify a key term:

WHAT IS AUTOMATION?

Economists do not agree among themselves on what "automation" means. Some writers use the term for any type of large-scale mechanization of industrial or administrative processes. Others, more plausibly, use it in referring to the mechanization of planning, supervision, and control.

(8) Biographical or personal comment worked organically into the introduction may help establish the *writer's qualifications* for dealing with his subject:

VICTORY AND AFTER

When I first came to Germany in November 1945, all the major cities seemed to be curiously alike. . . .

(9) An introduction may gain impetus by *attacking a currently accepted assumption:*

THE NEW ILLITERACY

We hear much about the reawakening interest in the humanities, the new appreciation of the generalness in the liberal arts, the growing dissatisfaction with overspecialization. Maybe so. But these signs are minute, I suggest, [compared with] those coming from the other direction. I offer the proposition that the trends that have been working against the humanities are likely to increase, not decrease, in the decade ahead. . . .—William H. Whyte, Jr., *Saturday Review*

(10) By *anticipating damaging objections,* the writer may disarm would-be critics:

THE HIGH COST OF MISFORTUNE

Nowadays anyone who advocates public health insurance is called a socialist. Thanks to years of skillful and well-financed publicity . . .

(11) A *controversial question,* concisely and provocatively worded, may stir up an apathetic reader:

LOYALTY BEGINS AT HOME

Should a man put loyalty to his country above loyalty to a friend? Does loyalty to the government come before loyalty to one's family? How we answer such a question depends on . . .

(12) An *amusing anecdote* may entertain the reader while at the same time conveying an important idea:

MEDICAL JOURNALISM—
WITH AND WITHOUT UPBEAT

As a veteran writer of medical and psychological articles for the mass-circulation "slicks," I have a fellow feeling for the violinist who rebelled after having been with an orchestra for thirty years. One day, so the story goes, he sat with his hands folded during rehearsal, and when the conductor rapped on the podium with his baton and demanded furiously, "Why aren't you playing?" replied, with a melancholy sigh, "Because I don't like music." Sometimes I feel like sitting at my typewriter with my hands folded. I don't like popularization. It has gone too far. The little learning—with illustrations—which the magazines have been pouring into a thirsty public has become a dangerous thing. . . .—Edith M. Stern, *Saturday Review*

Some common ways of introducing a theme are usually, though not necessarily always, ineffective:

(1) A *repetition,* often verbatim, *of the assignment.*

(2) A *vague, colorless summarizing statement:* "There are many qualities that the average college graduate looks for in a

job. Most of them probably consider the following most important. . . ."

(3) An *unsupported claim to interest:* "Migratory birds are a fascinating subject. Ever since I was a little child I have been interested in the migration of birds. Studying them has proved a wonderful hobby. . . ."

(4) An *unsubstantiated claim that the paper is going to deal with a burning issue:* "There has been much controversy over the question of whether public schools should give their students released time for religious instruction. This question has been debated many times. . . ."

(5) *Complaints about the subject:* "I find it hard to discuss prejudice in a paper of 500 words. Prejudice is a vast subject. . . ."

(6) *Apologies* for the writer's lack of qualifications: "I am really not very well qualified to write about the qualifications that good children's books should have. . . ."

(7) *Evasive or platitudinous remarks:* "Everyone feels differently about the merits of required courses. I think everyone has a right to his own opinion. . . ."

O 6c Conclusions. *An effective conclusion ties together different parts of a paper and reinforces its central message.* It may simply be an emphatic restatement of an important idea, an explicit assertion of what the writer has been hinting at. At the end of a fairly long and involved paper the conclusion may offer a convenient summary of major points. Often an essay concludes with a detail symbolic of the prevailing mood, or with an anecdote reaffirming the central idea in a witty or memorable way.

Here are some examples of effective conclusions:

(1) A *memorable restatement* of the central idea:

. . . Underneath our shiny fronts of stone, our fascination with gadgets and our new toys that can blow the earth into a million stars, we are still outside the doorway through which the great answers wait. Not all the cameras in Christendom nor all the tricky lights will move us one step closer to a better understanding of ourselves, but only, as it always was, the truly written word, the profoundly felt gesture, the naked and direct contemplation of man which is the enduring glamour of the stage.—Arthur Miller, "The American Theater," *Holiday*

(2) A *final anecdote* that reinforces the central idea without explicit restatement:

. . . Only once did I ever hear of an official football speech which met with my entire approval. It was made by a Harvard captain. His team had lost to Yale but by a smaller score than was expected. It had been a fast and interesting game. At the dinner when the team broke training the captain said, "We lost to Yale but I think we had a satisfactory season. We have had fun out of football and it seems to me that ought to be the very best reason for playing the game."

A shocked silence followed his remarks. He was never invited to come to Cambridge to assist in the coaching of any future Harvard eleven. His heresy was profound. He had practically intimated that being defeated was less than tragic.—Heywood Broun, "A Study in Sportsmanship," *Harper's*

(3) An apposite *final quotation:*

. . . Should there be codes of ethics for honesty in government? Must public men declare themselves in writing to be honest men just as some professors have been required to swear solemnly that they do not really intend to overthrow the Government of the United States? Personally, I have no faith in such oaths. A gentleman who much influenced my early life once told me:

"Son, by God, when I invite a man to dinner I do not propose to count the silver—before or after he leaves the table!"—William S. White, "The American Genius for Hypocrisy," *Harper's*

(4) A sober estimate of the *significance of the conclusions* reached:

. . . Criticism by outsiders will not miraculously transform the quality of network programs. But as long as criticism finds its way into print, and as long as network presidents take their critics seriously enough to cajole or denounce them, the cause of informative and satisfying television is not lost.

(5) A *forecast or warning* based on facts developed in the paper:

. . . In education we have not yet acquired that kind of will. But we need to acquire it, and we have no time to lose. We must acquire it in this decade. For if, in the crucial years which are coming, our people remain as unprepared as they are for their responsibilities and their mission, they may not be equal to the challenge, and if they do not succeed, they may never have a second chance to try.—Walter Lippmann, "The Shortage in Education," *Atlantic*

(6) An essential *condition for future progress:*

. . . When public relations people become as a group more forthright, less designing, more strict in their standards, and more respectful of the public, then—and only then—will the discerning public accept them as real professionals.—Vance Packard, "Public Relations: Good or Bad," *Atlantic*

(7) A suggestion for *remedial action:*

. . . If the leading citizens in a community would make it a point to visit their state prison, talk with the warden, then return to their communities with a better understanding of actual down-to-earth prison problems, they would have taken one of the most important and most effective steps toward a solution of our crime problem.—Erle Stanley Gardner, "Parole and the Prisons—An Opportunity Wasted," *Atlantic*

(8) A *return from the specific to the general,* relating the findings of the paper to a general trend:

(ex.)

. . . Inge's family plays constitute a kind of aesthetic isolationism upon which the world of outside—the world of moral choice, decision, and social pressures—never impinges. Although he has endowed the commonplace with some depth, it is not enough to engage serious attention. William Inge is yet another example of Broadway's reluctance or inability to deal intelligently with the American world at large.—Robert Brustein, "The Men-Taming Women of William Inge," *Harper's*

Here are some examples of lame, ineffective conclusions:

(1) The *noncommittal platitude:* "This problem deserves the serious attention of every right-thinking American."

(2) The *unfounded optimistic prediction:* "When things look their grimmest, a turn for the better is usually not far away."

(3) The *undeveloped panacea:* "The restoration of proper discipline in the nation's schools will make juvenile delinquency a thing of the past."

(4) The *conclusion raising problems* that weaken or distract from the point of the paper: "Of course, a small car has obvious disadvantages for a family with numerous children or for the traveler in need of luggage space."

NOTE: No separate conclusion is sometimes better than an anticlimactic one—a tacked-on paragraph that raises belated doubts or blurs the reader's understanding of important points.

EXERCISES

A. Describe the approach chosen in each of the following introductions and comment on the effectiveness of both introduction and title. Do they make the reader want to go on reading? Do they seem to lead clearly and directly into a specific subject? What kind of paper would you expect in each case?

1. HYDROPONICS IN THE HOME

Hydroponics is a subject about which many people have little or no knowledge, yet there is nothing really new or mysterious about it. It is merely a system by which plants are grown in water solutions containing the essential minerals for plant growth. The terms *water culture* and *water gardening* refer to this same system. . . .

2. THE LATEST STYLE

If you picked this paper up expecting a dissertation on frills, frocks, and new brassieres to dream in, you had best put it down again. I am concerned here with a new style in automotive power plants, the free-piston turbine engine. You may ride behind one sooner than you think. . . .

3. THE ESSENCE OF FOOTBALL

To write an account of the essential features of football by giving only a description of its rules and procedures and omitting consideration of its actual practice in American sports would be misleading. A dictionary definition of football does not meaningfully convey to a person totally unfamiliar with the game a genuine understanding. American football is a living thing, not an abstract concept. Thus, American football transcends its mere rules and procedures and must be described accordingly if its essentials are to be validly grasped. . . .

4. THE EDUCATED ANTI-INTELLECTUALS

It is a curious fact that the American people spend more per capita on the schooling of their children than any other people on this globe and yet they persist in proclaiming their anti-intellectualism. Consider the epithets "brain trusters" and "eggheads." Look at the general disdain for the very word "intellectual" . . .

5. BRUTE STRENGTH IS NOT ENOUGH

Football has often been called a game for men who are all muscle and have no brains. This charge may have been justified in the infant years of the game, when it consisted entirely of running plays and when the players used brute strength to crash through the opposing line. Today, a team may use as many as fifty different plays, involving complicated deception and a wide variety of passes. . . .

6. THE ROLE OF GOVERNMENT

The decision between a strong government which governs the people or a weak government is one of importance and one that needs careful thought and consideration. Throughout history, the proper role of government has been a subject of discussion. . . .

7. EXTRA! EXTRA!

Splotch! The sound of the *Ungi Bungi Evening News* careening against my little mud hut stimulates every cultural and educational drive of my little Ungi Bungian mind. Where else can I find such factual and unbiased accounts of history-shaping events? Without further ado I will unfurl the parchment to discover what great accomplishments the world has recorded today. . . .

8. THE BENT AND BLUNTED FREE LANCE

In the chivalry of the thirteenth century, an important figure was the free lance, an independent knight who sold his fighting skill to the highest bidder and, so legend says, tilted his bold weapon in defense of the helpless against all sorts of dragons and outrages. So far in the twentieth century an important adjunct to communication has been the free-lance writer who has made a living, and a considerable social impact, with his pen. . . .—Hartzell Spence, *Saturday Review*

B. Describe the function and estimate the probable effectiveness of the following conclusions:

1. (A paper describing the game of badminton)

. . . Badminton can be very exciting. If you are ever looking for a good time I suggest that you try this game. I know from experience that it can really be a lot of fun.

2. (A paper discussing a veteran's visit to his former high school)

. . . As I walked, alone, down the familiar and yet strangely different hall, I began to realize a truth that nostalgic people like myself find hard to learn: Distance gives glamor to the past.

3. (A paper defending women against the charge that they are poor drivers)

. . . that the woman driver, inexperienced and timid as she may be, is less of a highway menace than the arrogant, inconsiderate male. Of course, this is only one woman's opinion, and yours may be different from mine.

4. (A paper trying to demonstrate the futility of censoring comic books)

. . . the parents can do most to counteract the comic-book habit. If they read to their children from good books, if they teach their children to treat good books as treasured possessions, if they make it a habit to talk about good books in the home, the positive attraction of good literature may prove more effective than censorship possibly can.

5. (A paper discussing several examples of "tolerance")

. . . We thus conclude that by "tolerance" we mean allowing beliefs and actions of which we do not wholly approve. Since many of us approve wholeheartedly of only very few things, life without tolerance would be truly intolerable.

6. (A paper examining the proposition that "that government governs best that governs least")

. . . Government must effectively govern to be a true government, but it must govern with restraint and not to excess. The government that governs least is not necessarily the best one. I would rather say that the government that governs ablest, in the interest of most of its citizens, is the best government.

C. Examine the introduction or "lead" in five current articles from different general-interest magazines. Write a well-developed paragraph about each one. Describe the approach followed and evaluate its effectiveness.

O 7 Continuity

A writer must learn how to take his reader along from point to point.

In a competent piece of writing, sentence follows sentence, and paragraph follows paragraph, in a smooth, natural sequence. When such progression is lacking, the reader will soon start asking exasperated questions: Where are we going? How does this fit in? What are you leading up to?

O 7a Key Sentences. *A writer should learn to formulate clear and emphatic key sentences to serve as guideposts to the reader.* A **topic sentence** is a guide to the intention of a paragraph (See O 1a). A more comprehensive programmatic statement may provide the clue to the intention of a major division of a long essay. Here is an outline consisting of key questions and key sentences from an article exceptionally deliberate and clear-cut in its organizational scheme:

> *What are the students like?* They come from all sorts of backgrounds. . . .
>
> Only one thing they are certain to have in common: they are roughly in the same age group. . . .
>
> *Why do they come to college?* They come because it is assumed that they will come, because almost everyone they know does. . . .
>
> A second and related reason why students come is to make good contacts. . . .

Many come simply to learn to make a living. . . .

To have fun is still another motive. . . .

There are students who actually come because they want to learn. . . .

What happens to students in college? It is the students' first meeting, most likely, with a national and perhaps international group of men and women of their own age. . . .

Furthermore, college is the students' first encounter with live intellectuals. . . .

Students are surprised, too, at their first meeting with really violent political opinion of all possible varieties. . . .

It is in college, too, that the sharp bitter sting of failure is first experienced to any appreciable extent. . . .

What does the student learn? On the simplest level he has acquired a considerable amount of information. . . .

He will also have learned to question. . . .—James K. Feibleman, "What Happens in College," *Saturday Review*

O 7b Transitional Phrases. *An effective writer uses appropriate transitional phrases to help the reader move smoothly from one paragraph to the next.*

(1) In systematic formal exposition, the reader may be reminded of the relation of each paragraph to the main point by phrases placing it in a numerical sequence. Such **enumeration** is used in the following excerpt from a general discussion of language:

There are *five simple facts* about language in general which we must grasp before we can understand a specific language or pass judgment on a particular usage. . . .

In the first place, language is basically speech. . . .

In the second place, language is personal. . . .

The third fact about language is that it changes. . . .

The fourth great fact about language . . . is that its users are, in one way or another, isolated. . . .

The fifth great fact about language is that it is a historical growth of a specific kind. . . .—Donald J. Lloyd, "Snobs, Slobs, and the English Language," *The American Scholar*

When used in a perfunctory manner, enumeration makes for heavy, plodding reading. The next example, which also proceeds by enumeration, uses less obtrusive transitional expressions:

thesis	An arrangement of shapes is satisfying, or otherwise, to the human eye, because of certain elementary natural laws. *The most essential*
first point	*of these* is the law of balance. . . .
second point	A picture also demands harmony. . . .
summarizing definition	*In speaking* of the harmony, or unity, of a picture, *we mean* that . . .
further development of point 2	The colors, *too,* must be related harmoniously. . . .
summary of points 1 and 2	*Thus* we have balance and harmony as necessities in a picture.
third point	We must *also* have variety and subtlety. . . .
definition summarizing points 1 and 2	The design of a picture, which includes *these qualities of* balance, harmony, and variety, is its basis and essential skeleton. . . .—K. W. Maurer, "On the Appreciation of Paintings," *Queen's Quarterly*

(2) In an essay presenting a **logical argument**, transitional phrases are likely to be varied. A section of such an essay might proceed like this:

introduces main point	It is plain that . . .
begins to enumerate reasons	Here are some reasons for . . .
elaborates on one of several points	The second of these . . .
summarizes what precedes	In short, . . .
raises a possible objection	Yet . . .
concedes a point	It is true that . . .
returns to original trend of thought	Nevertheless, . . .
draws balanced conclusion	At the very least, . . .

Here are some other common transitional phrases: (**logical conclusion**) *accordingly, consequently, as a result, hence;* (**con-**

trast or objection) *but, however, on the other hand, conversely, on the contrary;* (**concession**) *granted that, no doubt, to be sure;* (**illustration**) *for example, for instance;* (**paraphrase or summary**) *in other words, to conclude, to sum up*. Often a complete sentence, and in longer papers a complete paragraph, may be needed to establish the transition from one major point to another. Overuse of transitional expressions like *however, therefore,* and *all things considered* can make a paper awkward and mechanical. On the other hand, when used sparingly and when varied to avoid monotony, they help to keep both writer and reader from leaving the tracks.

NOTE: *Avoid transitional expressions that are too vague to give the reader a sense of direction:* "One question that often arises is whether . . ."; "another interesting point is that . . ."; "we should also take a look at . . ."

O 7c Continuity of Thought. *A well-organized paper shows structural features that reflect continuity of thought.* Notice how the opening sentences of each paragraph in the following excerpt suggest well-planned, systematic forward movement. Notice the frequent use of a *this* or *these* pointing back to a preceding paragraph. Notice the use of a *the one . . . the other* pattern tying two paragraphs together:

thesis	The diversity of higher education in the United States is unprecedented. . . .
first major aspect of general topic is taken up; one alternative is considered	Consider the *question of size.* The small campus offers . . .
second alternative is considered	Others feel hemmed in by these very qualities. They welcome the *comparative anonymity and impersonality* of the big university. . . .
second major aspect of general topic is taken up; first alternative is considered	Another familiar question is whether the student should go to a *college next door, in the next city, or a thousand miles away.* By living at home . . .

second alternative is considered

Balanced against this, there are considerable advantages to a youngster in *seeing and living in an unfamiliar region* of the country. . . .

alternatives are weighed

But this question too must be decided in terms of the individual. . . .

third major aspect of general topic is taken up; first alternative is considered

Co-education poses still another problem. Those who favor it argue . . .

second alternative is weighed

Others believe that *young men and women* will work better if . . .

alternatives are weighed

There is no pat answer. It might be healthy for one youngster . . .

fourth major aspect of general topic is taken up

The so-called *"prestige" colleges and universities* present a special problem. . . .—John W. Gardner, "How to Choose a College, if Any," *Harper's*

In the following excerpt, notice how the *repetition of key terms* like *work, toil,* or *labor* suggests well-focused discussion:

What elements of the national character are attributable to this long-time agrarian environment? First and foremost is *the habit of work.* For the colonial farmer ceaseless striving constituted the price of survival. . . .

The *tradition of toil* so begun found new sustenance as settlers opened up the boundless stretches of the interior. "In the free States," wrote Harriet Martineau in 1837, *"labour* is more really and heartily honoured. . . ."

One source of Northern antagonism to the system of human bondage was the fear that it was jeopardizing this basic tenet of the American creed. "Wherever *labor* is mainly performed by slaves," Daniel Webster told the United States Senate, "it is regarded as . . ."

Probably no legacy from our farmer forebears has entered more deeply into the national psychology. If an American has no *purposeful work* on hand . . .

This *worship of work* has made it difficult for Americans to learn how to play. As Poor Richard saw it, "Leisure is . . ."

The first mitigations of the daily grind took the form of hunting, fishing, barn-raisings and logrollings—*activities that* had no social stigma because they *contributed to the basic needs of living. . . .*

The importance attached to *useful work* had the further effect of helping to make "this new man" indifferent to aesthetic considerations. . . .—Arthur M. Schlesinger, *Paths to the Present*

Continuity of thought may find its expression in a number of effective unifying devices:

(1) A writer may *ask a central question* in the title or in the introduction, proceed to discuss relevant facts, and then restate and answer the initial question in the conclusion.

(2) A writer may *present a topical anecdote* early in the paper, and then, after examining its implications, return to it at the end.

(3) A writer may *start by stating a series of propositions* and finish by restating them, in parallel form but with important qualifications.

Repetition of key phrases, of important metaphors, and of grammatical patterns may help give the reader a sense of purpose.

EXERCISE

In a page of expository prose selected by your instructor, point out all key sentences, transitional phrases, and words or devices making for continuity.

O 8 Outlines and Summaries

Practice in outlining and in summarizing helps a writer achieve a firm grasp of oganization.

O 8a Working Outlines. *Even in writing a short theme, you will do well to construct a working outline by jotting down major points in a tentative order.* The working outline for a library or research paper is usually a rather carefully developed chart, without which the investigator may lose his way.

Here is a first tentative outline for a short paper on anti-intellectualism in the high schools:

emphasis in high school on
    athletics
    social activities

little recognition for intellectual achievement
    honor roll
    debating society
    drama society ("intellectual"?)

attitude now changing?
    stress on college entrance

NOTE: A good outline, reworked and reorganized repeatedly as the paper progresses, resembles an architect's preliminary sketches rather than his finished blueprint. An outline helps the writer visualize and strengthen tentative connections. It helps him detect weaknesses after he has finished his first draft. It serves him as a guide in cutting sentences and paragraphs that turn out to be irrelevant.

O 8b Final Outlines. *The final outline, intended as a guide to the reader, usually follows one of several conventional forms.*

(1) The **topic outline** is most useful for quick reference. It presents, in logical order, the topics and subtopics that a paper covers. Like other outlines, it is often preceded by a thesis sentence summarizing the central idea of the paper:

WHY I WENT TO COLLEGE

THESIS: Going to college offered me both personal satisfactions and practical advantages.

I. Desire for independence
   A. Freedom from direct parental supervision
   B. Absence of demanding brothers and sisters

II. Attraction of changed surroundings
   A. Living in a congenial environment
      1. Quiet and dignity of college town
      2. Natural beauty of its surroundings
   B. Meeting people
      1. Classmates and fellow business majors
      2. Social acquaintances
   C. Participating in the cultural life of the college community

III. Satisfaction of working for a definite goal
   A. Choice of majors leading to a business career
   B. Opportunities for field work

(2) In a **sentence outline**, the writer sums up, in one complete sentence each, what he has to say on each topic and subtopic. The sentence outline thus forces him to think through his material thoroughly and systematically:

MAIN STREET ISN'T PENNSYLVANIA AVENUE

THESIS: A successful business career does not automatically qualify an executive for government work.

I. Prominent businessmen have often occupied high positions in the federal government.

II. Business executives often lack preparation for important aspects of government work.
   A. They tend to lack the tact and experience necessary for dealing with people from foreign cultures.
      1. They may alienate foreign diplomats.
      2. They tend to ignore public opinion abroad.
   B. They tend to lack the legal training required in interpreting and administering laws.
   C. They tend to be impatient with the delays inherent in democratic processes.

III. Businessmen often have qualifications that government officials tend to lack.
   A. They are in close contact with the wishes and opinions of the general public.
   B. They have thorough training in organizational problems.
      1. They are trained in administrative efficiency.
      2. They are cost-conscious.

IV. The personal qualifications of the individual executive are more important than his business background.

NOTE: The divisions of an outline do not always correspond exactly to the paragraph divisions in the paper. Several minor subdivisions may be treated in the same paragraph; one subdivision developed by detailed examples may spread through several paragraphs; short transitional paragraphs may intervene between subdivisions.

(3) A **paragraph outline** requires one summarizing statement for each paragraph. Usually these summarizing sentences are simply numbered consecutively, without an attempt to indicate the major divisions of the paper or the relative importance of different paragraphs.

Check your finished outlines against the following list of suggestions:

(1) *Be consistent* in the use of symbols, indention, and spacing.

(2) *Avoid using "Introduction," "Conclusion,"* etc., as substitutes for individual headings.

(3) *Avoid single subdivisions.* If there is a subdivision *A,* there should be a subdivision *B.* If there is a section numbered *1,* there should be a section numbered *2.* If a section covers only one major point or one major step, leave it undivided.

(4) *Avoid a long sequence of parallel elements* such as *I-X, A-F,* or *1-8.* Unless the subject matter justifies mere un-

differentiated enumeration, try to split the sequence into two or three major groups.

(5) *Use parallel grammatical structure* for headings of the same rank in order to emphasize their logical relation. For instance, if *A 1* reads "To revive the student's interest," *A 2* and *A 3* should also be worded as infinitives: "To promote the student's participation"; "To develop the student's independent judgment."

(6) Make sure that *subdivisions are relevant and logically subordinate to the main heading* under which they appear.

(7) Make sure that your thesis is specific rather than vague and that it represents the central idea of the paper. *Make sure the thesis is a complete statement*—not a question, not a phrase without a predicate, not a dependent clause.

(8) In a topic outline, *make each topic specific and informative.* In a sentence outline, make each subdivision a complete sentence. *Make each sentence sum up an idea* rather than merely indicate a topic.

O 8c Summaries. *Related to skill in outlining is skill in the writing of summaries*—of your own work or, more commonly, of the work of others.[1] To summarize a piece of writing, you need to grasp its organization. You can then state essential points and qualifications in the most concise possible form, omitting illustrations, lengthy explanations, and incidental comment. A summary can preserve the gist of an article or a paper for efficient study, for future reference, or for the use of a busy reader.

In writing a summary, you will have to observe several essential requirements.

(1) *Make sure you grasp the main trend of thought.*

[1] See Section 8 for detailed discussion of how to summarize and paraphrase quoted material.

Isolate key sentences; formulate the major point implied in a paragraph; distinguish between incidental comments and important steps in an argument.

(2) *Reduce explanation and illustration to the essential minimum.* Omit passages that are mere paraphrase. Preserve only the most important details, examples, statistics. Reduce or omit elaboration by metaphor, comparison, anecdote.

(3) *Use the most economical wording possible.* Use the simpler of two alternative terms, the shorter of two synonyms. If you can, substitute a single word for a phrase, a phrase for a clause.

Study the differences between the full text and the summary in the following pairs:

ORIGINAL: The invention of the process of printing from movable type, which occurred in Germany about the middle of the fifteenth century, was destined to exercise a far-reaching influence on all the vernacular languages of Europe. Introduced into England about 1476 by William Caxton, who had learned the art on the continent, printing made such rapid progress that a scant century later it was observed that manuscript books were seldom to be met with and almost never used. Some idea of the rapidity with which the new process swept forward may be had from the fact that in Europe the number of books printed before the year 1500 reaches the surprising figure of 35,000. The majority of these, it is true, were in Latin, whereas it is in the modern languages that the effect of the printing press was chiefly to be felt. But in England over 20,000 titles in English had appeared by 1640, ranging all the way from mere pamphlets to massive folios. The result was to bring books, which had formerly been the expensive luxury of the few, within the reach of all. More important, however, was the fact, so obvious today, that it was possible to reproduce a book in a thousand copies or a hundred thousand, every one exactly like the other. A powerful force thus existed for promoting a standard uniform language, and the means were now available for spreading that language throughout the territory in which it was understood.—Albert C. Baugh, *A History of the English Language*

SUMMARY: Printing from movable type, invented in Germany about 1450 and brought to England about 1476, had a far-reaching influence on all European languages. Within a hundred years, manuscript books had become rare. Though at first most printed books were in Latin, over 20,000 titles in English had appeared by 1640. Books were now within the reach of everyone and could exert a powerful standardizing influence upon language.

ORIGINAL: The tendency to erect "systems"—which are then marketed as a whole—affects particularly the less mature sciences of medicine and psychology. In these subjects we have had a succession of intellectual edifices originally made available only in their entirety. It is as if one cannot rent a room or even a suite in a new building, but must lease the whole or not enter. Starting with a substantial contribution to medicine the authors of such systems expand their theories to include ambitious explanations of matters far beyond the original validated observations. And after the first pioneer, later and usually lesser contributors to the system add further accretions of mingled fact and theory. Consequently systems of this kind—like homeopathy, phrenology, psychoanalysis, and conditioned reflexology (the last dominant for years in Russia)—eventually contain almost inextricable mixtures of sense and nonsense. They capture fervid adherents, and it may take a generation or several for those who preserve some objectivity to succeed in salvaging the best in them while discarding the dross.—Dr. Ian Stevenson, "Scientists with Half-Closed Minds," *Harper's*

SUMMARY: Medicine and psychology have produced a number of intellectual systems that one is asked to accept as a whole or not at all. The ambitious authors and adherents of such systems go beyond original valid findings to produce a mixture of truth and error that attracts enthusiastic supporters. Objective observers may not succeed in separating the valuable from the worthless till much later.

NOTE: Unless the original version is already severely condensed, a summary of about one third or one fourth the original length can usually preserve the essential points. However, the shorter the summary, the greater the danger of oversimplification or outright misrepresentation. You will have to be careful to preserve essential conditions and distinctions: *if-* and *unless-*clauses; differences between *is, will,* and *might;* qualifiers like *only, almost,* and *on the whole.* You will have to preserve the relative emphasis of the original, giving more prominence to a point treated at great length than to one mentioned in passing.

EXERCISES

A. Select a current magazine article whose organization you find exceptionally clear or effective. Prepare both a topic and a sentence outline. Your instructor may wish to suggest a maximum number of words for each outline.

B. Sort out the following material and arrange it in a topic outline:

EDUCATION WITHOUT REPRESENTATION

THESIS: Students would profit greatly from being given greater influence on curricula and teaching methods than they now have.

1. Training for citizenship through active participation
2. Present lack of student influence
3. Sense of belonging through participation
4. Attitudes toward elective as compared with required courses
5. Success of experimental programs
6. Attitude of night school and business college students toward freely chosen subjects
7. Training for adult responsibilities in business and family through participation
8. Improved motivation through active participation

C. Sort out the following material and arrange it in a sentence outline:

THE VALUE OF GROUP DISCUSSION

THESIS: Training in the techniques of group discussion is an indispensable part of the student's general education.

1. Discussion teaches us to look for evidence that will withstand criticism.

2. Discussion teaches us to control emotional reactions.

3. The primary goal of a discussion is to solve immediate problems.

4. Successful discussion requires ability to focus on the subject at hand.

5. In modern American society, more and more decisions are reached as the result of group discussion.

6. Successful discussion requires willingness to consider the viewpoints of others.

7. Discussion teaches us to estimate the reliability of evidence submitted by others.

8. Comparison of different views enables us to distinguish valid from invalid arguments.

9. The give-and-take of discussion is a humane alternative to one-sided propaganda and the use of force.

10. Discussion teaches us to get along with others.

11. Discussion teaches us to respect people whose knowledge or ability is superior to ours.

12. A successful discussion has educational value.

13. Discussion teaches us to be patient with people whom we assume to be wrong.

14. Discussion teaches us to evaluate evidence.

15. Successful discussion requires careful investigation of the relevant facts.

16. Discussion teaches us how to think.

17. Disagreement forces us to re-examine our views.

D. (**Review**) Outline each of the following student themes. Is there a thesis sentence? How adequate are restriction of subject, organization, and paragraph development? Comment on the effectiveness of title, introduction, and conclusion. Examine each theme for continuity.

(ex.)

1. CERAMICS—MY HOBBY

Have you ever picked up a piece of free-form earthenware and thought how very satisfying and enjoyable it must have been for the person who worked it up from mere earth and water? By "free form," I mean the potter's own creative idea modeled in clay. Such free-form modeling is rather an involved process—many times, it is true, heartbreaking, but nevertheless an enjoyable and thoroughly gratifying experience.

It is possible to dig one's own clay from the earth. By moistening it with water and adding certain chemicals, one can make the clay mass more elastic, more workable, and stronger. Then follows the mixing of a glaze which, according to a specialized formula, will have an affinity to the original clay body. This in itself can become a long and tedious procedure. So, unless one has a pioneering spirit, it is better to find a standard clay body and glazes which have already been processed according to the manufacturer's own formula.

Cutting, shaping and molding the clay mass into the desired form with one's own hands is one of the biggest thrills imaginable. It is surprising what can be done with moist clay! A creative spirit can really go "wild" and still come up with something both beautiful and practical—say a flower vase or planter in the exaggerated form of some sea shell.

When the piece is thoroughly dry, it is known as "greenware" and is very fragile, but it becomes hardened through firing in a kiln. The firing is done slowly. The heat goes up to about 2000°F. It is measured by a cone-shaped pin set in a clay base and made to melt at the desired temperature. This is known as the pyrometric cone. The entire firing period takes about eight hours. Then the kiln is cooled slowly. It should not be opened or disturbed during the cooling time, which may take twelve hours or more. The greenware is now referred to as "bisque."

Bisque may be painted in a variety of colors, called underglaze, and then dipped in a transparent glaze. It may be sprayed or brushed with or dipped in any of the colored glazes. A second firing to bring out the glaze effect is now necessary. Usually, this firing is slow too, with the temperature not as intense as before—about 1800°F. However, the pyrometric cone must be watched more closely than in the bisque firing, especially with certain glaze formulas.

Glazes are extremely difficult to control, and many unexpected effects are obtained—probably caused by moisture in the air, uneven firing elements, firing time, dirt particles, or some chemical reaction. Many unique and unusual effects can be obtained through experimentation with underglazes, overglazes, colored clay bodies, sifted sands, crushed colored glass and even salt! I remember my first experiment. I used sifted sand which I found in my backyard. I dusted the sand over the glaze coating and, after firing, found there were bright red and black raised granules throughout the glaze.

One can look at this hobby from a practical point of view. Gifts alone, especially at Christmas time, make it worth while. But it is the ideas and experiments that make it a truly fascinating and worthwhile hobby.

2. HAPPINESS IN THE FAMILY

It is a safe venture to say that no one is more familiar with any family than he is with his own, the one he was brought up in. This is certainly the case with me, and it is largely my own family experiences and conditions which have influenced my views of successful family life. I feel that I am fortunate in being part of a successful family and in having been brought up in a happy home environment. When I examine the reasons for our happiness, certain factors stand out, which I will attempt to explain.

Certainly not a prerequisite to family success, but a factor which has considerably influenced my family's happiness, is having many members in the family. I come from a family of eight. Although a large family has disadvantages, I feel that the advantages far outweigh the problems that arise. In a large family, for instance, there is rarely loneliness, and affection usually prevails. I can't exactly pinpoint the reason why there is such a warm atmosphere in large families, but it might partly be that, as in my family, there is always some little sister or brother who needs comforting from a mishap, or someone who needs advice or requires help in a task. The feeling of closeness is promoted so much that it becomes habitual.

Family activities are an integral part of successful family living. The family should take out time now and then to do things together as a group. This strengthens family unity and promotes common interests among the members. I always looked forward eagerly to such family excursions as occasional visits to the museum or outings to a duck pond for a picnic. It has also been a policy of my family to take an annual camping trip to a national park and spend a week "roughing it." We all enjoy such exploits and share a unanimous liking for the outdoors.

I have always been glad that my family lives in a relaxed, informal atmosphere. When strict, formal behavior is enforced in a home, the members sometimes feel constrained and may become reserved in manner. I remember the summer when I was twelve years old, during which I went to live with my aunt's family for four months. It wasn't long before I began to count the days until I was to leave. Not only were my cousins and I made to address my aunt exclusively as "Ma'am," but many other restrictions were imposed upon us. No pace faster than a walk was allowed in the house, no loud talking was permitted, and no discussions were tolerated at the dinner table except between the adults. Even such minor things as eating corn-on-the-cob were regulated. We were instructed to eat two rows of corn at a time and chew each bit twenty-two times. I was so busy regulating bits and counting chews that the distinctive pleasure of eating corn-on-the-cob was lost. I know my cousins were as frustrated by all these restrictions as I was. Spontaneous affection, which I think is a necessary part of family happiness, can hardly be cultivated in an atmosphere like this.

Religion plays an important role in family life. There should be a common religion among the members, and the religious customs should be observed if the religion is to have any meaning for all members. I know of one family in which the mother was of one religion and the father of another. The conflicting religious customs resulted in both parents dropping their own observances, and the children now have no religion at all. Aside from failing to provide each member with religious satisfaction, this family is missing out on the special unity brought about by a common religion.

I think that the conditions essential to a happy family life are those which promote unity among the members, open expression of affection, and the personal contentment of each individual. I hope I can achieve these goals in a family of my own someday, much as they have been achieved in the one in which I grew up.

3. SOMETHING NEW

Have you ever thought what a joy it would be to be thrilled at the idea of returning to college in the fall, to look forward with anxiety and zeal to your coming classes? If you are the way I am, you probably dread the thought of lugging those old school books down that foggy, cold path to the school buildings in the morning. After that, you fight to stay awake under the heat from the old radiator next to you and the monotonous drone of the econ-professor. Once through with your first-hour class, you wander aimlessly through a barrage of other uninteresting subjects. Then, finally, you are through with your last class for the day, and back you plod on the trail home. Not a very exciting day, is it?

That is what college holds for me—or did until recently. You see, I have just finished reading Herman Hundinger's essay, "Education at Beechcroft College." His description of the system that is used by this school has not only greatly aroused and interested me but has affected my entire outlook on college education.

Can you imagine going to school and not having a preselected and definite curriculum thrown at you with the command, "Do it or else!" Under the Beechcroft system you will be amazed when you find yourself telling your advisor or counselor just what courses and subjects you wish to pursue. Then too, if you are in doubt, you can test out certain fields of endeavor that you are curious about. In the days ahead, if you find the trial curriculums are not what you wished or expected, you are free to change your major objective. You are allowed two years to "find" yourself; you are given the freedom of every way and means that you need to master and learn your chosen field of study. To aid you in your learning, there will be your counselor, who will meet with you once a week and give you directions and guidance. Your counselor will show you the proper channels and areas that you will need to know; he will also give you encouragement when you are feeling down and praise you when you are accomplishing that next rung on the ladder to the culmination of your life's work.

Let us place you in an example that will be found in a school of the sort described. Suppose you had chosen Industrial Relations for your major (which incidentally is my present major). You would have on your schedule for the day the classes that you yourself had chosen. There is no power or force that compels you to attend these classes, but you do so of your own accord. Some days, instead of going to class, you might visit the library and fall victim to those overpowering stacks. You would probably be so absorbed in your quest for more and more knowledge, contained in those thousands of books, that lunch time would have passed by hours ago. I don't want to convey to you at this point that you will not gain any knowledge or information from attending your classes. On the contrary, during your independent research you will be encountering many difficulties and problems. These obstacles can be overcome with instructions and guidance by your professors; they can be thrashed out and dissected in a group laboratory, or with just the instructor alone. In this way you will acquire more accurate understanding and knowledge.

Then you might spend another day in doing field work. By field work, I mean going out into the world and encountering actual everyday experience. You might decide to visit all the retail department stores in your city and try to determine what harmony, if any, there is in the relations between management and labor. With your instructor's guidance in making charts and plotting curves to find the normal expected behavior, you will be able to make many new and interesting assumptions and conclusions.

This knowledge, that you are studying what you want, and learning facts that you want to learn, will force you (very much I'm afraid) to burn that midnight oil. I am sorry we do not have a system like this in my school today. Picture yourself tearing out of the house before having that second cup of coffee, racing helter-skelter to the college, and roaring with vim and vigor through the day's schedule! Perhaps my children may enjoy these privileges that I have been denied.

THEME TOPICS

OBSERVATION AND DESCRIPTION

1. Describe a fairly complicated piece of machinery or equipment, such as a radio or television set, a gasoline or diesel engine, refrigerating or air conditioning apparatus.
2. Compare two cars or pieces of equipment to show which you consider superior.
3. Describe some type of fairly complicated work or a hobby which requires a certain amount of knowledge or skill.
4. Describe a city which you remember as particularly memorable or as in some way different from what you take to be the average medium-sized or small American town.
5. Describe the countryside in an area comparatively untouched by city civilization.

PERSONAL EXPERIENCE

6. Write an account of the high school or college instructor who comes closest to your idea of an ideal teacher.
7. Write an account of the vocation or profession that you plan to follow or that interests you most.
8. Compare contrasting influences in your family background or early training.
9. What has your own experience taught you about the role or influence of women in American society?
10. What are some of the causes of misunderstanding between teen-agers and their parents?

OPINIONS ON COLLEGE LIFE

11. Was your high school training adequate preparation for the kind of work you are expected to do in college?

12. Weigh the advantages and disadvantages of being a member of a fraternity or sorority.
13. Is a part-time job an asset or a handicap?
14. Would students be better off if there were no required courses?
15. Is it true that college students are apathetic about social, political, or religious issues?

DEFINITION OF TERMS

16. Explain and illustrate your idea of a "tactful" person, a "perfect gentleman," or a "snob."
17. Can one draw a clear line between the "amateur" and the "professional" athlete?
18. Can college students be called more "mature" than high school students?
19. Define and illustrate "fair play," "tolerance," or "open-mindedness."
20. Explain what you mean by a "good actor," a "good play," a "good book."

GENERALIZATION AND INFERENCE

21. Explain and support a general conclusion you have reached about a group of people or a type of person.
22. What psychological factors make people buy one car rather than another?
23. What accounts for the popularity of a television or radio show, or a television or movie star?
24. Which qualities is a college-educated girl of your own age most likely to look for in a future husband?
25. What is the status of minority groups in your home town or in the schools that you have attended?

ARGUMENT AND CONTROVERSY

26. Should eighteen-year-olds have the right to vote?
27. Should comic books be subject to censorship?

28. Does the United States have a moral obligation to help underdeveloped countries?
29. Can a good patriot support world government?
30. Is the separation of church and state in the best interests of church and state?

READING AND WRITING

31. Describe as fully—and as frankly—as you can your favorite reading material.
32. Discuss a book by a modern writer to show what makes it "modern."
33. Explain your preferences or dislikes as regards poetry.
34. Should high school students be required to read Shakespeare?
35. Why do you (don't you) like to write?

6

MECHANICS AND SPELLING

M 1 Manuscript Mechanics

A writer must learn to submit neat and competently prepared copy.

Whenever you hand in a theme or a report, the outward appearance of your manuscript is the first thing to strike your reader. A good first impression is likely to put him in a tolerant and receptive mood. A bad first impression is likely to linger even after he discovers compensating virtues in the text.

M 1a Penmanship and Typing. *All copy, whether handwritten or typed, should be neat and legible.* To produce legible handwritten copy, use composition paper of standard size, preferably ruled in *wide lines,* and a reliable pen. You may find that you don't write fast enough, especially when you are asked to write in class. Don't try to develop speed by substituting a smudge for letters like *a, e,* or *i;* by running together combinations like *mm* or *mn;* or by substituting a vague scrawl for endings like *ing* and *tion*. Instead, practice speed writing while at the same time forcing yourself to make every *a* and *e* as distinct as your grade school penmanship book required. Dot all your *i*'s and cross all your *t*'s. Distinguish clearly between capitals and lower-case letters.

Prune your writing of flourishes that interfere with the immediate perception of the standard letters and symbols. Avoid excessive slanting or excessive crowding. Unconventional handwriting is much more likely to annoy than it is to impress the reader.

To prepare typewritten copy, use unlined paper of standard

size. Onionskin paper or semi-transparent sheets are for carbon copies; use solid, nontransparent paper of good quality for the copy you turn in. Change your typewriter ribbon at reasonable intervals.

Double-space all material except block quotations and footnotes. Leave two spaces after a period or other end punctuation; use two hyphens—with no space on either side—to make a dash. Proofread all typewritten copy carefully for typographical errors and for errors in transcription.

M 1b Corrections. *Last-minute corrections are permissible on the final copy, provided they are few in number, look neat, and conform to standard practice.* (On papers written outside class all major revisions are of course made on the rough draft.)

(1) Draw a line through words and phrases that you want to omit; *do not use parentheses or square brackets for this purpose.*

(2) To correct a word, draw a line through it and insert the corrected word in the space immediately above; avoid crossing out or inserting individual letters.

(3) To add a missing word, insert a caret (‸) and write the word immediately above.

M 1c Titles of Themes. *Titles of themes follow the general rules for the capitalization of words in titles of publications* (see SP 7b). Do *not* underline or put in quotation marks the title that you assign to one of your own themes. Use a question mark or exclamation mark after it where appropriate, but do *not* use a period even if your title is a complete sentence:

Chivalry Is Dead
Is Chivalry Dead?
Chivalry Is Dead!

M 1d Spacing and Syllabication. *Observe conventional spacing and syllabication.* Whether your papers are handwritten or typed, leave adequate margins. An inch and a half on the left and at the top, and an inch on the right and at the bottom are about standard. Indent the first lines of paragraphs, about an inch in longhand or five spaces in typed copy. To make a last-minute change in the paragraphing of a paper, insert the symbol ¶ to indicate an additional paragraph break. Insert *no* ¶ in the margin to indicate that an existing paragraph break should be ignored.

On the whole, a somewhat uneven right margin is preferable to the practice of dividing words at the end of every second or third line. Dictionaries generally use centered dots to indicate where a word may conventionally be divided (*com·pli·ment*). A few generally observed practices are worth remembering:

(1) The setting off of single letters saves little or no space and tends to confuse the reader. Do not divide words like *about, alone,* and *enough* or like *many* and *via.* Similarly, do not set off the ending *ed* in words like *complained* or *renewed.*

(2) Hyphenated words become confusing when divided at any other point than at the original hyphen. Do not break up the *American* in "un-American" or the *sister* in "sister-in-law."

(3) Do not divide the last word on a page.

M 1e Italics. Italics (or slanted type) are indicated in the handwritten or typed manuscript by underlining.

(1) *Italics identify technical terms and words borrowed from foreign languages.* (See P 8e.)

(2) *Italics serve to emphasize or call special attention to part of a sentence:*

> The judge told me to apologize *in person* to everyone who had sat down in the freshly painted pews.
>
> The company is not liable for accidents caused by the negligence of employees or *by mechanical defects.*

Like other means of procuring emphasis, such italics lose their value if overused.

(3) *Italics serve to set off the title of a publication from the text in which it is cited.* Italicize titles of periodicals and of works published as separate units. Use **quotation marks** to set off titles of articles, chapters, or poems that are merely a part of a complete publication:

Kipling's "Recessional" can be found in *A Treasury of Verse.*

For many years, Chicago has had one of the best book-review sections in the country in the *Tribune's* "Sunday Magazine of Books."

M 2 Abbreviations and Numbers

Avoid the overuse of abbreviations in ordinary expository prose.

Abbreviations save much time and space. Here as in other matters, however, formal written English discourages excessive short cuts. The short cuts are obviously excessive in a sentence like the following: "Chas. told his prof. that during the past 3 yrs. he had been working for the govt. in L.A."

M 2a Acceptable Abbreviations. *Some abbreviations are generally appropriate in expository writing:*

(1) Before or after names, the titles *Mr., Mrs., Dr., St.* (*Saint*); the abbreviations *Jr.* and *Sr.;* degrees like *M.D.* and *Ph.D.* (Mr. John J. Smith, Jr.; Dr. Alfred Joyce or Alfred Joyce, M.D.).

(2) Before or after numerals, the abbreviations *No.,* A.D. and B.C., A.M. and P.M.; and the symbol $ (in 1066 B.C.; at 5:30 A.M.; $275).

(3) Initials standing for the names of agencies, organizations, business firms, technical processes, chemical compounds,

and the like, when the full name is awkward or unfamiliar: *AFL-CIO, FBI, PTA, TVA, UNESCO, DDT, FM radio.*

(4) Some common Latin abbreviations: *e.g.* (for example), *etc.* (and so on), *i.e.* (that is), *viz.* (namely). However, the modern tendency is to prefer the corresponding English expressions.

M 2b Restricted Abbreviations. *Some abbreviations are appropriate in addresses, newspaper reports, technical reports, and other special contexts.* Most of these have to be written in full in ordinary expository prose:

(1) With a few exceptions, names of countries, states, streets, and the like, are spelled out in ordinary writing: *United States; Schenectady, New York; Union Street* (Exceptions: *USSR; Washington, D.C.*).

(2) The ampersand ("&") and abbreviations like *Inc.* and *Bros.* occur in ordinary writing only in references to organizations that employ those abbreviations in their official titles: *Smith & Company, Inc.*

(3) In ordinary expository prose, *lb.* (pound), *oz.* (ounce), *ft.* (foot), and *in.* (inch) are usually spelled out. Some units of measurement are more unwieldy and are abbreviated, provided they are used with figures: *45 mph, 1500 rpm.*

Check your dictionary whenever you are not sure of the use of capitals and periods with an abbreviation. Some dictionaries include common abbreviations in the main listing; others list them in a special appendix.

M 2c Numbers. *In ordinary expository prose, the use of figures is to some extent restricted.* They are generally appropriate in references to the date of the month (*May 13*), the year (*1917*), street numbers (*1014 Union Avenue*), and page numbers (*Chapter 7, page 18*). For other uses of numbers, the following conventions are widely observed:

(1) Numbers from one to ten, and *round numbers* requiring no more than two words, are usually spelled out (*three dollars a seat; five hundred years later; ten thousand copies*).

(2) Figures are used for *exact sums, technical measurements, decimals, and percentages,* as well as for references to time using A.M. or P.M. (*$7.22; 500,673 inhabitants; 57 per cent; 2:30* P.M.).

(3) Figures are avoided at the beginning of a sentence: "Fifteen out of 28 replied . . ." or "When questioned, 15 out of 28 replied . . ." Except in special situations like this one, changes from figures to words (and vice versa) in a series of numbers are generally avoided.

(4) When spelled out, *compound numbers* from 21 to 99 are hyphenated: *twenty-five; one hundred and forty-six.*

EXERCISE

Rewrite the following passage, using abbreviations and numerals in accordance with standard practice:

> Mister Geo. Brown had resided at Eighteen N. Washington St. since Feb. nineteen-hundred and forty-four. Though he weighed only one hundred and twenty-six lbs. and measured little more than 5 ft., he was an ardent devotee of the rugged life. He did his exercises every a. m. and refused to send for the Dr. when he had a cold. 3 yrs. after he moved here from Chicago, Ill., the Boy Scouts of America made him an honorary member, & he soon became known in scout circles for the many $ he contributed to the Boy Scout movement. One Sat. afternoon B. forgot to spell out the amount on a check for one-hundred and twenty-five dollars intended for a bldg. drive and payable to the B. S. of A. The treasurer, Bernard Simpson of Arlington, Va., wrote in 2 additional figures, spelled out the changed amount, and left the U. S. after withdrawing B.'s life savings of twelve-thousand five-hundred and fifty dollars from the local bank. "Ah," said Geo. when he found 2 $ and 36 cts. left in his account, "if I had only spelled out the No.'s and abbrev.!"

SP 1 Spelling Habits

Correct spelling is the result of good spelling habits, established by study and drill over the years.

The average high school graduate spells correctly most of the words he uses. According to recent studies, most of the trouble that college students have with spelling is caused by perhaps fewer than 250 words out of the 5,000 or 10,000 they are likely to use. The most common troublemakers are everyday words like *believe* or *definite*. The spelling of such a word may look right not because you have seen it in this particular word but because you have seen it in another word that is confusingly similar. Thus, you may spell the main syllable in *believe* like the main syllable in *receive*. You may spell the ending in *definite* like the ending in *ultimate*. To spell such a word correctly, you have to memorize it letter by letter, while at the same time seeing each letter as a part of the whole.

SP 1a Corrective Drill. Merely looking up misspelled words has little long-range effect. The following procedure has a good chance of producing favorable results:

(1) *Find out which words you tend to misspell.* Make a list of all spelling errors pointed out to you in your themes, quizzes, and exams. Work your way through a list of common spelling demons (such as the one printed under SP 4) and copy out those that you have found troublesome in your own writing.

(2) *Put in twenty minutes three times a week over a fairly long period of time.* Unless you work on your spelling regularly, you will make little progress. You cannot unlearn in two or three hours the spelling habits that you developed over many years.

(3) *Work out a definite routine and stick to it.* At each

sitting, take up a group of perhaps ten or twenty spelling words. If you are a "visualizer," place your spelling words before you in clear, legible handwriting. Try putting them on a set of small note cards that you can carry around with you. Run your eyes over each word until you can see both the individual letters and the whole word at the same time. Circle the letters that cause the most trouble. If you learn primarily by ear, read each word aloud. Then spell each letter individually: *Receive*—R-E-C-E-I-V-E. If you learn best when you can bring your nerves and muscles into play, try writing each word in large letters. Trace it over several times. Combine or alternate the three methods in the manner that seems to yield the best results.

(4) *Make use of memory devices like the following:*

MAC got ACquainted.
ALL RIGHT means ALL is RIGHT.
There's an INNING in begINNING.
Don't beLIEve LIEs.
There's a CRITIC in CRITICism.
There's IRON in the envIRONment.
Men who GOVERN are a GOVERNment.
There's a COG in reCOGnition.
There's a VILLA in VILLAin.

SP lb New Words. *Copy out difficult new terms and names that you encounter in your reading for various courses.* Study and memorize them. If you are a science major, master words like *enzyme, anesthesia, protein,* or *arteriosclerosis*. If you are taking a literature course, focus on the exact spelling of names like *Oedipus, Xanthippe,* or *Omar Khayyam.*

SP 2 Spelling Problems

Learn to identify and master recurrent spelling problems.

Some words can be conveniently grouped together because they share common characteristics. Others are best studied together because they need to be carefully distinguished from each other.

SP 2a Spelling and Pronunciation. *Some words become spelling problems because the gap between spelling and pronunciation is unusually wide.*

(1) Frequent causes of confusion are *vowels occurring in unstressed positions.* For instance, *a, e,* and *i* become indistinguishable in the endings *ate* and *ite, able* and *ible, ance* and *ence, ant* and *ent.* You can sometimes learn to choose the right ending by associating the word with a closely related one: *definite* (fin*i*sh, defin*i*tion); *separate* (separ*a*tion); *ultimate* (ultim*a*tum); *indispensable* (dispens*a*ry). For many other words no such crutches are available. Watch out for the following:

a: accept*able,* accept*ance,* attend*ance,* attend*ant,* brilli*ant,* perform*ance*

e: consist*ent,* excell*ence,* excell*ent,* exist*ence,* experi*ence,* independ*ent,* persist*ent,* tend*ency*

i: irresist*ible,* plaus*ible,* poss*ible,* suscept*ible*

(2) A number of words are difficult to spell because of *silent* or *slurred consonants.* Be sure to insert the silent consonants in "condem*n,*" "de*b*t," "dou*b*t," "forei*g*n," "mor*t*gage," and "sovereign." Some consonants are silent only in hasty or in nonstandard speech: "can*d*idate," "Feb*r*uary," "gover*n*ment," "lib*r*ary," "quan*t*ity."

(3) In unstressed positions, words like *have, can,* or *will* tend to appear in shortened forms. Do not substitute *of* for *have* in combinations like *could have been, might have been, should have seen.*

SP 2b Variant Forms. *Some words are confusing because they appear in a variety of forms.*

(1) Especially confusing are different spellings in variant forms of the *same root word:* "ti*ll*" but "unti*l*," "fo*u*r" and "fo*u*rteen" but "f*or*ty," "fo*r*ward" but "fo*re*most," "ni*ne*" and "ni*ne*ty" but "ni*n*th." Watch out for spelling differences in pairs of words representing different grammatical categories:

absor*b*—absor*p*tion, advi*s*e (v.)—advi*c*e (n.), conscien*c*e—con-scien*t*ious, court*eous*—court*e*sy, curi*ous*—curi*o*sity, dissen*t*—dissen*s*ion, gener*ous*—gener*o*sity, geni*us*—ingeni*ous*, proc*eed*—proc*e*dure, pron*ou*nce—pron*u*nciation, ren*ou*nce—ren*u*nciation

Notice the *ed* in "He *used* to come" and "He was prejudic*ed*."

(2) Sometimes a confusing change in spelling accompanies a *change in the grammatical form* of the same word. For instance, you "ch*oo*se" and "l*ea*d" in the present, but you "ch*o*se" and "l*e*d" in the past. Most nouns have distinctive forms for one of a kind (**singular**) and several of a kind (**plural**). These sometimes cause spelling difficulties: one *man* but several *men,* one *woman* but several *women.* Remember these especially:

SINGULAR:	hero	Negro	potato	tomato	wife
PLURAL:	hero*es*	Negro*es*	potato*es*	tomato*es*	wi*ves*
SINGULAR:	freshman	postman	life	veto	calf
PLURAL:	freshm*e*n	postm*e*n	li*ves*	veto*es*	cal*ves*

NOTE: Your dictionary lists the correct spelling of plural forms that are difficult or unusual. Sometimes it lists two acceptable forms: *buffalos* or *buffaloes, scarfs* or *scarves.*

SP 2c Confusing Words. *Some words need attention because they sound similar but differ in spelling or in meaning.* Here is partial list of these:

ACCEPT: to *acc*ept a bribe; to find something *acc*eptable; to make an *acc*eptance speech

EXCEPT: everyone *exc*ept Judy; to make an *exc*eption; to *exc*ept (exempt, exclude) present company

ADOPT: to ad*o*pt a proposal (in its present form); the ad*o*ption racket

ADAPT: to ad*a*pt it to our needs (to make it more suitable); an ad*a*ptable worker; an ad*a*ptation from a novel

CAPITAL: unused capit*a*l; modern capit*a*lism; the capit*a*l of France; capit*a*l letters

CAPITOL: the cupola of the Capit*o*l; remodeling the façade of the Capit*o*l

CENSOR: to cens*or* a reporter's dispatch; to object to cens*or*ship

CENSURE: to cens*ure* (blame, condemn) someone for his behavior; a vote of cens*ure*

CITE: *c*ited for bravery; to *c*ite many different authorities; a *c*itation for reckless driving

SITE: the *s*ite of the new high school (where it is *sit*uated or located)

CONSUL: the American c*o*nsul in Berlin; the French c*o*nsulate in New York

COUNCIL: the members of the city coun*ci*l; Coun*ci*lor Brown

COUNSEL: the coun*se*ling staff of the college; camp coun*se*lors

DESERT: he lost his way in the de*s*ert; he de*s*erted his family; he got his just de*s*erts

DESSERT: the dinner did not include a de*ss*ert

EFFECT: to *e*ffect (produce, bring about) a change; immediate *e*ffects; an *e*ffective speech

AFFECT: it *a*ffected (had an influence on) his grade; he spoke with an *a*ffected (artificial) British accent

LOOSE: l*oo*se and fast; l*oo*sen your grip

LOSE: win or l*o*se; a bad l*o*ser

PERSONAL: a perso*nal* appeal; speak to him perso*nal*ly
PERSONNEL: a perso*nnel* bureau; hire additional perso*nnel*

PRESENTS: visitors bearing presen*ts*
PRESENCE: your presen*ce* is requested; presen*ce* of mind

PRINCIPAL: his princip*al* (main) argument; the princip*al* of the school
PRINCIPLE: princip*les* (rules, standards) of conduct; the princip*les* of economics

QUIET: be qu*ie*t; a qu*ie*t neighborhood
QUITE: qu*ite* so; not qu*ite*

RIGHT: r*ight* and wrong; r*ight* and left; all r*ight*
RITE: savage r*ites* (ceremonies); the r*ites* of spring
-WRIGHT: a play*wright;* a wheel*wright* (a man who wrought, or made, wheels and carriages)

THAN: bigger th*a*n life; more trouble th*a*n it is worth
THEN: now and th*e*n; until th*e*n

THERE: here and th*ere;* th*ere* you are; no one was th*ere*
THEIR: they lost th*eir* appetite; mental ills and th*eir* cure

TO: go *to* bed, cut *to* pieces; easy *to* do, hard *to* deny
TOO: *too* good to be true; bring your children, *too*
TWO: *two* and *two* makes four

WHETHER: *whe*ther good or bad
WEATHER: bad *wea*ther; to *wea*ther the storm

EXERCISES

A. Insert the missing letter in each of the following words; accept__nce, attend__nce, brilli__nt, consist__ncy, defin__te, excell__nt, exist__nce, experi__nce, independ__nt, indispens__ble, occurr__nce, irresist__ble, perform__nce, persist__nt, separ__te, tend__ncy.

B. Look up the plural of *cargo, Eskimo, hoof, mosquito, motto, piano, solo, soprano, wharf, zero.*

C. Select the appropriate word in each of the numbered pairs:

1. After Jean-Pierre *(1)accepted/(2)excepted* our invitation to spend a month in the nation's *(3)capital/(4)Capitol,* he applied to the American *(5)consul/(6)counsel* for a visa. 2. The *(7)presence/(8)presents* of federal troops prevented further *(9)incidence/(10)incidents.* 3. The city's employees presented the members of the city *(11)council/(12)counsel* with a declaration of *(13)rights/(14)rites* and *(15)principals/(16)principles.* 4. My moral *(17)principals/(18)principles* do not permit a *(19)personal/(20)personnel* appearance at a play depicting *(21)loose/(22)lose* behavior. 5. Though he can *(23)cite/(24) site* no precedent, the city *(25)council/(26)counsel* advises us to *(27)adapt/(28)adopt* a motion providing for the *(29)censoring/(30)censuring* of foreign films. 6. After our *(31)censor/ (32)censure* of conditions at the plant, the owner *(33)affected/(34)effected* changes *(35)affecting/(36)effecting* most of his *(37)personal/(38)personnel.* 7. The teachers wanted to wait on the steps rather *(39)than/(40)then* enter the *(41) capital/(42)Capitol,* for all *(43)accept/(44)except* the *(45) principal/(46)principle* had already been *(47)their/(48)there.*

D. What is the difference in meaning between the words in each of the following pairs? Aid—aide, causal—casual, complimentary—complementary, costume—custom, emigrant—immigrant, eminent—imminent, isle—aisle, key—quay, meet—mete, rational—rationale, stationary—stationery, straight—strait.

SP 3 Spelling Rules

Spelling rules provide a key to a group of words that you would otherwise have to study individually.

The purpose of spelling rules is *not* to make English spelling appear more regular than it is but to help you memorize words that follow a common pattern.

SP 3a *I* before *E*. *Identical sounds are often spelled differently in different words.* For instance, *ie* and *ei* often stand for the same sound. If you sort out the words in question, you get the following:

ie: achieve, believe, chief, grief, niece, piece (of pie), relieve
cei: ceiling, conceited, conceive, perceive, receive, receipt

In the second group of words, the *ei* is regularly preceded by *c*. In other words, it is *i* before *e* except after *c*. About half a dozen words do not fit into this pattern:

ei: either, leisure, neither, seize, weird
cie: financier, species

SP 3b Doubled Consonant. *In many words a single final consonant is doubled before an ending* (or **suffix**) that begins with a vowel: *ed, er, est, ing*. Doubling occurs under the following conditions:

(1) The vowel preceding the final consonant *must be a single vowel,* not a double vowel (**diphthong**) indicated in writing by combinations like *oa, ea, ee,* and *ou* or by a silent final *e* (k*ite,* h*ope,* h*ate*). Note the differences in pronunciation and in spelling in the following pairs:

bar—barred	bare—bared
bat—batted	boat—boating
hop—hopping	hope—hoping
plan—planned	plane—planed
red—redder	read—reading
scrap—scrapped	scrape—scraped
slip—slipped	sleep—sleeping
stop—stopped	stoop—stooped

(2) In words of more than one syllable, the syllable immediately preceding the ending and containing the single vowel *must be the one stressed in pronunciation.* Sometimes a shift in stress will be reflected in a difference in the spelling of different forms of the same word. Compare the following groups:

adMIT, adMITTed, adMITTance	EDit, EDited, EDiting
forGET, forGETTing, forGETTable	BENefit, BENefited
beGIN, beGINNing, beGINNer	HARDen, HARDened
overLAP, overLAPPing	deVELop, deVELoping
reGRET, reGRETTed, reGRETTable	proHIBit, proHIBited, proHIBitive
preFER, preFERRed, preFERRing	PREFerence, PREFerable
reFER, reFERRed, reFERRing	REFerence

NOTE: There is doubling after the single vowel *i* in *equip—equipped* (the *u* does not combine with *i* but is part of the consonant *qu*); there is no doubling of the final *x* in *mix—mixed* (*x* is a double consonant).

SP 3c Y as a vowel. *Y* is sometimes used *as a consonant* (*y*ear, *y*outh), sometimes *as a vowel* (m*y*, dr*y*; hurr*y*, stud*y*). As a single final vowel, it changes to *ie* before *s*, to *i* before all other endings except *ing*.

ie: family—families, fly—flies, study—studies, try—tries, quantity—quantities

i: beauty—beautiful, bury—burial, busy—business, copy—copied, dry—drier, lively—livelihood, noisy—noisily

y: burying, copying, studying, trying, worrying

When it follows another vowel, *y* is usually preserved: *delays, joys, played, valleys.* A few common exceptions are *day—daily, gay—gaily, lay—laid, pay—paid, say—said.*

SP 3d Final E. *In some words a silent final vowel is omitted before an ending starting with a vowel.*

(1) A silent *e* at the end of a word is dropped before an ending that begins with a vowel; it is preserved before an ending that begins with a consonant:

bore	boring	boredom
hate	hating	hateful
like	liking, likable	likely
love	loving, lovable	lovely

The following words do *not* fit into this pattern: *argue—argument, due—duly, dye—dyeing* (as against *die—dying*), *mile—mileage, true—truly, whole—wholly.*

(2) A final *e* may signal the difference in pronunciation between the final consonants in *rag* and *rage* or in *aspic* and *notice*. Such a final *e* is preserved not only before a consonant but also before *a* or *o:*

ge: advantage—advantageous, change—changeable, courage—courageous, outrage—outrageous

ce: notice—noticeable, peace—peaceable

EXERCISES

A. Insert *ei* or *ie:* ach__vement, bel__ver, dec__tful, f__ld, inconc__vable, misch__f, perc__ve, rec__ving, rel__f, s__ze, w__rd, y__ld.

B. Select the appropriate word in each of the numbered pairs: *(1)bared/(2)barred* from office; his *(3)bating/(4)batting* average; *(5)caned/(6)canned* meat; a *(7)hatful/(8)hateful* task; *(9)hoping/(10) hopping* for the best; *(11)pined/(12)pinned* to the mat; a *(13)well-planed/(14)well-planned* outing; *(15)robed/(16)robbed* in white; a boy *(17)spiting/(18)spitting* his parents; *(19)taped/(20)tapped* him on the shoulder.

C. Combine the following words with the suggested endings: accompany—ed, advantage—ous, argue—ing, benefit—ed, carry—s, come—ing, confide—ing, differ—ing, excite—able, friendly—ness, lively—hood, occur—ing, prefer—ed, remit—ance, sad—er, satisfy—ed, shine—ing, sole—ly, study—ing, tragedy—s, try—s, use—ing, valley—s, whole—ly, write—ing.

SP 4 Words Often Misspelled

Studies of the words most frequently misspelled in student writing have resulted in substantial agreement on words most likely to cause spelling difficulties.

In addition to words listed in SP 1–3, the following list will repay careful study:

absence
abundance
accessible
accidentally
acclaim
accommodate
accompanied
accomplish
accumulate
accurately
accuses
accustom
achievement
acknowledgment
acquaintance
acquire
acquitted
across
actuality
address
adequate
admit
adolescence
advantageous
advertisement
afraid
against
aggravate
aggressive
alleviate
allotted
allowed
all right
altar
already
altogether
always
amateur
among
amount
analysis
analyze
annual
anticipate
anxiety
apologize
apology
apparatus
apparent
appearance
applies
applying
appreciate
approach
appropriate
approximately
area
argue
arguing
argument
arising
arrangement
article
artistically
ascend
assent
athlete
athletic
attendance
audience
authority
balance
basically
basis
beauty
becoming
before
beginning
belief
believe
beneficial
benefited
boundaries
breath
brilliant
Britain
business
buses
calendar
candidate
career
careless
carrying
category
ceiling
cemetery
challenge
changeable
character
characteristic
chief
choose
chose
clothes
coarse
column
comfortable
comfortably
coming
commission
committed
committee
companies
competition
competitive
completely

comprehension
conceivable
conceive
concentrate
condemn
confident
confidential
conscience
conscientious
conscious
considerably
consistent
continually
continuous
control
controlled
convenience
convenient
coolly
courageous
course
courteous
criticism
criticize
cruelty
curiosity
curriculum
dealt
deceit
deceive
decision
definite
definitely
definition
dependent
describe
description
desirability
desirable
despair
desperate

destruction
devastate
develop
development
device
difference
different
difficult
dilemma
dining
disappear
disappearance
disappoint
disastrous
discipline
disease
disgusted
dissatisfaction
dissatisfied
doesn't
dominant
due
during
ecstasy
efficiency
efficient
eighth
eliminate
embarrass
embarrassment
eminent
emphasize
endeavor
enforce
enough
entertain
environment
equipped
erroneous
especially
etc.

exaggerate
excellent
exceptionally
exercise
exhaust
exhilarate
existence
experience
explanation
extraordinary
extremely
familiar
families
fascinate
finally
financial
financier
foreign
forward
friend
fulfill
fundamentally
further
gaiety
generally
genius
government
governor
grammar
guaranteed
guidance
happily
happiness
height
heroes
heroine
hindrance
hopeful
huge
humorous
hundred

hurriedly
hypocrisy
hypocrite
ignorant
imaginary
imagination
immediately
immensely
incidentally
indefinite
independent
indispensable
inevitable
influence
ingenious
intellectual
intelligence
interest
interpret
interrupt
involve
irrelevant
irresistible
itself
jealous
knowledge
laboratory
laid
leisure
likelihood
literature
livelihood
loneliness
losing
magnificence
maintain
maintenance
manageable
manufacturer
marriage
mathematics

meant
medieval
merely
mileage
miniature
minute
mischievous
muscle
mysterious
naïve
necessarily
necessary
ninety
noticeable
obstacle
occasion
occasionally
occurred
occurrence
omit
operate
opinion
opponent
opportunity
optimism
original
paid
parallel
paralysis
paralyze
particularly
passed
past
peace
peculiar
perceive
perform
performance
permanent
persistent
persuade
pertain
phase
phenomenon
philosophy
physical
piece
pleasant
possess
possession
possible
practical
precede
prejudice
prepare
prevalent
privilege
probably
procedure
proceed
professor
prominent
propaganda
prophecy
psychology
pursue
quantity
really
recommend
regard
relief
relieve
religion
repetition
representative
resource
response
rhythm
ridiculous
roommate
safety
satisfactorily
schedule
seize
sense
separate
sergeant
shining
significance
similar
sincerely
sophomore
speech
sponsor
strength
stretch
strictly
subtle
succeed
successful
summarize
surprise
temperament
tendency
therefore
thorough
together
tragedy
transferred
tries
undoubtedly
unnecessary
useful
using
various
vengeance
villain
weird
writing

SP 5 The Apostrophe

The **apostrophe** *has no exact equivalent in speech and is therefore easily omitted or misplaced.*

SP 5a Contractions. *The apostrophe is used in contractions to indicate that one or more letters have been omitted* (*I'll* go now; *I'm* too tired; *we're* almost ready). It appears most frequently in contractions using a shortened form of *not: haven't, can't, wouldn't, won't, isn't.* Take care not to misspell *doesn't,* which is a shortened form of "*does* not."

A few contractions are easily confused with words of different spelling and different meaning. *It's,* meaning *it is,* differs from *its,* meaning "of it" or "belonging to it." *Who's,* meaning *who is,* differs from *whose,* which means "of whom" or "of which." *They're* means *they are* and differs from both *there* and *their:*

> *It's* time to give the cat *its* milk.
> *Who's* to say *whose* fault it is?
> If *their* lights are turned off, *they're* not *there.*

NOTE: Contractions are characteristic of informal conversation. Avoid them in formal reports, research papers, and letters of application. Some readers approve of contractions only in distinctly informal writing.

SP 5b Possessives. *The apostrophe designates a special form of nouns.* A person closely associated with something named by another noun often appears in the **possessive** form, usually produced by adding an apostrophe plus *s* to the plain form of a noun: *my sister's purse, Mr. Smith's garage, the student's notebook.* Often the possessive indicates where something belongs or who owns an article. However, it also indicates many other relationships between two closely associated nouns: *the boy's friends, the firemen's ball, a man's world, the child's innocence, the children's capers, the general's dismissal.* Possessives occur in many familiar expressions: *an hour's drive, the day's news, a moment's notice, a dollar's worth, tonight's paper.*

Note the following variations:

(1) Sometimes the plain form of a noun already ends in *s.* The possessive is then formed by adding an apostrophe only.

This applies especially to plural forms. Compare the following pairs:

the Turk's wives (one Turk)	the Turks' wives (several Turks)
the girl's swimming pool (one girl)	the girls' swimming pool (several girls)
a week's pay	two weeks' pay

Names of individuals do not always follow this rule. The writer may or may not add a second *s*, depending on whether he would expect an extra syllable in pronunciation: *Mr. Jones' car—Mr. Jones's car; Dolores' hair—Dolores's hair; Charles Dickens' first novel—Charles Dickens's first novel.*

(2) The apostrophe is *not* used in the *possessive forms of personal pronouns.* No apostrophe appears in *his, hers, its, ours, yours,* or *theirs.* It does appear in the possessive forms of such indefinite pronouns as *one* (one's friends), *everyone* (to everyone's surprise), *someone* (at someone's suggestion; also, at someone else's house).

SP 5c Plurals of Letters and Symbols. *The apostrophe is often used to separate the plural* s *from the name of a letter or a symbol or from a word named as a word* (two large 7's; if's and but's):

Those great big beautiful A's so avidly sought, those little miserly C's so often found, were meant for another time and another student body.—Oscar Handlin, "Are the Colleges Killing Education?" *Atlantic*

EXERCISE

Check for appropriate use of the apostrophe in choosing between the spellings in each of the following pairs.

1. When the mother and the father respect each *(1)other's/ (2)others'* opinions, children learn to live harmoniously by fol-

lowing their *(3)elders/(4)elders'* example. 2. Since the *(5) chairmans/(6)chairman's* resignation, the *(7)members/(8)member's* have been speculating about *(9)whose/(10)who's* going to succeed him. 3. *(11)Mrs. Beattys/(12)Mrs. Beatty's* husband still sends her *(13)flowers/(14)flower's* on *(15)Valentines/(16) Valentine's* Day. 4. We were all overjoyed when my *(17)sister's/(18)sisters'* baby took *(19)its/(20)it's* first faltering steps. 5. A *(21)student's/(22)students'* lack of interest is not always the *(23)teachers/(24)teacher's* fault. 6. *(25)Its/(26)It's* the *(27)parents/(28)parents'* responsibility to provide for their *(29)children's/(30)childrens'* religious education. 7. *(31)Lets/ (32)Let's* borrow *(33)someones/(34)someone's* car and go for an *(35)hour's/(36)hours'* drive. 8. *(37)Charles/(38) Charles's* father murmured audibly that the assembled *(39) relatives/(40)relative's* had consumed at least ten *(41)dollars/ (42)dollars'* worth of food.

SP 6 The Hyphen

Use of the **hyphen** *is the least uniform and the least stable feature of English spelling.* In doubtful cases, the most recent edition of a reputable dictionary is the best available guide.

SP 6a Compound Words. *Treatment varies for words habitually used together as a single expression.* Some compound words are clearly distinguished from ordinary combinations by differences in both writing and pronunciation: *black bird* (black BIRD) but *blackbird* (BLACKbird), *dark room* (dark ROOM) but *darkroom* (DARKroom). Such unmistakable compounds are *bellboy, bridesmaid, headache, highway, newsstand, summertime,* and *stepmother.* In many similar compounds, however, the parts are conventionally kept separate: *bus boy, commander in chief, goose flesh, high school, labor union, second cousin.* Still other compound words conventionally require a hyphen: *able-bodied, bull's-eye, cave-in, great-grandfather, merry-go-round, mother-in-law.*

NOTE: Be sure to spell *today, tomorrow, nevertheless,* and *nowadays* as single words. Be sure *not* to spell as single words *all right, a lot* (a lot of time), *be able,* and *no one.*

SP 6b Prefixes. *Many hyphenated compounds consist of a prefix, or introductory qualifier, and the word it precedes.*

(1) *All-, ex-* (in the sense of "former"), *quasi-, self-,* and sometimes *co-* require a hyphen: *all-knowing, ex-husband, quasi-judicial, self-contained, co-author.*

(2) All prefixes require a hyphen before words beginning with a capital letter: *all-American, anti-American, pro-American, un-American.*

(3) Often a hyphen prevents the meeting of two identical vowels: *anti-intellectual, re-election, semi-independent.*

NOTE: Sometimes a hyphen distinguishes an unfamiliar use of a prefix from a familiar one: *recover—re-cover* (make a new cover), *recreation—re-creation* (creating again or anew).

SP 6c Group Modifiers. *Several words may temporarily combine as a modifier preceding a noun.* They are then usually joined to each other by hyphens: *a flying-saucer hat, a middle-of-the-road policy, a question-and-answer period, a step-by-step account, a devil-may-care attitude.* No hyphens are used when the same combinations serve some other function in a sentence: *tend toward the middle of the road; explain a process step by step.*

NOTE: No hyphen is used when a modifier preceding a noun is in turn modified by an adverb ending in *ly: a fast-rising executive, a well-balanced account* but *a rapidly growing city, a carefully documented study.*

EXERCISE

Insert hyphens or combine elements where appropriate.

1. The prospective son in law listened self consciously to Mother's praise of the bride to be. 2. Those who denounced the parking privileges for out of town students were obviously not from out of town. 3. Both pro British and anti British Arabs were united in their contempt for ex king Farouk. 4. The anti intellectual local news paper had called our candidate an absent minded ex professor and a tool of the labor unions; never the less he was elected. 5. Now a days few self respecting candidates conduct old fashioned campaigns taking them into out of the way places. 6. Mr. Andrews and his co author have written a well documented account of the un democratic procedures followed by quasi judicial agencies.

SP 7 Capitals

Although practice varies on minor points, certain conventions of capitalization are widely observed.

SP 7a Proper Names. *Proper names are always capitalized.* Capitalize the names of persons, places, regions, historical periods, ships, days of the week, months (but not seasons), organizations, religions: *James, Brazil, the Middle Ages, S.S. Independence, Sunday, February, Buddhism.* Capitalize words derived from proper names: *English grammar, French pastry, German beer, Parisian fashions, Christian charity, Marxist ideas.*

Note the following difficulties:

(1) In some words the proper name involved has been lost sight of, and a lower-case letter is used: *guinea pig, india rubber, pasteurized milk.*

(2) The same word may apply to various examples of a

kind or serve as a proper name for a person, an institution, a place:

democratic (many institutions)	Democratic (name of the party)
orthodox (many attitudes)	Orthodox (name of the church)
history (general subject)	History 31 (specific course)
west (general direction)	Middle West (specific area)
my mother (common relationship)	Mother (name of the person)

(3) Generally applicable descriptions of a title, a family relationship, an institution, or a geographical feature are capitalized when they combine with a proper name: *Major Brown, Aunt Augusta, Sergeant Barnacle, Campbell High School, Indiana University, Tennessee Valley Authority, Medora Heights, Lake Erie.* Some titles refer to only one person and can take the place of the person's name: *the Pope, the Queen* (of England), *the President* (of the United States).

SP 7b Titles of Publications. *A capital letter marks the first and all major words in the title of a book, other publication, or work of art.* The only words not counting as major are articles (*a, an,* and *the*), prepositions (*at, in, on, of, from, with*), and connectives (*and, but, if when*). Prepositions and connectives are usually capitalized when they have five or more letters. Observe these conventions in writing the title of a theme:

My First Day on Campus
Life in a Dormitory
Get Rich Through Hypnosis
New Facts About the Common Cold

The same conventions apply to titles of publications cited in a sentence:

Several generations of Americans read *Sink or Swim, Phil the Fiddler, Mark the Match Boy,* and *From Canal Boy to President,* records of achievement which rewarded personal goodness with happiness and goods.—Saul Bellow, "The Writer as Moralist," *Atlantic*

EXERCISE

Revise the following passage to make it conform to the conventions governing the use of capitals.

> Boris was a young american pianist. His father came from a calvinistic new england family. His mother, who had been born in the caucasus, spoke french, german, and russian, as well as english and her native armenian. She had studied classical music in european cities like paris and vienna. Before he was ten, boris could play everything from viennese waltzes to presbyterian hymns. In high school he read books like *the life of beethoven, all about wagner,* and *brahms through the eyes of a friend.* At east bloomingdale city college, he took a course in music appreciation as well as a course entitled "the great composers." After he graduated, he spent the summer in california and the winter giving concerts in the middle west.
>
> Fame came to boris in march one year when, armed with his bible, he set off for a contest in a country dominated by marxist ideology but susceptible to capitalist music. Even orthodox socialists cheered wildly when boris was awarded the first prize. Back home, the united states senate promptly commended boris's achievement as a national triumph and a vindication of democratic principles. Only one democratic and two republican senators abstained. The national broadcasting company paid the back rent on boris's piano after he performed in a sunday morning concert given by the new york philharmonic orchestra and broadcast from carnegie hall. In june, *lifemanship* magazine had an article on boris in its section entitled "speaking of pianists." The article said: "So catholic is the appeal of music that it reconciles, for a time, yankees and southerners, protestants and catholics, russians and americans."

PUNCTUATION MARKS
Reference Chart

COMMA

before coordinating connectives	**P 3d**
with nonrestrictive adverbial clauses	**P 4b**
after introductory adverbial clauses	**P 4c**
with nonrestrictive modifiers (other than adverbial clauses)	**P 5b–c**
after introductory modifiers (other than adverbial clauses)	**P 5c**
with adverbial connectives	**P 3c**
with *especially, namely, for example,* etc.	**P 2b**
with *after all, of course,* and other sentence modifiers	**P 5c**
between items in a series	**P 6a**
in a series of parallel clauses	**P 3b**
between coordinate adjectives	**P 6b**
with dates and addresses, etc.	**P 6c**
with direct address and other light interrupters	**P 7c**
between repeated or contrasted elements	**P 6d**
with quotations	**P 8a–b, d**

SEMICOLON

between closely related sentences	**P 3a**
before adverbial connectives	**P 3c**
before coordinating connectives between clauses containing commas	**P 3d**
in a series with items containing commas	**P 6a**

COLON

to introduce a list or explanation	**P 2b**
to introduce a formal quotation	**P 8a**
between closely related sentences	**P 3a**

PERIOD

at end of sentence	**P 1c, P 2**
ellipsis	**P 8c**
with abbreviations	**M 2**

DASH

break in thought	**P 2a, P 7a**
before summary at end of sentence	**P 7a**

QUOTATION MARKS

with quotations	**P 8a–d**
quotation within quotation	**P 8a**
with terminal marks	**P 8b**
with slang or technical terms	**P 8e**
to set off titles	**M 1e**

EXCLAMATION MARK	**P 1a**
QUESTION MARK	**P 1b**
PARENTHESES	**P 7b**

7

PUNCTUATION

When we speak, we do more than put the right words together in the right order. We pause at the right times, raise our voices for emphasis. To the structures and forms we study in the grammar of the written sentence, speech adds **intonation**: differences in timing, pitch, and stress that make our words mean what we want them to mean. Such differences are further supplemented by facial expressions and gestures: the knowing wink that indicates irony, the raised forefinger that signals emphasis. When writing, we use punctuation marks for similar purposes.

The English system of punctuation has relatively few ways of indicating differences in emotion or attitude. In speech, "George is an honor student" can express many different shades of meaning. When we try to reproduce these differences in writing, we are soon reduced to devices frowned upon by conservative readers:

George is an honor student!
George is an honor student?
George is an honor student (!).
George is an honor (?) student.
George is an "honor" student.

English punctuation is best equipped to signal differences in structure. Punctuation marks may separate groups of words from each other. They may establish different kinds of connection between them. For instance, punctuation may show two closely related groups of words to be a general statement followed by detailed explanation:

The room was full of noisy men: ranchers, merchants, and lawyers.

It may show them to be an important statement followed by incidental additional information:

Richard inherited his uncle's estate, which had been in the family since 1632.

The conventional system of punctuation, like English spelling, developed in haphazard fashion. However, it has the great advantage of being readily understood by all educated readers. With minor variations, certain ways of doing things are repeated over and over in most of what you read. Besides, like conventional spelling, conventional punctuation is generally accepted as a symptom of literacy. Unconventionally punctuated sentences, though to a lesser degree than misspelled words, invite disapproval and ridicule.

P 1 End Punctuation

End punctuation puts a stop to an utterance that is grammatically complete.

Utterances terminated by end punctuation may have to become part of a coherent narrative or argument before their full meaning becomes clear. They do not need anything before them or after them to be complete as far as grammatical structure is concerned.

P 1a Exclamations. The **exclamation mark** terminates an utterance that has an unusual amount of energy or emphasis behind it. Such utterances range from a groan, curse, or shout to an order or command. *The exclamation mark can signal excitement, insistence, surprise, indignation, or fear:*

Ouch! Hurrah!
Silence! Get up! Close the book!

He loves me!
And this man wants to be President!

NOTE: Avoid using the exclamation mark as an easy way of making trivial things seem important. Avoid using more than one exclamation mark at a time.

P lb Questions. Whenever you raise your voice inquiringly at the end of something you say, you should terminate the written equivalent with a **question mark** (*Did you see my hat?*). However, not all questions are marked by intonation. *Use the question mark whenever an utterance is worded as a request for information:*

Who are you?
What did he want?

Many students forget to use question marks at the end of questions that are long or involved:

How is the student who enters college as a freshman supposed to find his way through the maze of instructions and regulations printed in small print in the college catalogue?

(1) Use question marks even after *rhetorical questions*. Rhetorical questions do not really ask for an answer but already indicate what the correct answer is supposed to be by the way they are worded:

Are you implying that our candidate is a liar?
Am I, life-long servant of this great republic, going to betray the trust placed in me by my constituents?

(2) You are free to omit the question mark after *requests phrased as questions* for the sake of politeness:

Will you please notify your clients of our decision?
Will you please notify your clients of our decision.

P 1c Statements. Statements are terminated by **periods**. *To use the period appropriately, you must be able to recognize the type of grammatically self-contained unit called a sentence.*[1] Some students use periods between units that are not complete sentences but merely **sentence fragments**. Others go to the opposite extreme by omitting the period between two complete sentences, thus producing what is called a **fused sentence**.

COMPLETE:	He is gone. *He left for Alaska.*
FRAGMENT:	He left yesterday. *For Alaska.*
FUSED:	You won't find him *he left for Alaska.*

P 2 Eliminating Fragments

The type of sentence fragment most common in student writing is caused by afterthoughts added to the main statement.

After making a statement (*I left home*), a writer may add an explanation without realizing that the addition is not a second complete sentence (*To go to college*). He may make a statement (*These are my relatives*) and add a comment (*A fine group of people*). He may make a statement (*I kept my eyes open for suspicious characters*) and add an example or illustration (*For example, policemen and store detectives*). Each of these afterthoughts is a sentence fragment when separated from the main statement by a period.

Grammatically, such fragments are of several common types:

APPOSITIVES:	A great man. My history teacher. Carts loaded with fruit.

[1] See G 2 for discussion of sentence structure and common sentence patterns.

ADJECTIVES, ADVERBS:	Beautiful in the morning sun. Carelessly as usual.
PREPOSITIONAL PHRASES:	For the last time. With great trepidation. On behalf of the management.
VERBALS, VERBAL PHRASES:	Leaving the car behind. Other things being equal.
DEPENDENT CLAUSES:	Because I did not study. Though nobody replied. Which came far too late. (See P 4a.)

Many such fragments can be joined to the main statement either without any punctuation at all (*I left home to go to college*) or by a comma (*These are my relatives, a fine group of people*). Whenever a fragment is pointed out to you try first to connect it with the main idea in such a way that the sentence flows smoothly, without interruption:

FRAGMENT: Be sure to be there. *At seven o'clock.*
REVISED: Be sure to be there *at seven o'clock.*

FRAGMENT: He bought a used car. *In spite of my warnings.*
REVISED: He bought a used car *in spite of my warnings.*

If the fragment cannot become part of either the preceding or the following statement, you may have to develop the material it contains into a complete sentence:

FRAGMENT: He appealed to a higher court. *Being a futile effort.*
REVISED: He appealed to a higher court. *The effort was futile.*

P 2a Breaks in Thought. *At times, material added to the main statement is kept clearly separate as an afterthought.* To indicate the break in thought, use a **dash** instead of a period:

These are my relatives—*a motley crew.*
He would close his eyes and talk into the dictaphone—*a strange way to write an English theme.*

Dashes can suggest the casual rambling of conversation or the jerky movement of an improvised speech. On the other hand, they can emphasize a break for ironic or dramatic effect.[2]

P 2b Explanation and Enumeration. *To establish a definite connection between an explanatory afterthought and the preceding statement, use a colon or a common transitional expression.*

(1) The **colon** serves to introduce a *list or description of* something that has already been mentioned in a more general way:

We have two excellent players this year: *Phil and Tom.*
She served an old-fashioned breakfast: *fishballs, brown bread, and baked beans.*
Your friend lacks an essential quality: *tact.*

The colon, like the period, ordinarily has a complete statement in front of it. Unlike the period, it may be followed by a group of words that is not a complete statement.

(2) Explanations or examples added to a complete statement are often introduced by expressions like *especially, such as, namely,* or *for example.* When they introduce material that is not a complete sentence, these expressions are usually preceded by a **comma**:

He took several courses in the humanities, *such as French Literature and Elementary Logic.*
Plato and Aristotle wrote in the same language, *namely Greek.*

In formal usage, another comma often keeps *namely, for example, for instance,* and *that is* separate from the explanations or examples they introduce:

[2] See P 7a.

Professor Miller objected to my system of punctuating, for example, my use of dashes.

Do not use another comma if the introductory expression is *especially* or *such as.*

P 2c Permissible Nonsentences. *Permissible fragments are common in speech and are used in writing for special effects.* Informal speech uses many fragmentary sentences whose meaning the listener can infer from gestures or from the context. When such fragmentary sentences occur in writing, most teachers and editors either consider them too informal for ordinary expository prose or simply take them as a sign of illiteracy. On the other hand, experienced writers use a number of permissible fragments, better called **nonsentences**, for special purposes. The following examples illustrate the most common of these:

(1) *Common transitional expressions.*

So much for past developments. *Now for* a look at our present problems.

(2) *Answers to questions,* suggesting the give-and-take of conversation or the rhetorical question-and-answer technique of the orator.

What did we gain? *Nothing.*

(3) *Descriptive passages,* especially when designed to give a static, pictorial effect.

We stood in the hot dry night air at one in the morning, waiting for a train at an Arizona station. *Nothing but the purple arc of sky and at the end of the platform the silhouette of a cottonwood tree lapped by a hot breeze. The stars big as sunflowers.*—Alistair Cooke, *One Man's America*

(4) In narrative, *passages suggesting random, disconnected thought.*

Fifty dollars to Dorothy's piano teacher. His sister. Another plain girl. She might as well learn how to play the piano.—Irwin Shaw, "Main Currents of American Thought"

(5) Transcripts of *conversation or dialogue.*

In one part of the picture you see five young men in white coats conferring around a microscope. The voice on the sound track rings out boldly, *"No geniuses here. Just a bunch of good Americans working together."*—William H. Whyte, Jr., "The New Illiteracy," *Saturday Review*

Most teachers discourage their students from experimenting with such incomplete sentences until they have learned to use complete sentences effectively and confidently.

EXERCISES

A. Check the following passages for conventional use of end punctuation. Label each passage *S* (satisfactory), *F* (unsatisfactory because containing a fragment), or *U* (unsatisfactory for some other reason).

1. Fred was collecting pictures of architectural marvels, such as Gothic cathedrals and Aztec pyramids. 2. The next summer I tried a new sales technique. With good results. 3. You will not be able to reach them. They left no address. 4. I remember the festive spirit of the Christmas season in my home town. The many colorful lights along the city streets. 5. When will parents realize that their children's education is not someone else's responsibility but their own. 6. He left school after two years. To take over his father's business. 7. The airline refused to transport his pet: a tame puma. 8. Rapidly growing housing tracts have created many problems. The most serious one being inadequate school facilities. 9. Why should I spend my time making excuses for an incor-

rigible liar. 10. He remembered his first glimpse of the United States. The Manhattan skyline. 11. Many of my friends were studying a foreign language, especially Spanish or French. 12. The club invited a well-known guest lecturer. An anthropologist from Cornell. 13. The osprey dives into the water to seize its prey. Plunging down from heights of up to one hundred feet. 14. Please stop at the post office. We need some stamps. 15. The gallery was showing the work of several French painters, especially Degas and Monet.

B. In the following passage, insert appropriate punctuation in the numbered spaces. Draw a diagonal line through inappropriate capitals (high ~~S~~chools). Leave a blank space where no punctuation is required.

Have you been to the circus lately___(1) What a change from old times___(2) Only one thing seems the same___(3) The tent___(4) Most of the performers seem to have lost their zest___(5) Especially the clowns and acrobats___(6) Where are the many hilariously funny clowns___(7) Of days gone by___(8) One of them used to drag into the arena___(9) A huge and complicated machine___(10) To serve as a cigarette lighter___(11) Acrobats used to fly from trapeze to trapeze___(12) Without a net___(13) The modern circus is half tiresome floats___(14) And half commercials___(15) How can spectators get into the true circus spirit___(16)

C. From your current writing and reading, select ten sample sentences that illustrate the various conventions of punctuation discussed in the preceding section.

P 3 Joining Independent Clauses

Semicolons and commas are the most important of the marks joining independent clauses in a sentence.

Your sentences will often contain not one subject-predicate group but several. The individual subject-predicate groups that can make up more complicated sentences are called **clauses**.

Next to end punctuation, the most important kind of punctuation is that which joins two or more clauses.

P 3a Closely Related Sentences. *A semicolon or colon may replace the period between two complete sentences.*

(1) The **semicolon** joins *complete sentences that are closely related.* Often two statements go together as related pieces of information, develop the same mood or point of view, line up related ideas for contrast. When a semicolon replaces the period between two such statements, the first word of the second statement is *not* capitalized:

The door was locked; the windows were closed.
Some librarians circulate books; others hoard them.
The Queen is not allowed to wear a crown; nothing less than a halo will suffice.—Kingsley Martin, "Strange Interlude," *Atlantic*

(2) In informal writing a **colon** often replaces the semicolon when the second statement gives the reader information or explanation that helps him understand the first one. Formal usage prefers the semicolon unless the *first statement clearly introduces the second:*

One thing was certain: he would never race again.

P 3b Comma Splice. *Commas join complete sentences only under special circumstances.*

(1) The **comma** generally indicates a less significant break than the semicolon. Next to the sentence fragment, the most noticeable departure from conventional punctuation is the "comma fault," the practice of rambling on from one complete statement to the other with only a comma to keep them apart. A group of statements spliced together by a comma is called a **comma splice** or, sometimes, a **run-on** sentence:

COMMA SPLICE: The doctor looked worn, he had stayed up all night.
REVISED: The doctor looked worn; he had stayed up all night.

(2) One permissible exception to the traditional rule against comma splices is a *sentence composed of three or more parallel clauses*. **Commas** may appear between clauses that are not only closely related in meaning but also similar in structure:

He came, he saw, he conquered.
The birds were chirping, the dogs were barking, the horses were neighing in the fields.

(3) When only two clauses are connected by a comma, the conventions of formal writing require the logical connection and similarity in structure to be especially close. This is often the case in clauses expressing a *carefully balanced contrast:*

Now, of course, there are no more contractors, only developers. And *they no longer build houses, they build homes.* And *they no longer build one at a time, they scorn to undertake less than eight hundred at a crack.*—Gerald W. Johnson, "Baltimore: The City Nobody Knows," *Atlantic*

NOTE: Some reputable writers use the comma in less obviously balanced sentences. This practice is often condemned as careless:

The grass is rich and matted, you cannot see the soil.—Alan Paton, *Cry, the Beloved Country*

Across the holy river is the foundation of a companion tomb which Shah Jenan had wanted to build for himself, only this one was to be of black marble.—Leslie C. Stevens, "The Grand Trunk Road to Agra," *Atlantic*

P 3c Adverbial Connectives. *Adverbial connectives overlap with other groups of connectives in meaning but differ from them in typically requiring a semicolon.* **Adverbial connectives** are *therefore, consequently, hence, accordingly, moreover, furthermore, besides, however, nevertheless, indeed,* and *in fact*. Since they show that two sentences are closely related, the sentences they join are typically separated by a **semicolon** rather than by a period. A period, nevertheless, would still be possible and acceptable:

Business was improving; *therefore,* we changed our plans.
Business was improving. *Therefore,* we changed our plans.

The hall was nearly empty; *nevertheless,* the curtain rose on time.
The hall was nearly empty. *Nevertheless,* the curtain rose on time.

Notice the following points:

(1) A connective of this group need not be placed at the point where the first statement ends and the second statement begins. You have to make sure that the *semicolon appears at the point where the two statements join,* regardless of the position of the connective:

Attendance is compulsory; *therefore,* the students have no choice.
Attendance is compulsory; the students, *therefore,* have no choice.
Attendance is compulsory; the students have no choice, *therefore.*

The possibility of a shift in position is a test that you can employ to identify members of this group. They share their freedom of movement with adverbs, a characteristic that explains their description as adverbial connectives or connective adverbs.

(2) Adverbial connectives are often *set off from the rest of the second statement* by **commas**, as in the examples already given. You then have to make sure that there is a punctuation mark both before and after the connective:

The food, *however,* was impossible.

NOTE: Whether you should set off an adverbial connective depends partly on the level of formality of your writing. Informal and journalistic writing tend toward **open punctuation**, using fewer commas than formal writing does. Accordingly, the authors of popular books and magazine articles tend not to separate adverbial connectives from the rest of a clause.

P 3d Coordinating Connectives. *Coordinating connectives typically require a comma. And, but, for, or, nor, so,* and *yet* establish a close relation between two clauses without making the one more important than the other. They are typically preceded by a **comma**:

> The bell finally rang, *and* George rushed out of the room.
> She saw me, *but* she did not recognize me.
> We went inside, *for* it had started to rain.
> You had better apologize, *or* she will not speak to you again.

Notice the reversal of subject and verb after *nor:*

> We cannot through the courts force parents to be kind, *nor can we force* men to be wise by the pressure of committees.—Dan Lacy, "Obscenity and Censorship," *The Christian Century*

Do not use the comma with these connectives when they join two words or two phrases rather than two clauses (came in *and* sat down, tired *but* happy, for cash *or* on credit).

Notice the following variations:

(1) *And, but,* and *or* are often used without a comma *when the clauses they join are short:*

> The wind was blowing *and* the water was cold.

Yet and *so* are often used with a **semicolon**:

> The critics praised Oliver's work; *yet* no one bought his paintings.

(2) Any coordinating connective may be used with a semicolon, especially if it joins *clauses that already contain commas* or that are unusually long:

Previously the river has always been accompanied by mountains near or far; *but* they lay generally parallel to its course. Now in the Big Bend the river encounters mountains in a new and extraordinary way; *for* they lie, chain after chain of them, directly across its way. —Paul Horgan, "Pages from a Rio Grande Notebook," *The New York Times Book Review*

(3) Unlike adverbial connectives, coordinating connectives *are not set off from the rest of the clause* they introduce; there is no comma after *and, but,* or *yet* unless it is required by some other convention of punctuation. Like adverbial connectives, however, coordinating connectives leave the clauses they join self-sufficient or independent grammatically. Thus, the clauses they connect may still be kept separate from each other by a **period**:

> I called your office twice. *But* nobody answered. *So* I left without you.

EXERCISES

A. Check the following passages for conventional use of punctuation marks in joining clauses. Label each passage *S* (satisfactory), *C* (unsatisfactory because of a comma splice), *U* (unsatisfactory for some other reason).

> 1. I asked my father for a car instead he gave me a bicycle. 2. I know the city very well; I used to live there, in fact. 3. In Europe family ties are close, the whole family does things together. 4. There is a growing audience for ballet, and the theater flourishes in half a dozen centers outside New York. 5. All the polls favored our candidate; the election, however, told a different story. 6. Previews consist of short selections from the movie being advertised, usually these are the most exciting or the most daring parts. 7. Children are

like tape recorders; they repeat everything they hear. 8. We had planned to look for driftwood on the beach, but the rain kept us indoors. 9. The horses must have been frightened by the crowd, for they started rearing and tugging nervously at their bridles. 10. High costs make orchestra deficits perennial, yet almost everywhere performances are sold out. 11. I hurriedly went downstairs for breakfast was ready. 12. His landlady did not know his whereabouts, nor could she name his companions. 13. A teacher cannot do everything for his students they must meet him half way. 14. Classes are large, therefore few students have a chance to participate in discussion. 15. Our school annual was to give many students a chance to participate; the captain of the football team, consequently, became our sports editor.

B. Insert appropriate punctuation in the numbered spaces. *Use no capitals or periods not already supplied in the text.* Leave a blank space where no punctuation is required.

Elia Kazan is best known as a director of motion pictures__(1) however__(2) he first worked in the theater__(3) and directed plays by Thornton Wilder__(4) and Arthur Miller. Kazan's life is an American success story__(5) of a familiar kind__(6) for he came to this country as the son of Greek immigrants__(7) at the age of five. He first lived in Manhattan__(8) later his parents moved to New Rochelle. Young Kazan long felt an outsider__(9) nevertheless__(10) he graduated with honors from Williams College__(11) and was soon highly praised as an actor. His numerous motion pictures have long since gained him lasting fame__(12) some critics__(13) indeed__(14) consider him the most powerful and distinctive of Hollywood directors.

P 4 Adverbial Clauses

A writer must distinguish between adverbial clauses set off by commas and those requiring no punctuation.

Adverbial connectives and coordinating connectives leave the clauses which they join independent. A third type of connective subordinates the second clause to the main clause of the sentence. It changes a self-sufficient, independent clause into a **dependent clause**, which normally cannot stand by itself. "If I were a boy" does not become a complete sentence until you answer the question "If you were a boy, then what?"

P 4a Subordinating Connectives. *Because of important differences in punctuation, subordinating connectives must be carefully distinguished from other types of connectives.* They normally introduce adverbial clauses, which tell us something about the circumstances of an action or event described in the main part of the sentence. *When, whenever, while, before, after, since, until, as long as,* and *where* introduce information about time and place. *Because, if, provided,* and *unless* introduce reasons or conditions.

(1) Subordinating connectives can turn a group of words into a sentence fragment even though the group has both a subject and a predicate. A complete sentence, in other words, normally contains a subject and a predicate *not* introduced by a subordinating connective. To put it more generally, *a complete sentence normally contains at least one independent clause.* Beware of dependent clauses added to a main statement as an explanatory afterthought:

FRAGMENT: He failed the test. *Because he did not study.*
REVISED: He failed the test *because he did not study.*

(2) To identify a subordinating connective, try to reverse the order of the two statements which it joins. *Subordinating connectives introduce material that may precede rather than follow the main clause:*

Vote for me *if you trust me.*
If you trust me, vote for me.

I drove more slowly *after I noticed the police car.*
After I noticed the police car, I drove more slowly.

P 4b Restrictive and Nonrestrictive Adverbial Clauses. *Restrictive adverbial clauses are typically not separated from the rest of the sentence; nonrestrictive ones are set off by a comma.*

(1) Adverbial clauses usually *restrict or qualify in a significant way the meaning of the clause to which they are joined.* Suppose a father tells his son, "I'll raise your allowance *after I strike oil.*" Without the proviso about striking oil, the sentence would sound like an immediate promise of more money. With the proviso, it means that the son will get more money only by a very remote chance. When they *follow* the main clause, such **restrictive** clauses are not set off by punctuation:

I consulted my notes *before I spoke.*
Do not sign anything *until you hear from me.*
We cannot keep you on the team *unless you improve.*

(2) Occasionally, the *time, place, or condition for an action or event is already indicated in the main clause.* In that case, the dependent clause may merely elaborate on the information already given. Such dependent clauses are called **nonrestrictive** and are separated from the main clause by a **comma**:

Bats were well developed *as far back as the Eocene, when man's ancestors were still in the trees.*

He was born *in California, where one can pick oranges during the Christmas holidays.*

A number of subordinating connectives usually introduce nonrestrictive material and as a result require a comma. The most important ones are *though, although,* and *whereas.* Rather than adding essential qualification, these words establish a *contrast between the statements they connect:*

I like the work, *though the salary is low.*
Her friend wore a sports shirt and slacks, *whereas the other men wore tuxedos.*

Combinations like *whether or not* and *no matter how* indicate that the main statement is true or applicable regardless of possibilities mentioned in the dependent clause:

> We are canceling the lease, *whether you like it or not.*
> She will never forgive you, *no matter what you do.*

(3) Some subordinating connectives introduce *either restrictive or nonrestrictive material, depending on the meaning of the sentence.* Notice the comma that signals the difference between the members of each of the following pairs:

Why are you going to town?
I am going to town *because I want to do some shopping.*
(The reason for your trip is the essential part of the sentence.)

What are you going to do?
I am going to town, because I want to do some shopping.
(The reason for your trip is added, nonrestrictive explanation.)

I am telling you this *so that* there will be no misunderstanding.
(*So that* reveals purpose or intention.)
The cafeteria was small, *so that* it was always overcrowded.
(*So that* introduces an unintended result.)

NOTE: Some connectives belong to different groups of connectives depending on their meaning in the sentence. *However* is normally an adverbial connective and requires a semicolon. It sometimes takes the place of the subordinating connective *no matter how* and requires a comma:

> I cannot please him; *however, I am trying hard.*
> I cannot please him, *however hard I try.*

Though, normally a subordinating connective, is often used in informal English as an adverbial connective placed in the middle or at the end of a clause:

I felt entitled to more freedom; *my parents, though, didn't agree with me.*

P 4c Introductory Adverbial Clauses. *An adverbial clause that precedes rather than follows the main clause is usually set off.* After an introductory adverbial clause, a **comma** normally indicates where the main clause starts:

If you want to do well, you will have to work hard.
Whenever there is a heavy rain, the area is threatened by floods and slides.

After restrictive introductory material, this comma is optional. Some writers consider it unnecessary after an introductory clause that is fairly short, provided the sentence would be clear without the optional punctuation.

NOTE: Subordinating connectives are not the only way of relating a dependent clause to another clause. Two other types of dependent clauses are treated under P 5. (See P 5a for noun clauses, P 5b for adjective clauses.)

EXERCISES

A. Check the following passages for conventional use of punctuation marks with subordinating connectives. Label each passage *S* (satisfactory), *F* (unsatisfactory because of a sentence fragment), or *U* (unsatisfactory for some other reason).

1. Though his paintings were truly remarkable, few of them found buyers among museums or private collectors. 2. Cleaning pots and pans looks easy on television. Whereas at home it takes a lot of hard work. 3. Unless a man has an unusual fondness for teaching grade school children are best taught by women. 4. Most of the animals were extremely shy, so that photographing them required much patience. 5. After the camera had followed the hero to his destination in the West, it switched back to the freshly plowed fields of Iowa. 6. The city is desperately short of hospital space because,

most people don't appreciate the need for adequate facilities. 7. Myrna has been afraid of heights since she was a small child. 8. Mountain climbing does not appeal to me; however exciting it may be to others. 9. Because many educated people in India know English, foreign visitors seldom learn Hindu. 10. If we didn't know the teacher usually supplied the answers in class. 11. In Mexico architecture seemed to flourish, whereas at home it had seemed a lost art. 12. The city relinquished one hundred acres of city-owned land so that the local baseball team could build a new stadium there. 13. Ralph was suspended last year. After he put war paint on the bronze Indian decorating the principal's lawn. 14. Our house is a shambles, whenever my uncle's family pays us a visit. 15. Ask me when you need advice; ask your father when you need money.

B. Insert appropriate punctuation in the numbered spaces. *Use no capitals or periods not already supplied in the text.* Leave a blank space where no punctuation is required.

If my own experience is typical___(1) high school students are reluctant readers___(2) because books play only a very minor role in their environment. Few teachers make their students explore the school library___(3) although it may contain everything from Chaucer to Sagan. The most popular students often read very little___(4) the newcomer___(5) therefore___(6) associates books with "longhairs" and intellectuals. When the student returns to his home___(7) the television set occupies the place of honor in the living room___(8) whereas___(9) the bookcase may stand as a dust catcher in a hidden corner.

C. From your current writing and reading, select ten sample sentences that illustrate the various conventions of punctuation discussed in P 3–4.

P 5 Punctuating Modifiers

A writer must learn to distinguish between modifiers set off by commas and those requiring no punctuation.

Often nouns and verbs are accompanied by further material that develops, embroiders, or modifies the meaning they convey. Such material is punctuated in accordance with its function and importance in the sentence.

P 5a Unnecessary Commas. *Unless extraneous material intervenes, there is no punctuation between basic elements of a sentence.* Do not put a comma between a subject and its verb, between a verb and its object, between a verb and a description of the subject, or between the two or three basic elements and the various phrases added to the sentence to describe circumstances, reasons, or conditions:

Andrew	studies	his textbooks	in bed.
Gaston	had been	a mess sergeant	during the war.
Jones	left	his wife	to shoot elephants.

The rule against punctuation breaking up the basic sentence pattern applies even when the place of the subject, the object, or the description of the subject is taken by a clause within a clause. Such clauses, which appear in positions frequently occupied by nouns, are called **noun clauses**. They become *part* of another clause and should not be confused with clauses which are *joined* to another clause:

NOUN (Subject):	*The writer*	knew your name.
NOUN CLAUSE:	*Whoever wrote it*	knew your name.
NOUN (Object):	John announced	*his plans.*
NOUN CLAUSE:	John announced	*that he would retire.*
NOUN (Description):	Your net gain is	*a small sum.*
NOUN CLAUSE:	Your net gain is	*what little remains after taxes.*

Be careful not to put a comma before or after a noun clause, especially one introduced by *that:*

We knew *that he is unreliable.*
That he failed to answer your letter is a bad sign.

P 5b Restrictive and Nonrestrictive Modifiers. *Restrictive modifiers are not separated from what they modify; nonrestrictive modifiers are set off by commas.* This convention applies especially to modifiers inserted after a noun (or noun equivalent) to clarify or develop its meaning:

The student, *a freshman,* studied the handbook.
The student, *looking weary,* studied the handbook.
The student, *who had little time,* studied the handbook.

He studied the handbook, *a fascinating volume.*
He studied the handbook, *a text required in the course.*

Modifiers become an essential part of the main statement if *used for the purpose of identification.* In that case, they are **restrictive**; they restrict or narrow down a generally applicable term like *student* to help the reader single out one particular student or one particular type of student. Restrictive modifiers are *not* set off:

Which student studied the book?
The student *wearing the red hunting cap* studied the book.

Which man took the money?
The man *dressed in the pink shirt* took it.

What kind of course appeals to you?
Courses *which require hard work* appeal to me.

Often information accompanying a noun is not necessary for the purpose of identification. It merely gives your reader *further information* about something on which he has already focused; it is **nonrestrictive**. Nonrestrictive material is set off from the rest of the sentence by a **comma**, or by a comma both before and after it if it occurs in the middle of the sentence:

He talked to his lawyer, *a well-known Boston attorney.*
His lawyer, *who is a very impatient man,* gathered up his papers and stalked out of the hall.

The commas used to set off nonrestrictive modifiers often make the difference between a very cautious and a very sweeping statement. "Americans *who do not speak French* need not apply" narrows down the scope of the statement to certain Americans, those that do not speak French. "Americans, *who do not speak French,* need not apply" is aimed at *all* Americans and at the same time makes a sweeping claim about their linguistic abilities. The commas used to signal the difference in meaning correspond to a break signaled in speech by a characteristic change in the tone of voice. You can train your ear to catch the distinction by going over the sample sentences already given and reading them out loud.

The following points should be noted:

(1) **Dashes** are occasionally used to set off a nonrestrictive *modifier that contains internal punctuation* and that would not be clearly marked without them:

His lawyer—*a gruff, stubborn, impatient man*—stalked out of the hall.

(2) A *proper name* is usually adequate identification; a modifier following the name usually becomes nonrestrictive and is set off by commas. Several such modifiers may succeed each other:

Mr. Smith, *my history teacher,* dismissed his class early.

In 1942, he joined the Actors' Theater, *a repertory company with strong political views.*

David Daiches, *English-born but Scottish-educated, formerly a professor at Chicago and Cornell, now at the University of Sussex,* chaired the meeting with the skill and courage of a lion-tamer.—Ralph W. Condee, "Bedlam at Edinburgh," *The Reporter*

Occasionally, a restrictive modifier is needed to help the reader distinguish between several people of the same name:

> I find it hard to distinguish between Holmes *the author* and Holmes *the Supreme Court justice.*

When your reader already knows whom you have in mind, even a proper name may be additional, nonrestrictive information:

> His oldest sister, *Martha,* has always helped him when he was in trouble.

(3) **Adjective clauses** modify a noun or noun equivalent and usually begin with *who, which,* or *that.* Clauses beginning with *when, where,* and *why* are also adjective clauses if they are used to modify a noun. Adjective clauses, like other modifiers, may be *either restrictive or nonrestrictive.* However, those beginning with *that* are always restrictive:

> The book *that you sent me* was very exciting reading.

Sometimes a noun is modified by a subject-predicate group from which a possible pronoun or connective has been omitted. Such abbreviated adjective clauses are always restrictive:

> Most of the things [*that*] *I like to eat* are fattening.
> She wrote a long passionate letter to the man [*whom*] *she loves.*

P 5c Sentence Modifiers. *Many sentence modifiers are set off by commas.* Modifiers may modify sentence elements other than nouns. They may also modify the sentence as a whole rather than any part of it.[3]

[3] Adverbial clauses, which can be classified as sentence modifiers, are treated under P 4.

(1) *Verbals and verbal phrases modifying a verb* may be either restrictive or nonrestrictive. Notice the **comma** indicating the difference:

RESTRICTIVE: He always came into the office *carrying a shirt box full of letters under his arm.*

NONRESTRICTIVE: Deadline newspaper writing is rapid because it cheats, *depending heavily on clichés and stock phrases.*

Verbal phrases modifying the sentence as a whole are always set off:

To tell you the truth, I don't even recall his name.
The business outlook being rosy, he invested his savings in highly speculative stocks.
Our new manager has done rather well, *considering his lack of experience.*

(2) If a *sentence is introduced by a long or substantial modifying phrase,* a **comma** usually indicates where the main sentence starts:

After an unusually solemn Sunday dinner, Father called me into his study.

Like all newspapermen of good faith, Mencken had long fumed at the low estate of the journalistic rank and file.—Philip M. Wagner, "Mencken Remembered," *The American Scholar*

Introductory verbals and verbal phrases are set off even when they are short:

Smiling, she dropped the match into the gas tank.
To start the motor, turn the ignition key.

The comma after an introductory modifier can be an important clue to the meaning of a sentence, and omitting it may cause serious misreading. Compare the following two sentences:

> *When hunting,* lions stay away from wooded areas.
> *When hunting lions,* stay away from wooded areas.

(3) Expressions like *after all, of course, unfortunately, on the whole, as a rule,* and *certainly* often do not modify the subject or the predicate of a sentence but establish a connection between one sentence and another. Depending on the amount of emphasis you would give such a modifier when reading, you can make it stand out from the rest of the sentence by a **comma**:

> *After all,* we are in business primarily for profit.
> *On the other hand,* the records may never be found.
> You will submit the usual reports, *of course.*

Sentence modifiers that are set off require two commas if they do not come first or last in the sentence:

> We do not, *as a rule,* solicit applications.
> A great many things, *to be sure,* could be said for him.

EXERCISES

A. Check the following passages for conventional punctuation of modifiers. Label each passage *S* (satisfactory), *F* (unsatisfactory because of a sentence fragment), or *U* (unsatisfactory for some other reason).

> 1. With only a cautious enthusiasm, newspapers are giving a little extra Sunday space to culture. 2. Despite the opposition of a crooked sheriff, the hero, a handsome screen cowboy on a $5,000 horse, succeeded in straightening things out. 3. The proctor—a waspish, restless man—kept his eye on the whispering students. 4. Everyone, who is physically able, should have some exercise each day. 5. The kind of history that we were taught dealt mainly with the pageantry

of princes and with the intrigues of empire. 6. Queen Victoria, brought from retirement by the skill of Disraeli, became the adored symbol of domestic virtue and imperial greatness. 7. Having swallowed enough water to last me all summer I decided to leave water skiing to those who had an aptitude for it. 8. My father who taught both in high school and in college gave me many helpful pointers on how to budget my time. 9. Major medical news—the discovery of a new surgical technique, the development of a cure for heart disease—is sometimes buried on the back pages. 10. Work after school can cut severely into study time, forcing the student to study late at night. 11. All kinds of opinion-makers—people who would never dream of insulting a Negro, Jew, Catholic, or Paiute Indian—delight in slipping their daily needle of sarcasm into the politician. 12. Usually a selfish person is a spoiled person. One who must have his way or else. 13. A good example of our neglect of public health problems, is the lack of hospital space for the mentally ill. 14. With print orders now running fourteen million monthly, the *Reader's Digest* faces no serious competition in its field. 15. Pontius Pilate, Procurator of Palestine, the highest judge and top administrator of the country, had few of the marks of greatness.

B. Insert appropriate punctuation in the numbered spaces. *Use no capitals or periods not already supplied in the text.* Leave a blank space where no punctuation is required.

1. Good television plays___(1) which are not very numerous___(2) do not have a predictable ending. The viewer cannot tell___(3) what will happen___(4) until the play is over. *Arts Theater*___(5) discontinued last June___(6) was a good example of a type of program___(7) appealing to the viewer's intelligence and curiosity. The play___(8) I remember best___(9) dealt with a punch-drunk prizefighter___(10) who fell in love with an attractive and well-educated girl. Until the very end of the play___(11) I did not know___(12) whether the fighter would win the girl.

2. My father___(1) the oldest child in a family with seven children___(2) grew up on a farm___(3) first cultivated by

my grandparents___(4) Swedish immigrants in Minnesota. My grandfather having died in an accident___(5) my father helped out at the local post office___(6) to help support his mother___(7) and the younger children. Being an unusually earnest young man___(8) he studied for an exam___(9) that would enable him___(10) to become an inspector. Having passed it with excellent grades___(11) he went to work investigating the activities of swindlers___(12) who used the mails to defraud the public.

P 6 Coordination

Important uses of the comma (and some other marks) occur in clauses where several elements of the same kind appear together.

P 6a Series. *Commas normally separate three or more items of the same kind appearing in a series.* The most common pattern separates the elements from each other by **commas**, with the last comma followed by a connective tying the whole group together:

Phil, Jim, and *Harry* came to see me.

After dinner, we *talked, laughed,* and *sang.*

The new students enter after a rigid selective process, *they present* few disciplinary problems, and *they arrive* after good and uniform preparation.—Oscar Handlin, "Are the Colleges Killing Education?" *Atlantic*

This basic *A, B, and C* pattern can be expanded to accommodate any number of elements:

The boys had spread out around them the homely tools of mischief—*the long wires, nails, hammers, pliers, string, flashlights, paraffin* saved from the tops of their mothers' jelly jars, *knives* for cutting a clothesline or carving out insults to the grown-up world, and *tin cans* filled with rocks for making a farewell noise after the damage was done.—Lois Phillips Hudson, "The Buggy on the Roof," *Atlantic*

Notice the following variations:

(1) Occasionally, you will want to arrange in a series *groups of words that already contain commas*. To prevent misreading, use **semicolons** instead of additional commas to indicate the major breaks:

Three persons were mentioned in her will: *John, her brother; Martin, her nephew;* and *Helen, her faithful nurse.*

(2) The last comma in a series is often left out in *informal and journalistic writing:*

Segregation, farm income and *foreign aid* are persistent issues in American politics.

More unusual is the practice of using commas only and leaving out the connective:

The idea was to pool all the needs of all those who had in one way or another been bested by their environment—*the crippled, the sick, the hungry, the ragged.*—John Lear, "The Business of Giving," *Saturday Review*

P 6b Coordinate Adjectives. *Adjectives are often separated by a comma corresponding to a characteristic break in speech.* Two adjectives describing different qualities of the same noun may be coordinated by a **comma** rather than by *and*. They are then called coordinative adjectives:

a *black* and *shaggy* dog	a *black, shaggy* dog
a *starved* and *exhausted* stranger	a *starved, exhausted* stranger
a *grand* and *awe-inspiring* sunset	a *grand, awe-inspiring* sunset

Not every sequence of adjectives falls into this pattern. Often an adjective combines with a noun to indicate a type of person or object (a *public* servant, a *short* story, a *black* market). An adjective preceding such a combination modifies the combination as a whole and should not be separated from it by a comma:

a *secretive* public servant
a *long* short story
a *lively* black market

NOTE: Often the most reliable method of distinguishing between the two kinds of adjective is to read the sentence out loud. This method will help especially with combinations where the difference in meaning is not obvious (a *tired, weary old man* but *an old, tired, weary man; chattering, giggling little girls* but *tiny, anemic, undernourished children*).

P 6c Dates and Addresses. *Commas are needed with dates, addresses, page references, and similar information consisting of three or four different parts.* The different items are kept separate from each other by a **comma**; the last item is followed by a comma unless it is at the same time the last word of the sentence:

The date was *Tuesday, December 16, 1952.*
Please send my mail to *483 Tulane Street, Jackson, Oklahoma,* starting the first of the month.
The quotation is from *Chapter V, page 43, line 7,* of the second volume.

Commas are also used to keep separate the different parts of *measurements* employing more than one unit of measurement, but the last item is usually not separated from the rest of the sentence:

The boy is now *five feet, seven inches* tall.
Nine pounds, three ounces is an unusual weight for this kind of fish.

P 6d Repetition and Contrast. *Commas are needed between expressions that either are identical or give two different versions of the same meaning.* Use the **comma** after a word or phrase to be repeated or to be followed by a definition or explanatory paraphrase:

Produce, produce! This is a law among artists, or rather it is their inner compulsion.—Malcolm Cowley, "Artists, Conscience, and Censors," *Saturday Review*

I am asking *whether you recall his exact language, whether you remember exactly what he said.*

Commas also separate words or groups of words that establish a *contrast:*

> *His wife, not his brother,* needs the money more.
> *The days were warm, the nights cool.*

EXERCISES

A. Check the following passages for conventional punctuation of coordinate or closely related elements. Label each passage *S* (satisfactory) or *U* (unsatisfactory).

> 1. Congress has the right to approve presidential appointments, to override presidential vetoes, and to impeach the President. 2. The old, the infirm and the widowed, are the most frequent victims of the confidence man's schemes. 3. While living there, I knew I was sharing a room with a friend, not just a roommate. 4. To my weary, apprehensive parents, November 12, 1947, was a momentous day. 5. More people than ever are painting pictures going to museums and listening to classical music. 6. The new hospital was faced partly with aluminum sun-breakers, partly with ceramic tile. 7. The alderman complained that the Henry E. Lee Memorial Library was a gigantic, white elephant. 8. Our editorial and executive offices are located in the Newsweek Building, Broadway and 42nd Street, New York 36, New York. 9. The ores of

the Comstock Lode not the natural beauty of the sierras had brought my family to Nevada. 10. Henry had not been heard from since he went to a carnival party in Munich Germany. 11. Ex-senators, ex-governors, ex-cabinet members, and distinguished private citizens have at times made good ambassadors. 12. The miles upon miles of small houses are new, spick-and-span, and highly sanitary, but they are also indistinguishable from those in Kankakee, Illinois; Lincoln, Nebraska; or Oakland, California.

B. In the following passages, insert appropriate punctuation in the numbered spaces. *Use no capitals or periods not already supplied in the text.* Leave a blank space where no punctuation is required.

1. In recent months___(1) senators___(2) ex-athletes___(3) and the clergy have added their voices to a mounting chorus of indignation. They agree with the many American___(4) physical___(5) education teachers___(6) who condemn Americans as flabby___(7) lazy___(8) and generally unfit. These people seem to fear___(9) that the Russians___(10) a race of tawny___(11) muscle-bound gymnasts___(12) will one day descend upon our shores and thresh each of us individually. My own fear is that the slender___(13) bony look in fashion among Americans today may be a handicap in the battle for the minds of men. How can the hungry___(14) human beings of other countries believe that a nation of gaunt___(15) emaciated people is as well off as it pretends to be?

2. The purpose of a quick___(1) warm___(2) synthesis between research___(3) thinking___(4) and writing is to attain the three prime qualities of historical composition___(5) clarity___(6) vigor___(7) and objectivity. You must think about your facts___(8) analyze your material___(9) and decide exactly what you mean. Most of the facts___(10) that you excavate from the archives___(11) are dumb things___(12) it is for you to make them speak by proper selection___(13) arrangement___(14) and emphasis.

P 7 Interrupters

Depending on their role and importance in the sentence, interrupters are set off by commas, parentheses, or dashes.

To some extent the conventions of internal punctuation follow the rhythms of speech. This is true of the practice of setting off interrupters, elements that are not part of the main structure of the sentence in which they occur.

P 7a Heavy Interrupters. *Some interrupters constitute a very definite break.* A speaker may stop in the middle of a sentence to supply some preliminary detail or clarification. Or he may pause to give special impact to a word or phrase. In writing, such material is set off from the rest of a sentence by **dashes**. Dashes tend to emphasize or dramatize the material they set off.

Four uses of such dashes are especially common:

(1) A *complete sentence is inserted into another sentence,* without a connective or relative pronoun to join them.

Lady Macbeth—*has this been noted?*—takes very little stock in the witches.—Mary McCarthy, "General Macbeth," *Harper's*

(2) A *list enumerating details or examples* interrupts rather than follows a clause.

Three of my friends—*Simp, Shnorkel, and Bip*—were waiting for me at the door.

(3) After a list of possible subjects, a sentence starts anew with a summarizing *all, these,* or *those.*

The visual essay, the rhythmic album, the invitation to drop in on a casual conversation—these are the idiosyncratic traits by which television, as television, has come to be recognized.—Walter Kerr, "What Good Is Television?" *Horizon*

(4) A word or phrase is made to stand out for emphasis or for a *climactic effect.*

After twenty-three years, he was leaving Newston jail—*a free man.*

P 7b Parenthetic Material. *Some interrupters, though constituting a definite break, supply relatively unimportant data or are mere asides.* The place of dashes may then be taken by **parentheses**:

Fatal accidents (*we had three of them last year in a town of 5,000 people*) can often be traced to excessive speed.

Kazan directed the rest of his considerable steam into studying English (*he graduated with honors*), waiting on tables, and joining as many extracurricular campus clubs as he could.—Thomas B. Morgan, "Elia Kazan's Great Expectations," *Harper's*

Parentheses are commonly used to enclose dates, addresses, page references, chemical formulas, and similar information if it might be of interest to some readers but is not an essential part of the text. Here are some typical examples: (*p. 34*) (*first published in 1910*) (*now called Market Street*).

NOTE: When inserted into another sentence, a sentence in parentheses, like a sentence set off by dashes, usually begins with a lower-case letter and has no end punctuation. When a sentence in parentheses begins *after* end punctuation, end punctuation is required inside the final parenthesis:

Select your purchases with care. (*No refunds are permitted.*)

P 7c Light Interrupters. *Many interrupters blend into the sentence they interrupt, producing only a slight break.* Such interrupters are set off by **commas**.

(1) Use commas when you interrupt a statement to *address the reader* or to *comment* on the source, validity, or plausibility of what you are saying:

> Marriage, *dear boy,* is a serious business.
> Politicians, *you will agree,* were never popular in this part of the country.
> Our candidate, *it seems,* is not very well known.

(2) Commas set off the *introductory greetings and exclamations,* as well as the introductory *yes* and *no,* which frequently precede a statement in conversation and in informal writing:

> *Why,* I don't even know that man.
> *Yes,* you can now buy Pinko napkins in different colors.
> *Well,* you can't have everything.

(3) Commas set off the *shortened questions* often added to a statement to elicit agreement or confirmation:

> You are my friend, *aren't you?*
> So he says he is sick, *does he?*

(4) Commas may take the place of dashes to set off a word for emphasis. They can suggest a *thoughtful pause* rather than a dramatic break:

> We should act, *and suffer,* in accordance with our principles.
> People cannot, *or will not,* put down the facts.

(5) Slight breaks corresponding to those caused by light interrupters are sometimes caused by *sentence elements that have changed their usual position in the sentence:*

> Laws, *to be cheerfully obeyed,* must be both just and practicable.

(ex.)

Philip, *for no apparent reason at all,* got up and left the room. Marriage, *unless it is to be a failure,* must be completely voluntary.

EXERCISES

A. Check the following passages for conventional punctuation of interrupters. Label each passage *S* (satisfactory) or U (unsatisfactory).

1. Photography, you will agree, is not yet generally accepted as an art form. 2. For years, English Methodists have debated the merits of reunion with the Anglican Church (2,922,000 members). 3. Many fine programs though presented mainly for entertainment, supplement what the child learns in school. 4. Painter Du Bois—his work is represented in Manhattan's Metropolitan Museum of Art—resisted the modern trend toward abstraction. 5. The lone rider, the barroom fight, and the gingham-clad heroine—these are the indispensable ingredients of the third-rate cowboy movie. 6. At one time President Wilson was a university president wasn't he? 7. A dozen last-inning victories (six of them since July 4) have given hometown fans something to cheer about. 8. He reports that political independents—his term is the mugwumps—have ejected the old-line party hacks from the city government. 9. Why if I were you Alice I would see a lawyer first thing tomorrow morning. 10. Peter Minuit I am sure you remember bought Manhattan Island from the Indians for a handful of trinkets. 11. The government, many businessmen feel, should insure foreign investments against expropriation. 12. A trip abroad, to be truly enjoyable, should be carefully planned.

B. From your current writing and reading, select ten sample sentences that illustrate the various conventions of punctuation discussed in P 5–7.

P 8 Quotation

Different ways of handling quoted material require different uses of quotation marks and other punctuation.

Often, you will need to indicate that you are reproducing information or ideas derived from a specific source, that you are quoting something first said or observed by someone else.

P 8a Direct Quotation. *In repeating someone's exact words, distinguish them clearly from your own text.* Such direct quotations are enclosed in **quotation marks**. They are usually separated by a **comma** from the credit tag (the statement identifying the source):

> She said, "Leave me alone."
> "I don't care," he said.

Often the *credit tag interrupts the quotation* instead of introducing or concluding it. You then need **commas** both before and after the credit tag if it splits one complete sentence. You need a comma before and a period after the credit tag if it comes between two complete sentences:

> "All men," Aristotle wrote, "naturally desire knowledge."
> "All men are curious," Aristotle wrote. "They naturally desire knowledge."

The following variations are important:

(1) No comma is required with extremely *short quotations* or with *quotations worked into the pattern of a sentence* that is not a mere credit tag:

Your saying "I am sorry" was not enough to soothe his wounded pride.

The clatter of dishes and tableware, mingled with lusty shouts of "Seconds here!" and "Please pass the butter!", will resound across the country.—John Crawford, "A Plea for Physical Fatness," *Atlantic*

No comma is required when the credit tag follows a question or an exclamation:

"Is everbody all right?" he shouted at the top of his voice.

(2) *Long or formal quotations* are often introduced by a **colon** instead of a comma. Whether you use a comma or a colon, capitalize the first word of the quotation if it was capitalized in the original source (or if it would have been capitalized if written down).

Saarinen's definition of architecture's purposes describes his work: "To shelter and enhance man's life on earth and to fulfill his belief in the nobility of his existence."

(3) *Long quotations* (more than ten typed lines) should be set off from the rest of a paper *not* by quotation marks but by indention and single-spacing. The same applies to quotations consisting of more than a full line of poetry. See Section 8 and the sample paper that follows it for examples of such **block quotations**.

(4) Indicate when the person you are quoting is quoting someone else. In a quotation marked by the conventional set of double quotation marks, **single quotation marks** signal a *quotation within a quotation:*

He said, "Our Congressman's constant cry of 'Cut that budget!' deceives no one."

In the words of Chester Bowles, "In our national efforts to prove that we are 'realists' who do not 'go off half-cocked,' we have developed an appalling gap between the moral beliefs to which we subscribe and our day-to-day performance."

P 8b Terminal Marks in Quotations. *Observe conventional sequence when quotation marks coincide with other marks of punctuation.*

(1) Commas conventionally precede the final quotation mark, whereas *semicolons and colons conventionally follow it.*

As he said, "Don't worry about me," the ship pulled away from the quay.
You said, "I don't need your sympathy"; therefore, I didn't offer any.

(2) End punctuation usually precedes the final quotation marks, as in all the examples given so far. Sometimes, however, you will have to use a *question mark or an exclamation mark after the quotation has formally ended.* This means that the quotation itself is not a question or an exclamation. Rather, you are asking a question or exclaiming about the quotation.

Who said, "We are strangers here; the world is from of old"?
Don't ever tell a girl, "There'll never be another woman like my mother"!

NOTE: *A terminal mark is not duplicated at the end of a quotation* even when logic might seem to require its repetition. For instance, use only one question mark even when you are asking a question about a question:

Were you the student who asked, "Could we hold the class on the lawn?"

P 8c Insertions and Omissions. *In direct quotation, any changes you make in the original text should be clearly indicated to your reader.*

(1) If for any reason you insert *explanations or comments of your own,* you should set them off from the quoted material by **square brackets**:

As Dr. Habenichts observes, "Again and again, they [the Indians] saw themselves deprived of lands of whose possession they had been assured with solemn oaths."

The note read: "Left Camp B Wednesday, April 3 [actually April 4]. Are trying to reach Camp C before we run out of supplies."

A comment sometimes inserted in a quotation is *sic,* the Latin word for "thus," which indicates that a passage that seems questionable or contains errors was transcribed exactly the way it occurred in the original source.

The police records contained this short entry: "The accomplices of the suspect is [*sic*] unknown."

(2) If you want to *omit unnecessary or irrelevant material* from a quotation, you have to indicate the omission by three consecutive periods, adding up to a total of four if the omission occurs after a period in the original text:

The report concluded on an optimistic note: "All three of the patients . . . are making remarkable progress toward recovery."

"To be a bird is to be alive more intensely than any other living creature, man included. . . . They live in a world that is always present, mostly full of joy." So wrote N. J. Berrill, Professor of Zoology at McGill University.—Joseph Wood Krutch, "If You Don't Mind My Saying So," *The American Scholar*

To indicate extensive omissions (a line or more of poetry, a paragraph or more of prose), you may use a single typed line of spaced periods.

NOTE: Periods indicating an omission are called an **ellipsis**. An ellipsis can easily distort or falsify a quotation by omitting important details or qualifications. A testimonial reading "This might have been a good book if it had been more carefully planned" should not be shortened to read ". . . a good book."

P 8d Indirect Quotation. *In indirect quotations, you reproduce someone else's ideas or thoughts but translate them into your own words.* Indirect quotations are *not* enclosed in quotation marks:

Aristotle stated *that all men naturally desire knowledge.*
General Grant replied *that he doubted the wisdom of such a move.*
The artist asked me *which of the drawings I liked best.*

(1) Indirectly quoted statements often take the form of noun clauses introduced by *that;* indirectly quoted questions, the form of noun clauses introduced by words like *whether, why, how,* or *which.* Such clauses are *not* separated from the statement indicating the source by a comma or colon. The following passage, by contrast, shows ways of *working the source statement into the indirect quotation as an interrupter,* requiring **commas**:

As Gandhi remarked, the first consequence of nonviolent action is to harden the heart of those who are being assaulted by charity. But, *he continued,* all the while they are being driven to a frenzy of rage, they are haunted by the terrible knowledge of how wrong they are. —Michael Harrington, "Whence Comes Their Passion," *The Reporter*

(2) Even in an indirect quotation, you may reproduce some words or phrases exactly as they were used by the person you quote. To indicate that you are *preserving part of the original wording,* you should enclose such directly quoted words and phrases—but not any other part of the quotation—in **quotation marks**:

The author felt that students could not be "tricked or coerced into thinking."

The government radio referred to the accused men as "bandits" and "murderers" and promised that justice would be upheld "regardless of the cost."

P 8e Words Set Off from Context. *Quotation marks sometimes indicate that a writer is using words and phrases that are not part of the vocabulary he would normally employ.* In other words, he is using expressions that are not his own, even though he may not be quoting them from any specific source.

(1) **Quotation marks** may identify words that are employed for *local color or comical effect.* They enable a writer to show irony by holding an expression as it were at arm's length:

At the school I attended, a girl who did not go on "dates" or take an interest in "fellows" was not accepted as a normal human being.

It would seem that every modern child's pleasure must have its "constructive aspects."—Lois Phillips Hudson, "The Buggy on the Roof," *Atlantic*

Avoid using such quotation marks as a way of evading responsibility for undesirable or inappropriate expressions.

(2) Either quotation marks or italicized print—which corresponds to underlining in a typed manuscript—identifies *technical terms* presumably new to the reader and *words discussed as words,* as in a discussion of grammar or meaning.

She wore a "Mother Hubbard," a loose, full gown long since out of fashion.

In logic, the term *inference* refers to a conclusion or deduction arrived at by reasoning.

The word *mob* was attacked as slang by some eighteenth-century writers.

(3) **Italics** rather than quotation marks identify *words that have been borrowed from foreign languages* and have not become part of the generally accepted vocabulary of the English language:

Logrolling and back scratching are his exercises; *Quid pro quo* and *Cui bono?* are his mottoes.—William Lee Miller, "Confessions of a Conferencegoer," *The Reporter*

Many legal and scientific terms borrowed from Latin belong in this category:

A writ of *certiorari* is issued by a superior court to obtain judicial records from an inferior court or quasi-judicial agency.

The sperm whale, *Physeter macrocephalus,* is valuable for its oil and spermaceti.

EXERCISES

A. Check the following passages for conventional punctuation of quotations. Label each passage *S* (satisfactory) or *U* (unsatisfactory).

1. "Everything has already been said," wrote André Gide, "but since nobody ever listens we always have to start all over again."

2. "I am Grace Anders," she said, "do you mind if I come in?"

3. "Terrible!" the director shouted. "Let's take that passage again, starting from 'O, that this too too solid flesh would melt . . .' "

4. Newspaper veterans turned the phrases "culture beat" and "culture editor" over in their mouths with the gusto of a man biting into an unripe olive.

5. The lady from Buffalo kept asking the guide "what he meant by primitive?"

6. Wild applause and shouts of "Encore!" greeted us when the curtain parted.

7. Instead of congratulating me, John said, "Beauty contests—what a farce!"

8. According to one irate bystander, the murderer deserved no more sympathy than a "rabid dog."

9. "I'm all right," said my uncle, "just watch what you are doing the next time."

10. The speaker charged "that the television audience resembled the ancient Romans, who liked to see gladiators do battle to the death."

11. The speaker quoted Jefferson as saying that "our new circumstances" require "new words, new phrases, and the transfer of old words to new objects."

12. The constant war cry of my high school English teachers was give an example!

B. In the following passage, insert appropriate punctuation in the numbered spaces. Underline lower-case letters that should be replaced with capitals (english). Leave a blank space where no punctuation is required.

The article points out___(1) that many commercials are directed at the younger and more impressionable among television fans___(2) for instance___(3) a commercial might go like this___(4) Harry the Bat eats Bang Cereal every morning to grow big and strong___(5) so why don't you kiddies have your mom buy some today___(6) Mom is then plagued by the___(7) kiddies___(8) until she buys the cereal___(9) wasn't it Edgar Guest who said___(10) none but the hard of heart can resist the pleading look of a child___(11) this technique takes unfair advantage of the parents___(12) for___(13) as a friend of mine recently put it___(14) children are often even more gullible than adults___(15).

C. From your current writing and reading, select ten sample sentences that illustrate the various conventions of punctuation discussed in the preceding section.

D. (**Review of punctuation**) Explain the use of punctuation marks in each of the following passages. Point out sentences that you would have punctuated differently and explain why. Explain effects achieved by unconventional punctuation.

1. In recent years it has been possible to make motion-picture films of events on the surface of the sun, and by speed-

ing them up several hundred times to project on the screen the life story of cataclysmic solar events which may occupy hours of time and quadrillions of cubic miles of space. Some of these films are awe-inspiring: they show immense fountains of flame spurting to heights of a hundred thousand miles from the sun's edge; bridges of fire, which could span a dozen earths, forming and crumbling; exact replicas of A-bomb bursts—but a thousand times as large—shooting up into space.—Arthur C. Clarke, "The Secret of the Sun," *Holiday*

2. Many of the greatest classics were written, assuredly, without children in mind, and were taken over by children who cheerfuly disregarded what they could not understand and cherished what they could. Thus Defoe, old and cantankerous, did not mean to write for children, but they adopted Robinson Crusoe and own him still; soon Crusoe spread all over the globe; he was celebrated in every language; he suffered one metamorphosis after another, most famously in "Swiss Family Robinson," but in dozens of others as well. After two hundred years he is read avidly by children in Montana and Tasmania and Norway, and very little by their parents. Nor did the harsh and embittered Jonathan Swift mean to write for the young, but he could not help himself either, it seems. The children took over Gulliver and went with him on his travels, they made him into a fairy-story character. —Henry Steele Commager, "When Majors Wrote for Minors," *Saturday Review*

3. Men are brought to these conferences, regularly, in a sort of balanced ticket: one Jew, one Catholic, one Protestant; one labor leader to every businessman; one Republican to every Democrat; very carefully, a Negro and a woman; an economist with the Economist's View, a psychoanalyst with the Psychoanalytical View, a philosopher with the Standpoint of Philosophy. In my earliest conferencegoing days I myself was a College Student, attending as representative decoration conferences composed mainly of older people. Invariably there would come a golden moment when—since I then had sense enough to keep my mouth shut and would not have spoken—the chairman would pounce: "But let us hear from the Student Mind"; or "And how does this sound to Young People?"—William Lee Miller, "Confessions of a Conferencegoer," *The Reporter*

8

THE RESEARCH PAPER

Every writer must learn to assemble, interpret, and correlate material from a variety of sources. He must learn to build on the work of previous investigators. He must present his findings in such a way that they will be accepted as the result of detailed and comprehensive exploration, conducted by a competent and responsible observer.

Choosing a Subject

Select a subject limited in scope and suitable for objective investigation.

As a student writing a research paper, you need to produce definite results in a limited time. The result of whatever research you do is supposed to be a substantial and coherent paper. Your first task, therefore, is to select a subject that you can profitably treat within the time and with the materials at your disposal. Obviously, you will avoid subjects for which you are completely unprepared. For instance, recent developments in the natural sciences or in medicine make interesting subjects, but most of them call for a knowledge of mathematics, physics, or chemistry that many college freshmen do not have. If you can, try to start from a foothold of previously acquired knowledge. If you grew up in the South, you might be prepared to investigate the ideas or the influence of a Confederate leader like Jefferson Davis. If your home state is known for its Indian reservations, you might profitably investigate the cultural traditions of an Indian tribe.

On the other hand, many subjects of general interest pro-

vide fruitful topics for a paper of this kind. A research paper will give you a chance to focus on a familiar idea and to assess its validity or significance. For instance, you might trace the concept of "rugged individualism" in the speeches and writings of Herbert Hoover. Or you might compare Mahatma Gandhi's concept of nonviolence with Western ideas of passive resistance.

Select a subject that will allow you to observe a number of basic requirements for a successful paper:

(1) *The paper should center on one limited aspect of a general subject.* If it is designed to establish a thesis, it should concentrate on establishing one or two main points. Avoid subjects that would lead you to compile miscellaneous information. Many research papers are unsuccessful because they cover too much ground. They are too broad in scope, too shallow in treatment. Restrict your general subject area until you arrive at something that you can explore in detail. "The early history of American universities" is a general subject area; "the training of Puritan divines at Harvard" is a specific subject.

(2) *The paper should show that the author has made detailed use of several different sources.* Avoid subjects that would tempt you to summarize preassembled information from one main source. Avoid subjects that are conclusively and satisfactorily treated in a textbook or in an encyclopedia. By definition, a research paper is more than a condensation of easily accessible material. Whatever points you make should require careful sifting and comparing of evidence from different, and possibly conflicting, sources.

(3) *The conclusions elaborated in the paper should stay close to the evidence actually presented.* Avoid subjects whose discussion might bring into play a large measure of partisan allegiance or personal preference.

Here are some general areas for research:

1. The past history and future prospects of English spelling; reasons for its irregularity; causes that led to standardization; attempts at spelling reform.

2. The history of dictionary making; the principles and practices of lexicographers like Samuel Johnson or Noah Webster; the history of the *Oxford English Dictionary;* problems of lexicography.

3. The nature and history of Basic English; the purposes it was designed to serve; arguments for or against its use; the obstacles it encountered.

4. The state of foreign-language teaching in American public schools; arguments for and against the study of Latin; current trends toward increased study of foreign languages; public-school offerings in Russian and other languages not often taught.

5. The need for an international language; the arguments for or against such projected world languages as Esperanto or Interlingua; the obstacles encountered by advocates of an international language.

6. The history or the extent of the censorship of imaginative literature in the United States; standards applied by critics, courts of law, civic groups; legal means and indirect pressures at the disposal of would-be censors.

7. The early history of some outstanding American universities or colleges; the philosophical, religious, or political motives of their founders; the purposes, vocational or otherwise, for which the institutions were originally intended; the educational principles of their founders or of their original faculties.

8. The education or the reading of a prominent early American; books that influenced Washington, Jefferson, Franklin, or Madison; the influence of the classics or of contemporary trends of of thought.

9. The present state of the American theater; the extent, quality, or reception of theatrical activity; the role of professional companies, amateur groups, drama festivals; economic and social status of actors and playwrights.

10. Religious trends in the United States; the growth of Catholicism, the spread and influence of evangelistic movements, the prospects for closer association of the various Protestant de-

nominations, tendencies within American Judaism; interest in religious subjects among high school or college students.

Using the Library

Learn to use the resources of your college library.

In an adequate college library, every imaginable subject is covered by books, articles, and reports that are often the result of painstaking and comprehensive study.

General Reference Works. *A writer must learn to use the reference tools available to every investigator regardless of his specific subject.*

ENCYCLOPEDIAS. Whatever your subject, you can start by looking it up in an encyclopedia. A general encyclopedia is a survey of reliable information in every field of study. It is written for laymen, usually with a minimum of technical terminology and of editorial bias.

The *Encyclopaedia Britannica,* as its name implies, is exceptionally full in its coverage of various aspects of British life, such as the British monarchy. Although you would normally consult the most up-to-date edition, you will sometimes find references to the earlier Eleventh Edition, which contained a number of valuable scholarly articles not retained in later revisions.

The Encyclopedia Americana, like the *Britannica,* is compiled with the help of outstanding authorities in academic and public life.

The *New International Encyclopaedia* is an older work of comparable standing (now out of print). Each of these major encyclopedias is supplemented annually by a yearbook dealing with the events and discoveries of the preceding year.

The one-volume *Columbia Encyclopedia* provides a bird's-eye view of many subjects that the more comprehensive encyclopedias treat in greater detail.

BIBLIOGRAPHIES. At the end of many encyclopedia entries you will find a short bibliography, a list of important books and other sources of information. The encyclopedia may suggest only very general books, but these in turn will often contain more detailed bibliographical listings or direct you to book-length bibliographies. Any general survey of a subject is likely to provide information about more detailed studies. College textbooks often provide a short bibliography at the end of each chapter.

Take up first those books that a bibliography labels "standard," "indispensable," or "the best introduction" to your subject. If the bibliographies you have consulted merely *list* books, take up those that are most frequently mentioned. Study their tables of contents, prefaces, introductory or concluding chapters. Find out what each book is trying to do and whether all or parts of it would be useful for your project.

The *Book Review Digest* contains short selections from book reviews written shortly after publication of the book reviewed. These can give you an idea of the intention and importance of books on subjects of general interest.

PERIODICAL INDEXES. When writing on a current problem, you may have to rely primarily on articles in both general and technical magazines. Often a well-written magazine article is the most convenient survey of and guide to information on a subject. Often magazine articles contain detailed discussion of points treated very briefly in available books. Since the card catalogue of your library lists magazines but not individual magazine articles, you will have to locate the latter in the so-called periodical indexes. These are published in monthly or semimonthly installments and then combined in huge volumes, each listing articles for a period of one or more years.

The *Readers' Guide to Periodical Literature* indexes magazines written for the general reader. If you are writing on American policy in the Far East, the *Readers' Guide* will direct you to speeches by government officials reprinted in full in *Vital Speeches of the Day* or in the *U.S. News and World Report.* It will direct you to detailed discussions of American foreign policy in such magazines as *Newsweek* or *The Reporter.*

The *International Index to Periodicals* lists articles in technical or scholarly magazines. If you are writing on the status of the American Negro, this index will direct you to articles in sociological and psychological journals. For a paper on cancer research, it will direct you to articles written by outstanding authorities.

Poole's Index to Periodical Literature lists articles published between 1802 and 1906. For instance, it can help you find contemporary reviews of Noah Webster's dictionary or of the novels of James Fenimore Cooper.

NOTE: Whatever index—or bibliography—you use, read its introductory pages and study its list of abbreviations. Study the list of the periodicals indexed—it may not include a magazine that you have seen mentioned elsewhere and that you know to be important. Look at sample entries to study the listing of individual articles (usually by subject) and the system of cross references.

Specialized Reference Works. *A writer must learn to use the reference tools of his special area of study.* Every major area, such as education, history, or art, has its own specialized reference guides: yearbooks, specialized encyclopedias, dictionaries of names and technical terms, general bibliographies.

To find specialized reference works relevant to your research project, turn to Constance M. Winchell's *Guide to Reference Books,* including the supplements bringing it up to date. It lists the standard sources of information for all major fields of study and contains many helpful hints for the inexperienced research worker.

BIOGRAPHY. One type of library project that is often assigned in writing classes is the biographical or quasi-biographical paper. In addition to the biographical entries in the major encyclopedias, most libraries have ample material for this kind of project.

Who's Who in America, a biographical dictionary of notable living men and women, provides a brief summary of dates and details on important contemporaries.

The *Dictionary of American Biography* contains a more detailed account of the lives of important persons. (The British counterparts of these two volumes are *Who's Who* and the *Dictionary of National Biography.*)

The *Biography Index* is a guide to biographical material in books *and* magazines. By consulting both recent and earlier volumes, you can compile a comprehensive bibliography of material on the married life of George Washington or on the evangelistic campaigns of Billy Graham.

LITERATURE. Courses that stress reading and discussion of imaginative literature may include a library project on a subject from literary history—an author's schooling or early reading, recurrent themes in the books of a well-known novelist, the contemporary reputation of a nineteenth-century American poet.

The fifteen-volume *Cambridge History of English Literature* and the *Cambridge Bibliography of English Literature* provide comprehensive information about English authors and literary movements.

The Spiller-Thorp-Johnson-Canby *Literary History of the United States,* with the bibliography published as its third volume, lists as its contributors an impressive and representative roster of contemporary American literary scholars.

Harper's Dictionary of Classical Literature and Antiquities is a comprehensive scholarly guide to Greek and Roman history and civilization. (Robert Graves' *The Greek Myths* and Edith Hamilton's *Mythology,* both available as paperbacks, provide an introduction to famous names and stories.)

CURRENT EVENTS. A number of special reference guides are useful for papers on a political subject or on current events.

Facts on File (published since 1941) is a weekly digest of world news, with an annual index. It gives a summary of news reports and comments with excerpts from important documents and speeches. It can serve as a convenient review of day-to-day happenings in politics, foreign affairs, entertainment, sports, science, and education.

The *New York Times Index* (published since 1913) is a guide to news stories published in the *New York Times*. By looking up an event or a controversy in either one of these indexes, you can ascertain the approximate dates for relevant articles in newspapers and magazines.

The annual index to the *Monthly Catalog of the United States Government Publications* lists reports and documents published by all branches of the federal government.

Sifting Evidence. *A writer must learn to evaluate conflicting evidence.* An inexperienced writer often shows an uncritical acceptance of other writers' views. He tends to accept statements as factual or true on the say-so of a single source: "The teaching of grammar has no appreciable effect on a student's writing" (because Professor X says so). "Economic rivalry between Germany and Great Britain was the primary cause of World War I" (because a book I have just read developed this theory). An experienced writer will accept such conclusions only after comparing the evidence offered by different authoritative sources. He is likely to consider such points as the following:

(1) Is the author an *authority on his subject* or merely a

casual observer? If you can, find out whether a book was written by an economist whose specialty is Russian agriculture or by a columnist who spent four weeks surveying Russian agriculture from the windows of a train.

(2) Does the author have an *established reputation in his field?* Keep an eye open for comments on the background and the scholarly competence of authors you are reading, or on the reputation of institutions and organizations with which they are connected.

(3) Does the publisher of the book or magazine represent a *tradition of scholarly and serious work?* Does he have a reputation to maintain? Know whether your material comes from a university press or from a popular book club, from a technical journal or from a mass-circulation magazine.

(4) Regardless of the reputation of the author and the publisher, *is the present work a thorough and carefully documented study* or a sketchy, improvised survey of the topic? Is it short on opinion and long on evidence, or vice versa? Does it weigh the findings of other authorities, or simply ignore them?

(5) Does the author settle important questions by *referring to primary sources*—that is, legal documents, letters, diaries, eyewitness reports, transcripts of speeches and interviews, reports on experiments, statistical surveys? Or does he rely exclusively on *secondary sources*—other authors' accounts and interpretations of primary materials?

(6) Is the work *recent enough to have profited from current scholarship?* If it was originally published ten or twenty years ago, is the current version a revised edition? Consider the possibility that an author's views may have been invalidated by new findings and changing theories in a rapidly expanding field of study.

EXERCISES

A. Select one of the three major encyclopedias discussed in this section and one other encyclopedia not mentioned here. Compare their treatment of *one* of the following subjects: atonality, cybernetics, Gestalt psychology, impressionism, semantics, stream-of-consciousness technique, surrealism, transcendentalism.

B. Study the general scheme of the *Book Review Digest* and check it for reviews of books you have read. Describe its treatment of one or two of the books.

C. Study the general scheme and sample entries of *one* of the following reference works: *American Universities and Colleges, Art Index, Cambridge Modern History, Catholic Encyclopedia, Concise Dictionary of American History, Dictionary of World Literature, Education Index, Grove's Dictionary of Music and Musicians, Standard Jewish Encyclopedia, Van Nostrand's Scientific Encyclopedia.* Report your findings, commenting on the scope, usefulness, and possible limitations of the work.

D. Select *one* of the following books and study its preface, table of contents, bibliography (if any), and introductory or concluding sections. Study its treatment of one or two limited topics. Then write a brief report on the intention, scope, level of difficulty, and special features of the book: (1) Ruth Benedict, *Patterns of Culture;* (2) James B. Conant, *On Understanding Science;* (3) Donald J. Lloyd and Harry R. Warfel, *American English in Its Cultural Setting;* (4) Erwin Panofsky, *Meaning in the Visual Arts;* (5) Robert C. Pooley, *Teaching English Grammar;* (6) David Riesman, *The Lonely Crowd;* (7) W. W. Rostov, *The Dynamics of Soviet Society;* (8) René Wellek and Austin Warren, *Theory of Literature.*

E. Study the general scheme of Constance M. Winchell's *Guide to Reference Books* and report on its treatment of a field that is of special interest to you, such as journalism, medicine, business, folklore, or religion.

F. Consult the *Readers' Guide* and find recent articles on *one* of the following: Benjamin Franklin, Alexander Hamilton, Andrew Jackson, Thomas Jefferson, Thomas Paine, George Washington. Compare the intention, tone, and level of difficulty of articles taken from three different periodicals.

G. Consult the *International Index* to find a scholarly article on *one* of the following: (1) the hypothetical parent language of all Indo-European languages; (2) the historical background of Homer's epics; (3) the Roman occupation of ancient Britain; (4) the earliest extant versions of the Old Testament; (5) the origins of medieval drama; (6) Freud's view of imaginative literature. Examine the author's use and identification of the source materials on which he has drawn.

Using Bibliographical Information

A writer should learn to make competent use of bibliographical information.

When you make extensive use of printed sources, you will realize the usefulness of systems of description and classification that help you to identify and to locate books. You will have to be able to interpret information about books that describes their origin, authorship, publication, content, and the like.

Library Catalogues. *A writer should learn to make efficient use of the card catalogue.* Your research projects will ordinarily be geared to the resources of your college library. Its central card catalogue is a complete alphabetical index of the materials available to you.

In most card catalogues, the same book is listed several times: by *author* (under the author's last name), by *title* (under the first word of the title, not counting *The, A,* or *An*), and by *subject*. Often, a card lists the several major *subject headings* under which the book can be found. For instance, a catalogue

card for a sociological study of a town in the Middle West may carry the following notation concerning various headings under which it is listed:

1. U.S.—Social conditions. 2. Cities and Towns—U.S. 3. Cost and standard of living—U.S. 4. U.S.—Religion. 5. Social surveys. 6. Community life.

Subject cards can direct you to many books that are relevant to your topic. Look for subject headings under which books on your topic might be listed. Books on progressive education might appear under *Education—Aims and Objectives,* under *Education—Experimental Methods,* or under *Educational Psychology.* Books on the Civil War might appear under *U. S.—History—Civil War,* under *U. S.—History—Military,* under *Slavery in the United States,* or under *Abolitionists.*

A card for a general-interest book brought out by a commercial publisher will look something like this:

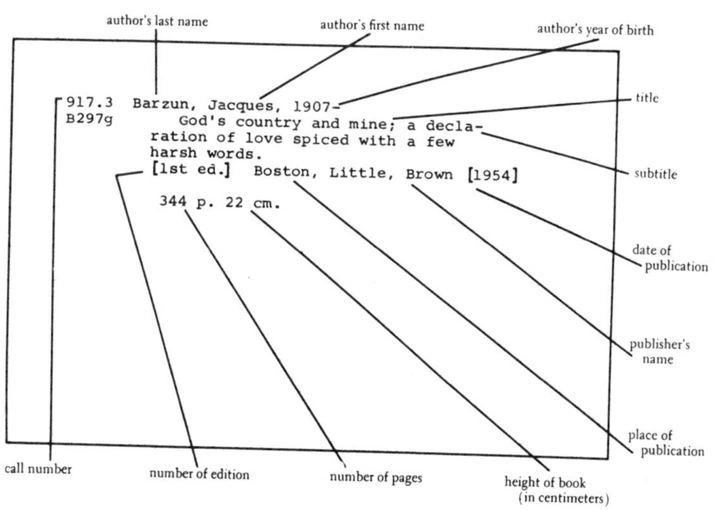

Such cards give you several kinds of information:

(1) After the *full name of the author,* you will find the *date of his birth* and, if applicable, of his death.

(2) After the title of the book, you will find *the number or description of the edition.* If the catalogue lists both the original edition and another one marked "2nd ed." or "Rev. ed.," you will generally choose the one that is most nearly up to date.

(3) The *name and location of the publisher* can be a clue to the nature of a book. For instance, a book published by one of the numerous university presses is more likely to be a scholarly and specialized study than a book published by a commercial publisher. The *date of publication* is especially important for books on scientific, technological, or medical subjects, since new scientific discoveries can rapidly invalidate old theories.

(4) The *number of pages,* with the number of introductory pages given as a lower-case Roman numeral, can indicate whether you are concerned with a short pamphlet or a full-scale treatment of the subject. If the book contains *illustrations* or a *bibliography,* the card will carry a notation to that effect.

Once you decide that you should consult a book, copy its call number. The **call number** is the group of letters and numbers usually found in the upper-left-hand corner of the card. It directs you, or the librarian, to the shelf where the book is located. Your library may use either of two numbering systems: the Library of Congress system or the Dewey decimal system. The **Library of Congress system** divides books into categories identified by letters of the alphabet. It then uses additional letters and numerals to subdivide each main category. For instance, the call number of a book on religion would start with a capital *B;* the call number of a book on education starts with a capital *L.* The more widely used **Dewey decimal system** uses numerals to identify the main categories. For instance, 400–499 covers books on language, 800–899 books on literature. The

800 range is then further subdivided into American literature (810–819), English literature (820–829), and so on. Additional numerals and letters distinguish among individual authors and among individual works by the same author.

Along with the call number, you may find a notation directing you to a special section of the library. The book you are looking for may be located in a reference room where encyclopedias, dictionaries, and other reference works are kept. It may be located in a special reading room where books for a particular field of study are on reserve. Although the card catalogue will list magazines and newspapers, most libraries have a separate, compact catalogue for periodicals. It lists, in alphabetical order, all periodicals to which the library subscribes. For each periodical it indicates the location of recent issues (often on the shelves of a separate periodical room) as well as of back issues (usually in bound volumes in the book stacks of the library).

Bibliography Cards. *Make your own card catalogue of all materials that seem promising or worthy of investigation.* Include a separate note card for each book, pamphlet, or magazine article you intend to use. Your instructor may suggest a minimum number of sources he wants you to consult. Your preliminary bibliography should have more than the minimum.

On each bibliography card, include the library call number or the place in the library where the publication is to be found. (This information is for your own personal use; do not reproduce it in your finished paper.) Other entries on your cards will serve as the basis for references to a source in your final manuscript. Check all entries carefully against the title page of the book or the heading of the magazine article in order to correct discrepancies. Be especially careful to get the *exact spelling* of unfamiliar names.

Usually, the first item you record is the *full name of the author.* Put the last name first to facilitate alphabetizing. If a work has been collected or arranged by a person other than the author (or the authors), you may start with that person's name, followed by "ed." for "editor." Ordinarily, however, the name of an editor or of a translater (followed by "trans.") appears on a separate line below the title. If an article in an encyclopedia is identified only by the author's initials, you may be able to find his full name by checking the initials against a list of contributors.

Start a new line for the *full title of the publication,* including a subtitle, if any. Underline the title of a book, pamphlet, or other work published as a separate entity. Underlining in a typed manuscript corresponds to italics in print. Put the title of an article or short poem in quotation marks and underline the title of the magazine, collection, or encyclopedia of which it forms a part.

Use a separate line for the *facts of publication.* For a book or pamphlet these may include a number of different items:

(1) The *number or description of the edition* (unless a book has not been re-edited since publication).

(2) The *number of volumes* (if a work consists of several, and all are relevant to your investigation).

(3) The *place of publication* (usually the location of the main office of the publishing house, or of the first branch office listed if several are given).

(4) The *name of the publisher.*

(5) The *date of publication* (not always given on the title page, though it can usually be inferred from the copyright date, found on the reverse side of the title page).

(6) The *number of the specific volume used* (if only one of several volumes is relevant to your investigation).

Often, a bibliography card for a book need list no more than the following information:

509 Conant, James Bryant
C743o *On Understanding Science: An Historical Approach*
New Haven: Yale University Press, 1947

For a magazine or newspaper article, the facts of publication ordinarily do *not* include the name of the publisher and the place of publication, though the latter is sometimes needed to identify a small-town journal. The pages of most professional or technical magazines are numbered consecutively through the several issues comprising one volume, usually the issues published during one year. For an article in such a magazine, record the *number of the volume* (preferably in Roman numerals), the *date of the issue,* and the *page numbers of the article.* For articles in other magazines and in newspapers, record the date of the issue and the page numbers. If the pages in separate sections of a newspaper are not numbered consecutively, identify the section where the article is to be found.

A bibliography card for an article is likely to contain something like the following:

Periodical Room	Whyte, Lancelot Law "Can We Grow Geniuses in Science?" *Harper's Magazine,* CCXIV (June 1957), 46–50

Annotation. *You will greatly increase the usefulness of your bibliography cards by annotation.* Write down brief reminders concerning characteristic features of your sources. Thus, you might note that an article on atomic energy is extremely technical; perhaps it requires more knowledge of physics than you command. Another article on the same subject may be a popularized treatment and give none of the specific data you need. Or you may want to note that a book has a glossary of technical terms, or an annotated bibliography, or a convenient summary of historical facts. (See annotated card on p. 306.)

NOTE: If your project is to provide the basis for further study on the part of your reader, you can help him by annotating the final bibliography which you furnish with your paper.

(ex.)

```
Humanities   Neville, Mark A.
Room         "Who Killed Poetry?"
             The English Journal, XLVII (March 1958),
                                   133-138

   Examines, with examples, conventional methods
of teaching poetry in high schools.  Concludes
that teachers of poetry should stress appreciation
and enjoyment rather than the study of versifica-
tion.
```

EXERCISES

A. Study the arrangement of cards in the central card catalogue of your college library in order to answer the following questions: (1) What are the major subdivisions for subject cards under the heading "Education"? (2) Where would you find a book by an author named John McMillan (under *Mc, Mac, Mi?*), George St. John (under *St., Sa, Jo?*), Antoine de Saint-Exupéry (under *De, Sa, St.?*)? (3) Do subject cards for books on the Civil War precede or follow cards for books on the War of Independence? Is the arrangement alphabetical or chronological? (4) Are books about George Washington listed before or after books about the State of Washington, or about Washington, D. C.? (5) Check under *John Keats:* What is the relative order of the author's individual works, his collected works, and books about the author?

B. Transcribe and explain the information that the card catalogue of your college library provides concerning *one* of the following books: Leonard Bloomfield, *Language;* H. W. Fowler, *A Dictionary of Modern English Usage;* Otto Jespersen, *Modern*

English Grammar; H. L. Mencken, *The American Language;* Stuart Robertson, *The Development of Modern English.*

The Technique of Note-Taking

A writer must learn how to take efficient and usable notes.

While you are investigating source materials, your reading will be primarily exploratory. You may read an article in an encyclopedia or a chapter in a textbook. You may glance through introductory material and selected chapters in a number of promising books. Even at this stage you may be jotting down tentative questions and observations. However, it will be some time before you have a clear idea of the scope and point of your paper. Only then will you be ready to start taking notes in a thorough and systematic manner.

Gathering Material. *Select material for its relevance to tentative generalizations that you formulate as you go along.* Ideally, you should become better able to decide what material is relevant to your purpose with every step in your investigation.

Suppose you are writing a research paper on trends toward increased teaching of foreign languages in the public schools. You are consulting a number of books published in the late fifties and early sixties and devoted to the improvement of American public education. By glancing over the table of contents and consulting the index of each book, you locate a number of discussions bearing on your subject. The following passages seem particularly relevant:

The school board should be ready to offer a third and fourth year of a foreign language, no matter how few students enroll. . . . I have met no teachers of foreign language who felt that anything approaching mastery could be obtained by the study of a foreign language for only two years in high school, nor have the students felt that two years of study had given them any real working knowledge of the

doc

language. Four years of study, on the other hand, will yield dividends for those capable of handling foreign languages. This is the recommendation of the foreign language panel of the NEA Conference on the Identification and Education of the Academically Talented held in Washington in February, 1958.

Almost without exception, I found a deplorable state of affairs in regard to foreign languages. . . .—James B. Conant, *The American High School Today*, p. 69.

. . . In the third field of importance today—foreign languages —the situation is even more serious. One consequence is that we have a diplomatic service where only 50 per cent now have command of a foreign language and where—still worse—a mere 30 per cent of the incoming recruits speak any foreign language; clear evidence of the deterioration of foreign-language teaching in the last generation. . . .

Progressive education must be blamed in large part for our neglect of foreign-language teaching. . . . We are the only major country which neglects the early years when a child can learn foreign languages most easily—from 10 onward.—H. G. Rickover, *Education and Freedom*, p. 109 and App., p. 65.

The American attitude toward the study of foreign languages has changed remarkably in the last decade. Twenty years ago, the future for these subjects seemed bleak indeed. Greek was gone, Latin was going, and enrollments in French and German were steadily declining. . . . In the early fifties, the Modern Language Association of America received from the Rockefeller Foundation a substantial grant for the purpose of setting up a Foreign Language Program. . . . It collected and disseminated information of all sorts and tried with some success to persuade the nation that a revival of foreign languages was in the national interest. The movement called FLES—Foreign Languages in the Elementary Schools—was greatly encouraged by this project.

The shudder that the launching of the Russian satellite sent through the world accelerated the swing back to foreign languages, as to other solid subjects. . . . The most dramatic response was the National Defense Education Act of 1958, which provided funds

for the improvement and expansion of instruction in science, mathematics, and modern foreign languages.—Albert R. Kitzhaber e.a., *Education for College,* pp. 113–116.[1]

From these and related passages, a number of tentative areas of agreement emerge. The first is the relatively low state of foreign-language teaching in the past. The second is a growing concern in the last one or two decades with the improvement of foreign-language instruction, reflected in the recommendations of educational authorities like Dr. Conant, in the efforts of professional organizations, and in government support. In further reading, you will look for material that will support or clarify these tentative points. At the same time, these passages suggest avenues for further exploration: You will try to find some of the "information of all sorts" disseminated by the Modern Language Association, some of it likely to be found in its official quarterly, *PMLA*. You will try to find out more about the role of the National Education Association (NEA), again perhaps turning first to an official publication like the *NEA Journal.* You will try to locate authoritative accounts of the original National Defense Education Act, both its original intent and its impact on the schools.

Recording Material. While recording information and ideas, you will have to employ a combination of techniques:

(1) *Learn to extricate important points from long passages,* to *summarize or condense lengthy quotations.* A formal abridgment, sometimes called a **précis**, preserves all essential generalizations and qualifications while curtailing or omitting altogether such material as explanations, examples, and incidental com-

[1] Albert R. Kitzhaber, Robert M. Gorrell, and Paul Roberts, *Education for College: Improving the High School Curriculum.* Copyright © 1961 The Ronald Press Company.

ments. It uses the most economical kind of wording, substituting one-word equivalents for lengthy phrases wherever possible. (See O 8.)

When you condense material for reproduction in the finished paper, you are likely to be more selective than in preparing a formal précis. You will pick out only those points of a report or of an argument that are directly relevant to your investigation. For instance, you may be investigating Woodrow Wilson's unsuccessful defense of the Treaty of Versailles and the League of Nations in 1919. After reading several pages of a historical study that reviews relevant political facts, you may decide to summarize them for use in an introductory paragraph. Your note might look something like this:

```
American Politics 1918-1920

     Election of Republican Congress in 1918.
Bitter opposition to President's role in peace
conference from such men as ex-President
Roosevelt and Senator Lodge.  Unprecedented
Republican majority in congressional elections
of 1920.  Final rejection of treaty and of
League of Nations  by U.S. Senate in March
1920.


Commager, History, pp. 411-413
```

(2) *Learn to translate information and ideas into your own words.* Many of the notes you will take for a research project will record information fairly specifically and fully. A

flexible method of recording such material is the **paraphrase**. This method enables you to select and emphasize points you consider important while at the same time working them smoothly into your text:

> Wilson's Campaign in Support of League
>
> Speech at Pueblo, Colorado, shows that Wilson is very much aware of the activities of men creating what he considers erroneous impressions concerning the League of Nations. Speech is designed to dispel mistaken impressions created in the public's mind.
>
> The proposed peace treaty is based not on the desire for territorial acquisition but on the principle that people should freely choose their own governments. The League of Nations is needed to mobilize the united moral force of the great nations of the world in support of the principles of nonaggression and of self-determination for all nations.
>
> Heffner, Documents, p. 235

(3) *Use well-chosen quotations to pinpoint key ideas or to clinch an argument.* Preserve characteristic phrases that give an insight into the personality of an author, whether by illustrating his aspirations, his sense of humor, or his style. The following note reproduces verbatim an author's position on a debatable point:

```
Dangers of Conformity

     "The idea that men are created free and
equal is both true and misleading: men are
created different; they lose their social
freedom and their individual autonomy in
seeking to become like each other."


Riesman, Lonely Crowd, p. 349
```

Use **direct quotation** sparingly or not at all in reproducing information, in outlining an author's argument, and in covering minor or noncontroversial points. Unselective recording of verbatim material in your notes is likely to lead to the kind of paper that consists primarily of lengthy excerpts from the original sources, held together by a thin tissue of phrases like "He further says . . ." and "We should also remember that . . ." Frequent use of undigested direct quotations tempts the reader to skip the quoted material and to look in the accompanying text for your main point.

NOTE: Make sure that your notes differentiate clearly between paraphrase or indirect quotation on the one hand and direct quotation on the other. In other words, *use quotation marks to identify all material quoted verbatim.*

Note Cards. *Separate note cards enable you to sort out and reshuffle information.* Most composition instructors require that their students take notes for a research project on 3x5 or 4x6

cards. Observing the following suggestions will help you make efficient use of your cards:

(1) Each card should record either *one single item of information or material so closely related that there is no chance of your having to separate it* in order to use it in different parts of your paper. However, generalizations should be accompanied by the specific detail that you will need to illustrate or support them in a paragraph. Include selected examples, statistical figures, definitions of difficult terms.

(2) The *material on each card should be full and clear enough* to make sense to you even after the context in which it originally appeared is no longer fresh in your mind. Of course, you will try to keep your notes free of unnecessary ballast. But excessive use of condensation and of abbreviations may make notes worthless later.

(3) The *material on each card should be representative* of the source from which it was taken. Be careful not to copy, as bare assertion, statements that are modified or qualified by the context in which they originally appeared.

(4) Each card should clearly *identify the source of the material recorded.* Use either a shortened form of the author's name and of the title of the work, or a code number that you have assigned the work in your preliminary bibliography. *Include the exact page reference.*

(5) If you have arrived at tentative subdivisions for your paper, the *heading to which the material on the card relates* should appear at the top of the card. Use headings that will divide your material into sizable but convenient units. Having too many cards per heading will make your notes unwieldy. Having too few cards per heading will make your notes confusing.

EXERCISE

Select an article (or chapter from a book) for its possible relevance to a future research project. Prepare a dozen note cards, grouped around two or three related headings and illustrating the various techniques of note-taking.

Writing and Revising the First Draft

A writer must learn to organize and adapt material from his note cards for use in his finished text.

By taking notes on separate cards, you can sort your notes into tentative categories while you are still studying your sources. When you have done most of the necessary reading, you should review your note cards to consider the main divisions they suggest.

Organizing the Research Paper. *The major weakness of many research papers is that the connections between the recorded facts are not clearly worked out.* Make sure your finished paper will not strike the reader as a collection of loosely connected bits of information. Group together cards that contain related material. Often a group of cards will record details pointing to a common generalization, evidence backing up the same major point. Often a group of cards will record related causes combining to produce a common result. Two related groups of cards may contain parallel sets of data for detailed comparison. Set aside cards containing material not relevant to the major points you are trying to establish.

The more definite shape your paper assumes in your mind, the more clearly should a unifying purpose or a unifying **thesis** emerge from your collection of data. Suppose you are writing a paper on the present state of gambling in the United States.

coh

Your main problem will be to keep your paper from becoming a repository of miscellaneous facts about gambling laws, famous gamblers, different games of chance, and tourist life in Las Vegas. To unify your paper, you might concentrate on the legal aspects of gambling. You could then review in some detail the laws of Nevada as exceptions to anti-gambling laws in other states, the legal status of horse and dog races, the question of lotteries and games conducted for charitable purposes. Another way of unifying your paper might be to concentrate on the extent and variety of gambling in this country. You could assemble statistics showing that gambling in one form or another plays a role in the lives of perhaps fifty million Americans.

Outlining the Paper. *After arranging your cards in a tentative sequence, write a preliminary outline that reflects their order.* Formulate a tentative thesis sentence summarizing the conclusion that your paper seems to suggest. Your outline and your thesis sentence will enable you to decide which of your note cards contain unnecessary or irrelevant material and should be set aside. They will also help you to decide in which areas your notes need to be supplemented by further reading. A definitive outline preceding the final paper usually shows whether the paper has a unifying purpose, whether the major subdivisions of the paper contribute to that purpose, and whether unrelated odds and ends have been eliminated.[2]

Once you have a preliminary outline, you can start writing a first rough draft of your paper. Keep your eyes on your overall plan and decide to be temporarily satisfied with less than perfection in details. Where necessary, modify your plan or reorganize your note cards as you proceed. If you notice unanswered questions or missing evidence, note the inadequacies in the margin and follow them up later.

[2] For forms of outlines see O 8.

Using Quoted Material. The most obvious difference between a short theme and a research paper is the need for working into the text an often considerable amount of quoted material. The following examples illustrate ways of incorporating material from a source into the text of a paper:

(1) *Extensive quotation—to be used sparingly.*

such a view. In an article in Fortune that has been frequently reprinted, Adlai Stevenson stated his belief that American postwar prosperity was due to the cooperation of business and government:

> It is a curious thing that the two institutional forces in the democratic capitalistic society that contributed most directly to this emergence of the powerful consumer during this quarter-century seemed to snarl at each other every step of their common way. The bounding prosperity of postwar America has been due in large measure to processes in which government and business have in effect played complementary and cooperative roles. The New Deal legislation of the Thirties helped to provide a "built-in" consumer demand that business could then work to satisfy, and the increase of 70 per cent in the scale of the American economy between 1939 and 1944 was achieved by the closest cooperation between government and industry in America's war effort.[7]

---

[7]Adlai E. Stevenson, "My Faith in Democratic Capitalism," Fortune, October 1955, p. 126.

In this example, a lengthy excerpt from a source is used to buttress an important point. The excerpt is indented and set off from the text as a **block quotation**—*no quotation marks, single-spaced lines.* The sentence introducing the excerpt gives credit to author and publication; the footnote numeral at the end directs the reader to the footnote providing the name of the article and an exact page reference. *The introductory sentence* *also summarizes the main point or the significance of the quotation.* A reader easily becomes bored and discouraged if he cannot make out why he is given numerous lengthy quotations.

(2) *Plagiarized version—illegitimate, unacknowledged paraphrase.*

```
has had lasting effects.  But it is surprising that the
two forces in our society that contributed most to the
emergence of the powerful consumer seemed to snarl at each
other every step of the way.  The prosperity of postwar
America has been due to the fact that government and
business have played complementary and cooperative roles.
The New Deal legislation of the Thirties provided a built-in
consumer demand for business to satisfy.  The increase of
70 per cent in the American economy was achieved by the
cooperation between government and industry in America's
war effort.
```

Much **plagiarism** takes this form: a slightly abridged version of the original source. Even if the source were identified, this way of adapting the material would be unsatisfactory. It preserves far too much of the original author's way of putting things—without using direct quotation. Sentence structure corresponds closely to that of the original. Much of the characteristic phrasing is preserved ("emergence of the powerful consumer," "seemed to snarl," "complementary and cooperative roles"). The only changes are the omission or shortening of incidental phrases. As in much hasty adaptation, qualifications that made the original cautious have been lost ("due to" for "due *in large measure* to"; "provided" for "*helped* to provide").

(3) *Legitimate paraphrase—attributed to the original author.*

Like other observers, Mr. Stevenson points out the irony in the apparent hostility of the two major institutions that made the American consumer a powerful force in the nation's economy. He attributes the rapidly growing prosperity of postwar America at least partly to the cooperation, intentional or unintentional, of government and business. Thus, legislation enacted under the Roosevelt administration helped to increase consumer purchasing power. Similarly, the extraordinary growth of the American economy between 1939 and 1944 was the result of government and industry working together in building up the country's military strength.[7]

This **paraphrase**, documented by a footnote, preserves the essential meaning of the original. At the same time, by translating the passage into his own words, the adapter shows that he has understood it. He shows how he interprets phrases that are in any way unusual or metaphorical. For instance, he takes the phrase "a curious thing" to express irony. For the graphic "seemed to snarl" he substitutes its literal equivalent, "apparent hostility." Instead of using percentage points, the adapter describes the growth of the economy as "extraordinary." Though general, this term does justice to the intention of the original. Although some of the sentences are roughly parallel to the original in grammatical construction, others—for instance, the first and second ones—are completely reorganized. This kind of close paraphrase is useful when detailed interpretation and evaluation of a source is desirable.

(4) *Part paraphrase, part direct quotation—worked closely into the text.*

Like economists and sociologists before him, Mr. Stevenson emphasizes that government and business in this country have in effect worked together in assuring postwar prosperity--even though they "seemed to snarl at each other every step of their common way." As he implies but does not directly state, business has never openly acknowledged that "New Deal legislation . . . helped to provide a 'built-in' consumer demand that business could then work to satisfy." He attributes an "increase of 70 per cent in the scale of the American economy between 1939 and 1944" to "the closest cooperation" between government and industry.[7]

This technique is the most flexible and most generally useful one for adapting source material to the adapter's own use. He condenses, restates, and interprets the material he has selected, while at the same time using brief direct quotations for important points and characteristic phrases. Competent use of this technique can effectively break up the deadly "So-and-So says such-and-such" pattern found in many library papers.

(5) *Legitimate summary.*

Mr. Stevenson feels that postwar prosperity in this country was to a large extent the result of cooperation between government and business. Specifically he refers to the role of New Deal legislation in restoring consumer demand and to the joint participation of government and industry in the war effort.[7]

This **summary** gets at the gist of the passage. At the same time it lists briefly arguments or details supporting the main point in the original.

doc

Form of Quotations. *Review carefully the conventions governing the punctuation of quoted material.* Pay special attention to the distinction between direct and indirect quotation, to differences in handling long and short passages, and to ways of indicating omissions and insertions.[3]

(1) If a quotation is only *part of a complete sentence,* you need to work it into the grammatical pattern of the sentence that introduces it, *without* changing the original wording of the material enclosed in quotation marks:

UNSATISFACTORY: Pope Pius described a just war in this way: "If it has been forced upon one by an evident and extremely grave injustice that in no way can be avoided."

SATISFACTORY: Pope Pius stated that a war is just "if it has been forced upon one by an evident and extremely grave injustice that in no way can be avoided."

UNSATISFACTORY: The writer suggests that Whittaker Chambers, "Having experienced at first hand the evils of communism, he now sees himself clad in shining armor, engaged in deadly combat with that evil."

SATISFACTORY: The writer says of Whittaker Chambers that "having experienced at first hand the evils of communism, he now sees himself clad in shining armor, engaged in deadly combat with that evil."

(2) Quotations must be *logically complete;* they should not require explanations that you do not provide. Suppose you quote Albert Schweitzer as saying, "I therefore stand and work in the world, as one who aims at making men less shallow and morally better by making them think." To keep the quotation from being

[3] See P 8.

logically incomplete, you will have to let your reader know what the "therefore" stands for. If you don't want to include the reasons to which it refers, you will have to shorten or paraphrase the quotation in such a way as to omit it.

(3) Your text should *differentiate clearly between your opinions and the opinions of authors you are investigating.* There is considerable difference between "Capitalism is a moribund system" and "According to Marx, capitalism is a moribund system." If you are citing several authors, make sure that references like "he," "this author," or "the writer" point clearly to the person you have in mind.

Revision. *Careful revision of the first draft is an essential step, and your timetable should make adequate allowance for it.* A first draft usually makes jerky reading. The writer is likely to have concentrated on arranging his material in the most logical or the most convenient order without always explaining to his readers how he got from one paragraph to the other. He is likely to have concentrated on getting the main body of the paper into shape, providing no more than a routine introduction and allowing the paper to run out without a definite conclusion.

In revising your first draft, you will make changes ranging from the substitution of a semicolon for a comma to the rearrangement of major sections of your paper. However, regardless of the specific improvements needed, your revision should concern itself with several basic requirements for a successful paper:

(1) Check for *adequacy of detail.* See to it that individual points are clearly stated and well illustrated or documented. Make sure that the evidence you present in support of your generalizations is adequate to prevent questions such as "Is this really so?" "Is this merely a superficial impression?" or "Do the experts agree on this point?"

(2) Check for *clarity of explanation.* Many papers suffer

from too much quotation, too much paraphrase, too much summary, and not enough explanation and comparison. Examine key terms to see whether they need to be more explicitly defined. Explain terms like *Hellenistic, psychosomatic,* or *lingua franca.*

(3) Check for *adequate paragraph structure.* Avoid sequences of short paragraphs that give bits of information or quotation from different sources. Instead, work material from different note cards into a coherent paragraph that coordinates, compares, contrasts. Choppy paragraphing makes continuous reading difficult, if not impossible.

(4) Check for *clear attribution.* If you are comparing different sources, keep your reader from getting hopelessly confused about who says what. Constant repetition of phrases like "according to Dewey" or "as his biographer observes" can make a paper seem heavy-handed. However, awkward but exact identification is preferable to elegant but misleading continuity of discussion.

(5) Check for *coherence.* Make your reader see the relationship between different parts of your paper. Anticipate and answer the questions of a reader mired in a mass of details: "How did this get in here?" "Why do I have to study this particular set of statistics?" Make sure there is a clear **transition**, implied or explicitly stated, from paragraph to paragraph. Inserting a *therefore,* a *nevertheless,* or a *for instance* in a few strategic places can help transform a rambling discussion into a tightly knit argument. Check the organization of the paper against your tentative outline and adjust your outline to reflect any changes you made while writing the first draft and while revising it.

(6) Check for *clarity of over-all intention.* Make sure that the main points you are trying to bring out are not merely implied but clearly and fully stated. State them preferably at the beginning of the paper following your introduction or, if more appropriate, toward the end of the paper in the form of a sum-

mary. Don't take it for granted that your reader will automatically arrive at the same conclusions that you did if you merely present "the facts."

EXERCISE

Select a passage of paragraph length from an article or book relevant to a future research project. Illustrate various legitimate ways of quoting, excerpting, or summarizing it in the text of a research paper.

Footnotes and Bibliographies

A writer must be familiar with the style used for footnotes and bibliographies in his major area of study.

Documentation enables your readers to identify and check your sources. Its purpose should not be to impress your readers but to provide exact and comprehensive information in condensed form.

Footnotes. *In your own paper, the main purpose of footnotes will be to document your sources.* You will use footnotes to indicate the origin of facts, opinions, and illustrative material, whether you quote them directly, paraphrase them, or summarize them. However, footnotes are not used exclusively for the purpose of documentation. **Explanatory footnotes** may define technical terms unfamiliar only to some of the readers. They may provide information not necessary to an understanding of the main trend of the argument. They may contain reservations needed to satisfy an exceptionally critical reader. Use such incidental material sparingly. Many readers check all footnotes to make sure they miss nothing of importance. Do not make them interrupt their reading for the sake of something trivial or irrelevant.

doc

Current practice favors consecutive numbering of all footnotes for a paper, article, or chapter of a book. In other words, footnotes are not indicated by asterisks or similar symbols. Nor do the footnote numbers start anew on each individual page. The **footnote number** is placed outside whatever punctuation goes with the item to which it refers. The footnote itself is indented like a paragraph and is introduced by a raised numeral; the numeral is *not* followed by a period or other punctuation. The footnote begins with a capital letter and ends with appropriate terminal punctuation, most commonly a period.

In printed publications, the footnotes for each page appear in small print at the bottom of each page. In typed manuscripts, footnotes are usually single-spaced and placed in one of three possible positions:

(1) Footnotes may be placed *between two unbroken lines immediately below the line of typed material* to which they belong. This system, when permitted by the instructor, helps the inexperienced researcher to make the right footnote go with the right portion of the text.[4]

---

[4] Even when a different system of placing footnotes is required in the final paper, students may find the system of which this footnote is an illustration the most convenient one to follow in the first draft. It prevents errors when footnotes have to be renumbered because of changes in the manuscript.

---

(2) Footnotes may be placed *at the bottom of the page,* separated from the text by an unbroken line or by triple spacing. This system is convenient for the reader, who is used to a similar arrangement in printed material, but it is hard on the amateur typist. It requires him to type his footnotes on a separate sheet of paper so that he can estimate the amount of space needed for each and leave exactly enough space at the bottom of each page for the footnotes that go with it.

doc,p

(3) Footnotes may appear *on a separate sheet at the end of the paper.* This system is usually required when a manuscript is submitted for publication.

First References. *The most common type of footnote gives full information about a source when the text cites it*—that is, quotes it or refers to it—*for the first time.*

Here are some examples of the standard form for a **first reference** to books and articles:

[6] Albert C. Baugh, *A History of the English Language* (New York, 1935), p. 450.

[4] Irving H. Anderson and Walter F. Dearborn, *The Psychology of Teaching Reading* (New York, 1952), pp. 70–72.

[7] Harold Taylor, "The Aims of Education," *College English,* XVIII (February 1957), 250–251.

[3] "U.S. Asked to Aid Youth Exchanges," *The New York Times,* June 15, 1964, p. 8, col. 1.

[2] Jeanne Contini, "The Illiterate Poets of Somalia," *The Reporter,* March 14, 1963, p. 36.

In its standard form, such a footnote contains the following information:

(1) *The first name, middle initial, and last name of the author.* Some names of well-known authors usually contain initials for first and middle names: T. S. Eliot, W. H. Auden, I. A. Richards. However, initials used with common names like Brown, Douglas, or Smith may force the reader to hunt through several hundred catalogue entries for publications by Smiths whose first names have the same initial. (Note that a footnote, unlike a bibliography or other alphabetical listing, puts the first name first.)

(2) *The title,* separated from what precedes it by a comma, or appearing first if the author's name is unknown. Titles of books, magazines, and newspapers are underlined (or italicized

in print). Titles of articles published in magazines and newspapers or as parts of books are enclosed in quotation marks and separated by a comma from the title of the publication in which they appeared: "How to Deep-Freeze Bait," *The Fisherman's Monthly.*

(3) *The circumstances of publication.* The title of a book is usually followed by place and year of publication, separated from each other by a comma and enclosed in parentheses, but not separated from what precedes them by other punctuation: (New York, 1958). The title of a magazine or newspaper may be followed by the date of the issue, separated from what precedes and follows it by commas. The volume number is usually given as a capital Roman numeral, separated from the title by a comma and, if appropriate, followed by the date of the issue in parentheses.

(4) *The page reference,* separated from the rest of the footnote by a comma. Page numbers are preceded by the abbreviation "p." for a single page and "pp." for several pages: pp. 163–168. These abbreviations are omitted if the page reference is signaled by a volume number given as a Roman numeral: XV (March 1958), 53.

NOTE: *Pay special attention to the way punctuation marks are used in the sample footnotes in this section.* Use commas, periods, parentheses, and quotation marks as here illustrated unless you are otherwise instructed by the teacher or editor who is to pass judgment on your work.

Variations from Standard Form. *Special situations require variations from standard footnote form.* You may have to omit from a footnote elements usually included or add elements not always applicable.

(1) If the *text of your paper gives the author's full name,* or both his full name and the full title of the work, do not repeat

them in the footnote. The footnote will then start either with the title or with the facts of publication:

[5] *A History of the English Language* (New York, 1935), p. 450.

[6] New York, 1935, p. 450.

(2) If the work you cite has a *subtitle,* separate it from the title by a colon unless the original has other punctuation. Underline the subtitle of a book; enclose both the title and the subtitle of an article in the same set of quotation marks:

[3] Lionel Trilling, *The Liberal Imagination: Essays on Literature and Society* (New York, 1950), p. 47.

[1] John J. Gross, "The Writer in America: A Search for Community," *Queen's Quarterly,* LXIII (Autumn 1956), 387.

(3) If the author's work has been selected, arranged, or translated by someone else, insert the *editor's or translator's name* after the title, separating it from the title by a comma and introducing it with the abbreviation "ed." or "trans." In references to collections of letters, to the work of unknown authors, or to selections from many different authors, the editor's name may take the place of the author's name:

[2] H. L. Mencken, *The Vintage Mencken,* ed. Alistair Cooke (New York, 1956), p. 49.

[8] André Siegfried, *America at Mid-Century,* trans. Margaret Ledésert (New York, 1955), p. 227.

[5] Kenneth Sisam, ed. *Fourteenth Century Verse and Prose* (London, 1948), p. 14.

(4) If a work has been revised or re-edited since its original publication, indicate the *number of the edition* you are using.

Place it before the facts of publication, separating it from what precedes it by a comma:

[2] Albert C. Baugh, *A History of the English Language,* 2nd ed. (New York, 1957), pp. 7–8.

[9] M. B. Forman, ed. *The Letters of John Keats,* 3rd ed. (London, 1948), pp. 67–68.

(5) If a work consists of several volumes, insert the *number of the volume* you are citing. Use a capital Roman numeral, insert it after the facts of publication, and separate it from what precedes and follows it by commas. Remember that after a volume number "p." and "pp." are omitted:

[3] Vernon Louis Parrington, *Main Currents in American Thought: An Interpretation of American Literature from the Beginnings to 1920* (New York, 1930), III, 355.

Subsequent References. *Subsequent references should not repeat the full name of the author, the full title, and the facts of publication.* You should aim at saving time and space while at the same time making the **shortened reference** identify the work clearly each time you mention it.

(1) When you are using only *one work of an author,* subsequent references may consist of the author's last name, separated from the page reference by a comma:

[11] Baugh, p. 9.

(2) When you are using *several works by the same author,* subsequent references may consist of the author's last name, a shortened form of the title, and the page reference, with the different items kept separate by commas:

[11] Baugh, *History,* p. 9.

doc, p

(3) An alternative system for shortened reference, making use of **Latin abbreviations**, is no longer in frequent use. Instead of repeating, in a shortened form, the author's name or the title, the writer may use *ibid.*, an abbrevation of Latin *ibidem*, meaning "in the same place." When used by itself, without a page reference, it means "in the last publication cited, on the same page." When used with a page reference, it means "in the last publication cited, on the page indicated." Like other Latin abbreviations used in footnotes, *ibid.* is no longer commonly italicized. It can refer only to *the last source cited:*

[1] G. B. Harrison, *Introducing Shakespeare* (New York, 1947), p. 28.

[2] Ibid., p. 37.

A work other than the last one mentioned may be identified by the author's name followed by *op. cit.*, short for *opere citato*, meaning "in the work already cited." This abbreviation is ambiguous and inappropriate if the writer has already cited more than one work by the same author.

[1] G. B. Harrison, *Introducing Shakespeare* (New York, 1947), p. 28.

[2] B. Ifor Evans, *A Short History of English Drama* (Hammondsworth, Middlesex, 1948), pp. 51–69.

[3] Harrison, op. cit., p. 37.

NOTE: Try to avoid a long string of footnotes giving different page references to the same work. If two or three quotations from the same portion of a work follow one another in one paragraph of your paper, you can sometimes *incorporate the different page references in a single footnote:*

[11] Harrison, pp. 8–9, 12.

doc, p

Frequently Cited Sources. *A number of well-known and frequently cited sources do not require detailed identification.*

(1) *References to standard encyclopedias* usually do not mention the names of the editors or the place of publication. Page numbers are unnecessary for short entries, because articles arranged in alphabetical order can be easily located. However, references to encyclopedias usually include the date or the number of the edition used, since the frequent revisions of major encyclopedias often omit or modify articles contained in earlier editions:

[2] M. J. Politis, "Greek Music," *Encyclopedia Americana,* 1956.

(2) *References to the Bible* usually identify only the book, the chapter, and the verse. The edition used is not mentioned unless the differences in wording between different translations are important. Notice that the name of a book of the Bible is not underlined or put in quotation marks:

[4] Judges 13:5. or [4] Judges xiii.5.

(3) *First references to literary classics* available in many different editions usually note the edition used. However, they often supplement page references by indicating the location of a passage in other ways for the benefit of readers using a different edition. References to a play usually indicate act, scene, and line; references to an epic poem, such subdivisions as books, cantos, and individual stanzas. After the edition used has been identified upon first reference, a reference to a passage from a Shakespeare play might look like this:

[7] *Hamlet* II.ii. 311–322.

Such abbreviated identification of passages from the Bible

or from literary classics is often inserted in the text immediately following the passage itself.

(4) No identification is necessary for *well-known or proverbial lines* like "The quality of mercy is not strained" or "A little learning is a dangerous thing." Burdening the reader with detailed identification of an overworked quotation merely compounds the injury.

Abbreviations. *Footnotes in scholarly books and articles employ a variety of abbreviations and technical terms in addition to those you will regularly use in your own work.* The meaning of many of these will be clear from their context or position; for example, *anon.* for "anonymous," *ch.* and *chs.* for "chapter" and "chapters," *col.* and *cols.* for "column" and columns," *l.* and *ll.* for "line" and "lines," *n.* and *nn.* for "note" and "notes." Others are not self-explanatory:

c. or ca.	Latin *circa,* "approximately"; used for approximate dates and figures (*c.* 1952)
cf.	Latin *confer,* "compare"; often used loosely instead of *see* in the sense of "consult for further relevant material" (Cf. Ecclesiastes xii.12)
et al.	Latin *et alii,* "and others"; used in references to books by several authors (G. B. Harrison et al.)
f., ff.	"and the following page," "and the following pages" (See pp. 16f.)
loc. cit.	Latin *loco citato,* "in the place cited"; used without page reference (Baugh, loc. cit.)
MS, MSS	manuscript, manuscripts
n.d.	"no date," date of publication unknown
passim	Latin for "throughout"; "in various places in the work under discussion" (See pp. 54–56 et passim)
q.v.	Latin *quod vide;* "which you should consult"

doc, p

Final Bibliography. *The final bibliography, based on your bibliography cards, includes all the information required to identify a source when first cited.* Its main purpose is to describe in one single alphabetical list all sources you have used. You may include sources that you have found helpful or enlightening but have not had occasion to quote from in your paper. However, do *not* list every book or article whose title you have come across during your investigation.

Entries in the bibliography differ from footnotes both in the arrangement and in the punctuation of the material presented:

(1) The *last name of the author* (or of the first author listed when a book has several authors) is placed first. His full name is separated from what follows by a period.

(2) The *facts of publication* for a book usually include the publisher's name. They are *not* enclosed in parentheses and are separated from what precedes and what follows by periods.

(3) Entries for books do not include page references; entries for parts of books or items in magazines give the *inclusive page numbers* for the whole selection.

In a typed manuscript, single-space each individual item but leave a double space between items. Indent two spaces for the second and for subsequent lines of each item. If you list *several publications by the same author,* substitute a line composed of six consecutive hyphens for his name in second and subsequent entries. If *no name of author or editor is known to you,* list the publication alphabetically by the first letter of the title, not counting "The," "A," or "An."

The following might be the final bibliography for a paper investigating theatrical conventions and stage techniques in the time of Shakespeare:

doc,p

BIBLIOGRAPHY

Adams, John Cranford. The Globe Playhouse: Its Design and Equipment. Cambridge, Mass.: Harvard University Press, 1942.

Bailey, Margery. "Shakespeare in Action," College English, XV (March 1954), 307-315.

Brooke, C. F. Tucker. "The Renaissance," in A Literary History of England, ed. Albert C. Baugh. New York: Appleton-Century-Crofts, Inc., 1948.

Chambers, E. K. The Elizabethan Stage. 4 vols. Oxford: The Clarendon Press, 1923.

Davies, W. Robertson. Shakespeare's Boy Actors. London: J. M. Dent & Sons, Ltd., 1939.

Granville-Barker, Harley, and G. B. Harrison, eds. A Companion to Shakespeare Studies. New York: The Macmillan Company, 1934.

Greg, W. W., ed. Henslowe's Diary. 2 vols. London: A. H. Gullen, 1904-1908.

Harbage, Alfred. Shakespeare's Audience. New York: Columbia University Press, 1941.

------. Theatre for Shakespeare. Toronto: University of Toronto Press, 1955.

"A New Shakespearean Festival," The Oakland Herald, August 12, 1958, p. 7, col. 2.

Rosenberg, Marvin. "Elizabethan Actors: Men or Marionettes?" PMLA, LXIX (September 1954), 915-927.

EXERCISE

A. Interpret the information provided in the following footnotes:

(ex.)

[3] Robert E. Spiller et al., *Literary History of the United States,* rev. ed. (New York, 1953), p. 1343.

[1] James Brown, "Eight Types of Puns," *PMLA,* LXXI (March 1956), 20.

[9] Euripides, *The Trojan Women,* trans. Richmond Lattimore, in *Greek Plays in Modern Translation,* ed. Dudley Fitts (New York, 1947), p. 161.

[2] "America—the Beautiful?" *Life,* June 3, 1957, p. 34.

[8] Kenneth Muir, ed. *Collected Poems of Sir Thomas Wyatt* (Cambridge, Mass., 1950), p. xx.

[7] I Corinthians iii.18–20.

[12] Cf. *The Complete Works of William Hazlitt,* ed. P. P. Howe (London, 1932), XI, 88ff.

B. Study the style of documentation followed in a scholarly journal in your major field of interest. Determine to what extent its style coincides with that outlined in the preceding discussion and in what respects it differs from it.

C. The following sample paper, adapted from a longer, student-written research paper, illustrates different ways of presenting and documenting evidence. Study the way it reproduces factual information, opinion, and lines of verse. Compare the different kinds of footnotes it employs. Compare the way sources are identified in footnotes and in the final bibliography.

BYRON'S INTEREST IN ANIMALS

by

Richard P. Dean

English 2, Section 8

March 25, 1964

OUTLINE

Thesis: Byron had a continuing interest in animals that helps illuminate his character.

I. Byron's menagerie on the road

II. Byron's critical reputation

III. Byron's animals at Newstead Abbey

    A. The Boatswain episode

    B. Wild animals

IV. Byron in Italy

    A. The Italian menageries

    B. The maddened elephant

    C. Byron's attitude toward hunting and fishing

V. Animals in Byron's poetry

VI. Byron's love of freedom

BYRON'S INTEREST IN ANIMALS

From Ravenna to Venice, in Italy, is a hundred miles through the lush green of the Po valley, and it is a hundred miles again along the road back from Venice to Ravenna. And from Ravenna to Pisa is a long hundred miles, each way, and the road is high and twisted across the backbone of Italy. Here, the tall slim spires of the Lombardy poplars, outlining the roads of the Po valley, give way to the hardy oaks of the Apennines.

In the early nineteenth century, the miles were the same as they are now--some seventeen hundred and sixty yards in length--but they were measured, then, not in the unmufflered roar of sports cars or the squeal of tires on a mountain turn, but by the hooves of horses set patiently down, one after another, again and again and again. And in time, the miles were not measured in minutes, but in long days--days in which there was time enough to absorb the beauty of the plain and of the mountains, time enough, also, to accumulate an intricate film of dust in the ears and nostrils, and to acquire bloodshot eyes and frazzled nerves, and to suffer the carriage-induced curse of constipation.

A stranger, pausing in some small village on the Ravenna road, during that slower time, for a drink of cool water or a glass of warm wine, might have witnessed a most amazing procession. Heralded, perhaps, by the cries of small boys, a splendid team of horses would have first come into view, to be followed by carriage after carriage drawn by equally splendid teams. The carriages were loaded, in large part, with animals and birds, caged and uncaged.[1]

Although the inventory of this menagerie would hardly have re-

---

[1]G. Wilson Knight, Lord Byron: Christian Virtues (New York, 1953), p. 4.

mained constant, we have a good indication of the variety of its probable make-up. One inventory lists eight immense dogs, three monkeys, five cats, an eagle, a crow, a falcon, five peacocks, two guinea hens, and an Egyptian crane. Another account adds a fox and a wolf to this list.[2] This astonishing caravan, with its horses, its attendants, and its master, would have constituted a problem in logistics in any day or time. There had to be meat for the wolf and the fox, for the dogs and the cats, and for the eagle and the falcon. Grain would suffice for the other birds, and fruit and nuts, perhaps, for the monkeys. There had to be nosebags of grain and night grazing for the horses, and there had to be water for all. Added to the feeding problem would have been the care and maintenance of the gear and of the carriages themselves. Obviously, the master of the caravan had to be a man of energy and patience.

Could this procession have been a small circus, or, perhaps, a large group of performing animals? Of course it was neither. It was merely a poet passing by--a poet shifting his household from one city to another. This poet was George Gordon Lord Byron, until his death in 1824 the most flamboyant among the younger generation of English Romantic poets.

Byron was, and continues to be, a controversial figure. His colorful aristocratic ancestry, his reckless and defiant spirit, his scandalous separation from his wife and subsequent exile in Italy, his death after joining the Greek revolutionaries in their fight against Turkey--all these have supplied his biographers and critics with plen-

---

[2]Knight, p. 4. See also Peter Quennell, Byron in Italy (New York, 1941), pp. 185-186.

tiful ammunition for conjecture and recrimination.[3] Some of his critics go so far as to say that his work survived only on the strength of the scandal connected with his personal life, that "Byron the poet depended entirely upon the glamour of Byron the man, who was Byron the rake, the daredevil, the rebel."[4] His champions, notably G. Wilson Knight, have tried to demonstrate "Byron's true greatness, his generosity and kindliness, his chivalry, courtesy, humility, and courage."[5] They have found in his poetry a "tough-minded realism and a trenchant satire often hilarious but always grounded in a basic sanity and a knowledge of human nature."[6]

It is not my purpose to plunge into the controversies over Byron's moral and literary qualifications. Rather I propose to explore one limited facet of his life that indirectly sheds light on both his character and his poetry. I intend to show Byron's constant interest in the animal world--an interest epitomized in the picture of Byron's menagerie trekking across the Italian mountains.

Boatswain, the great Newfoundland dog of Byron's youth, is the best known of all his animals. This is unfortunate, in a way, for the affair of Boatswain's death and burial, though lauded by dog lovers, has been derided and picked to pieces by others. When the dog was dying of rabies, Byron tended him, sponging the foaming jaws with ungloved hands. Boatswain did not offer to bite his master but buried his fangs

---

[3]The best-known biography of Byron is André Maurois, Byron, trans. Hamish Miles (New York, 1930). Leslie A. Marchand, Byron: A Biography, 3 vols. (New York, 1957), makes use of recent scholarship and of documents not previously accessible.

[4]Ernest Boyd, Literary Blasphemies (New York, 1927), p. 119.

[5]Lord Byron, p. 29.

[6]Leslie A. Marchand, ed. Selected Poetry of Lord Byron (New York, 1951), p. v.

time and again in his own tormented body.[7]

This display of loyalty and courage did not make Byron more lovable and human in the eyes of many of his critics, for it led to the "excessively misanthropic"[8] inscription that young Byron placed on Boatswain's tomb:

NEAR THIS SPOT
ARE DEPOSITED THE REMAINS OF ONE
WHO POSSESSED BEAUTY WITHOUT VANITY
STRENGTH WITHOUT INSOLENCE
COURAGE WITHOUT FEROCITY
AND ALL THE VIRTUES OF MAN WITHOUT HIS VICES.
THIS PRAISE WHICH WOULD BE UNMEANING FLATTERY
IF INSCRIBED OVER HUMAN ASHES
IS BUT A JUST TRIBUTE TO THE MEMORY OF
BOATSWAIN, A DOG
WHO WAS BORN AT NEWFOUNDLAND, MAY 1803,
AND WHO DIED AT NEWSTEAD ABBEY, NOVEMBER 18, 1808.[9]

More than one critic has accused Byron of theatrical insincerity in this episode. One of them cites as evidence that the inscription for the tomb was composed eighteen days before the dog's death and that Byron wrote a letter on November 18 claiming that the dog had been dead for ten days.[10] So the Boatswain incident must still be regarded as controversial insofar as it pertains to Byron's character.

At Newstead Abbey, the Byrons' grand and gloomy family seat, there were other animals whose presence seems more characteristic of Byron's later interests. During the spring following Boatswain's death, one of Byron's friends wrote from the Abbey describing how one might encounter a bear or a wolf in the halls, roaming freely.[11] One can imagine sleeping in a house where a snuffling in the night did not necessarily

---

[7]Maurois, p. 113.

[8]George E. Brandes, Main Currents in Nineteenth Century Literature (New York, 1906), IV, 263.

[9]Maurois, p. 114.

[10]B. R. McElderry Jr., "Byron's Epitaph to Boatswain," Modern Language Notes, LVIII (November 1943), 553-554.

[11]Knight, p. 4.

mean that someone had a cold! Among other wild, but less fierce, creatures at the Abbey were the hedgehogs and tortoises which Byron had brought back from his early travels in Greece. Byron included information concerning the well-being of these and other animals in his letters to his friends. He mentioned their illnesses and their indispositions in his conversations.[12] To him, the animals were not merely brute creatures but sentient beings worthy of his concern and consideration.

It was in Italy, however, that the full blossoming of Byron's relationship with animals occurred. In Ravenna, Venice, Pisa, and Genoa he maintained his overflowing and ebullient menageries. In Ravenna, all the animals except the horses had free run of the mansion, which virtually exploded now and again under the impact of their unsupervised quarrels.[13] In Venice, the menagerie occupied the ground floor of the Palazzo Mocenigo, along with the stored carriages. As in other pretentious Venetian residences this bottom floor was unfurnished because of its dankness and smell of the sea. Byron, passing to his gondola, would stop to feed the animals and to watch their antics.[14]

On his Italian travels, Byron was always accompanied by his dogs and, according to one of his biographers, usually by his geese. The latter joined Byron's household as a result of his tenacious hold upon the rural English customs of his childhood. These dictated roast goose for Michaelmas. After acquiring a somewhat thin goose a month before the holiday, Byron began to feed it by hand. He soon developed a regard for it that prevented its gracing his table. Instead, the goose became

---

[12]Knight, pp. 7-8.
[13]Quennell, pp. 185-186.
[14]Quennell, p. 118.

his constant companion and the ruler of his courtyard. Later he obtained a companion for it, and the flock eventually grew to four.[15]

Though Byron respected such lesser lights as tortoises and geese, it was at fiercer fires that he warmed his soul. In Venice, for instance, he followed a maddened elephant, which, after breaking loose and killing its keeper, wrecked a fruit shop and finally invaded a church. It was eventually killed by a charge from a cannon. At one spot the elephant showered Byron with flying beams, and the poet gloried in the wild energy expended.[16] Given the space and the opportunity, he would doubtless have welcomed the elephant into his Venetian menagerie.

Although Byron participated in some sports, he condemned many others, including all those that tormented, wounded, or destroyed animals. He castigated the clergy for their fox-hunting vicars.[17] He refused to participate in live target shooting when practicing marksmanship with Italian revolutionaries, although it would have benefited his reputation if he had shown himself to be of sterner stuff. This weakness was the "weakness of a great heart," observed the Countess Guiccioli, Byron's one truly congenial female companion.[18] G. Wilson Knight quotes the passage from Byron's Don Juan that expresses the poet's contempt for the fisherman:

> And angling, too, that solitary vice,
> Whatever Isaac Walton sings or says;
> The quaint, old, cruel coxcomb, in his gullet
> Should have a hook, and a small trout to pull it.[19]
> (XIII, cvi, 845-848)

---

[15]Ernest J. Lovell Jr., ed. His Very Self and Voice: Collected Conversations of Lord Byron (New York, 1954), p. 251.

[16]Knight, pp. 6-7.

[17]For a typical reference see Lovell, p. 474.

[18]Knight, p. 13.

[19]Knight, p. 12. Line references are to The Complete Poetical Works of Lord Byron, ed. Paul Elmer More (Boston, 1905).

All of the many facets of Byron's relationship with animals come to light in his poetry. In his essay on Byron in The Burning Oracle, G. Wilson Knight lists some of the passages from Byron's poetry that show the poet's insight into animal life and energy.[20] They range from the description of the butterfly in The Giaour,

> . . . rising on its purple wing
> The insect queen of eastern Spring
> (388-389)

to the account of the wild horses in Mazeppa, with

> Wide nostrils never stretched with pain,
> Mouths bloodless to the bit and rein.
> (XVII, 680-681)

Byron's sense of animal companionship is implicit in the lines from The Prisoner of Chillon that describe the prisoner's feelings upon his release after years of solitary confinement:

> And half I felt as they were come
> To tear me from my second home.
> With spiders I had friendship made,
> And watched them in their sullen trade;
> Had seen the mice by moonlight play,
> And why should I feel less than they?
> (XIV, 379-384)

Byron liked animals. The word liked is the key to his relationship with them. It is also, to an extent, a key to his character. He was not an "animal lover" in the usual sentimental sense, except perhaps in the case of Boatswain. He had for the others--the representative creatures in his menageries, and their counterparts in the world at large--a vast and genuine liking. Byron must be remembered as a major contributor to the liberation of nineteenth-century Greece from the Turks, and as an advocate and tireless worker in the cause of freedom

---

[20]New York, 1939, pp. 200, 204.

all of his short life. As man, worshipper of light and of the sun, has imprisoned portions of each in lamps and bulbs and in fire-places and stoves, so, possibly, Byron surrounded himself with bits of freedom which shone, for him, through the bars and fretwork of the cages of his animals, and which blazed forth in sudden spurts of wild energy. Byron's interest in animals was an inspiriting and inspiring thing, and without his untimely death it might have emerged as more than just another eccentricity of the Romantic age.

BIBLIOGRAPHY

Boyd, Ernest. Literary Blasphemies. New York: Harper and Brothers, 1927.

Brandes, George E. Main Currents in Nineteenth Century Literature. 6 vols. New York: The Macmillan Company, 1906.

Knight, George Wilson. Lord Byron: Christian Virtues. New York: Oxford University Press, 1953.

------. The Burning Oracle: Studies in the Poetry of Action. New York: Oxford University Press, 1939.

Lovell, Ernest J. Jr., ed. His Very Self and Voice: Collected Conversations of Lord Byron. New York: The Macmillan Company, 1954.

Marchand, Leslie A. Byron: A Biography. 3 vols. New York: Alfred A. Knopf, 1957.

------, ed. Selected Poetry of Lord Byron. "Modern Library College Editions." New York: Random House, Inc., 1951.

Maurois, Andre. Byron, trans. Hamish Miles. New York: D. Appleton and Company, 1930.

McElderry, B. R. Jr. "Byron's Epitaph to Boatswain," Modern Language Notes, LVIII (November 1943), 553-554.

More, Paul Elmer, ed. The Complete Poetical Works of Lord Byron. "Cambridge Edition." Boston: Houghton Mifflin Company, 1905.

Quennell, Peter. Byron in Italy. New York: The Viking Press, 1941.

9

GLOSSARY OF USAGE

NOTE: The following glossary reviews the status of words, word forms, and constructions that are frequently criticized as careless, illogical, excessively informal, or otherwise restricted in appropriateness and effectiveness. The glossary is limited to information that goes beyond the scope of the ordinary dictionary entry or that tends to be lost in the wealth of other information a dictionary provides.[1]

a, an. The *a* should appear only before words that begin with a consonant *when pronounced: a desk, a chair, a house, a year, a* C, *a university*. The *an* should appear before words that begin with a vowel when pronounced (though in writing, the first letter may be a consonant): *an eye, an essay question, an honest man, an* A, *an* M, *an uninformed reader*. In the latter position, *a* is nonstandard.

above, above-mentioned, aforementioned, aforesaid. Avoid the use of *above, above-mentioned, aforementioned,* and the like, to refer to something previously mentioned. These phrases suggest the wooden, bureaucratic style of some business letters, many government publications, and most legal documents. Use a less mechanical, less obtrusive expression like "this point," "this fact," "these considerations." If a *this* would not be clear, restate or summarize the point to which you wish to refer.

[1] For confusing words often included in a Glossary of Usage, see SP 2c; for a list of idiomatic prepositions, see D 1e.

allusion, illusion. An "allusion" is a hint or indirect reference (to call an athlete a "Goliath" is to use a Biblical allusion). An "illusion" is a deceptive sense impression or a mistaken belief. When an illusion is serious and persistent enough, it may become a "delusion."

amount, number. *Amount* is sometimes used loosely instead of *number* in reference to things counted individually and as separate units:

SATISFACTORY: A large *number* (not *amount*) of people were waiting.

SATISFACTORY: The *number* (not *amount*) of unsold cars on dealers' lots was growing steadily.

***and* and *but* at the beginning of a sentence.** When *and* and *but* are used at the beginning of a sentence, or at the beginning of a paragraph, they have the effect of partly canceling out the pause signaled by the period or by the paragraph break. They can therefore suggest a sudden or important afterthought. But many modern writers start sentences with *and* or *but* merely to avoid heavier, more formal connectives like *moreover, furthermore, however,* and *nevertheless.*

and/or. *And/or* is an awkward combination sometimes necessary in commercial or official documents. Its use in ordinary expository prose is an annoying mannerism.

angle, approach, slant. *Angle, approach,* and *slant* are currently overused as synonyms for "attitude," "point of view," "position," or procedure."

apt, liable, prone. In informal speech and writing, *apt, liable,* and *prone* all appear in the sense of "likely." In formal usage, *apt* suggests that something is likely because of someone's aptitude ("he is apt to become a successful artist"); *liable* suggests that what is likely is burdensome or undesirable ("he is liable to break his leg"); *prone* suggests that something is almost inevitable because of strong habit or predisposition ("he is prone to suspect others").

as. *As* as a substitute for *that* or *whether* ("I don't know *as* I can come") or as a substitute for *who* ("Those *as* knew her avoided her") is nonstandard. As a substitute for *because* or *while, as* is often criticized as ambiguous, unemphatic, or overused (see D 7b).

attenuate, extenuate. Both *attenuate* and *extenuate* basically mean "to thin out." *Extenuate* is the legal term: "Extenuating circumstances" make a crime seem less serious or contemptible than it originally appeared.

attribute, contribute. *Contribute* means "to give one's share" or "to have a share" in something; *attribute* means "to trace or ascribe something to a cause or source" ("He *attributed* the crossing of the letters in the mail to the intervention of a supernatural power").

being as, being that. As substitutes for *because* or *since, being as* and *being that* ("*being that* I was ill") are nonstandard.

between, among. *Between* is historically related to *twain,* which in turn is a variant of *two.* As a result, grammarians have often restricted *between* to references to two of a kind (distinguish *between* right and wrong) and required *among* in references to more than two (distinguish *among* different shades of color). *Between* is also appropriate when more than two things can be considered in pairs of two:

He had sand *between* his toes.
Bilateral trade agreements exist *between* many European countries.

Indiscriminate substitution of *between* for *among* invites avoidable criticism.

blame for, blame on. There are two idiomatic uses of the word *blame:* "He blamed the passenger *for* the accident" or "He blamed the accident *on* the passenger." The first of these is preferred in formal English.

calculate, reckon, expect, guess. In formal written English, *calculate* and *reckon* usually imply computing or systematic reasoning; *expect* implies expectation or anticipation; *guess* implies conjecture. In the sense of "think," "suppose," or "consider," these verbs are colloquial or dialectal.

***can* and *may*.** Formal English uses *can* in the sense of "be able to" or "be capable of," *may* to indicate permission. The use of *can* to indicate permission, increasingly common in speech and writing, is generally considered colloquial:

FORMAL: You *may* (have my permission to) take as much as you *can* (are able to) eat.
COLLOQUIAL: *Can* I speak to you for a minute?

cannot help but. Although occasionally found in writing, *cannot help but* is widely criticized as an illogical or confused variant of *cannot help:*

SATISFACTORY: I *cannot help* wishing that I had never met you.
SATISFACTORY: I *cannot but* wish that I had never met you.

childish, childlike. "Childish gesture" and "childlike gesture" both remind us of children; but the former suggests silliness or immaturity, the latter endearing innocence.

compare with, compare to. We compare two cities *with* each other to see what they have in common, but we compare a city *to* an anthill to show what a city is like.

continual, continuous. To be "continuous," something must extend without interruption in space or in time. People may keep up a "continual" conversation, interrupted because they have to pause for breath.

couple of. In formal writing, *couple* refers to two of a kind, a pair. Used in the sense of "several" or "a few," it is colloquial. Used before a plural noun without a connecting *of,* it is nonstandard.

COLLOQUIAL: We had to wait *a couple of* minutes.
NONSTANDARD: We had only *a couple* dollars left.

credible, credulous, creditable. Stories may be credible or incredible; the people who read them may be credulous or incredulous. An act that does someone credit is a creditable act.

cute, great, lovely, wonderful, swell. Words like *cute, great, lovely,* and *wonderful* so often express thoughtless or insincere praise that their use in formal writing can suggest immaturity. *Cute* is colloquial. *Swell* is slang.

different than. *Different from* is characteristic of formal written English. Nevertheless, *different than,* widely used in speech, is becoming acceptable in writing. Recent writers on usage point out that it is the more economical way of introducing a clause:

ECONOMICAL: We tried a different method *than* we had used last year.
LESS ECONOMICAL: We tried a different method *from the one* we had used last year.

disinterested, uninterested. In formal writing, *disinterested* usually means "unswayed by personal, selfish interest" or "impartial." The word is used especially to indicate the absence of a financial interest or of personal ambition: "We were sure he would be a *disinterested* judge." The use of *disinterested* in the sense of "uninterested" or "indifferent" is colloquial.

do form for emphasis. Verb forms with *do, does,* or *did* can serve as emphatic variants of the simple present and the simple past: "She may not wear the latest fashions, but she *does know* how to cook." In student writing, the emphatic *do* is sometimes overused:

OVERDONE:	I really *did appreciate* the teacher's help an awful lot.
BETTER:	I *appreciated* the teacher's help.

double comparative, double superlative. Short adjectives usually form the comparative by adding the suffix *er* (*cheaper*), the superlative by adding the suffix *est* (*cheapest*). Long adjectives and adverbs ending in *ly* usually employ the intensifiers *more* and *most* instead (*more expensive, most expensive*). Forms using both the suffix and the intensifier are nonstandard (*more cheaper, most cheapest*).

double negative. Double and triple negatives—the use of additional negative words to reinforce a negation already expressed—are nonstandard: "I *didn't* do *nothing*." "*Nobody* comes to see me *no more*."

due to as a preposition. *Due to* is generally accepted as an adjective: "His absence was *due to* ill health." "His absence, *due to* ill health, upset our schedule." As a preposition meaning "because of," *due to* is often criticized:

OBJECTIONABLE:	He canceled his lecture *due to* ill health.
SAFE:	He canceled his lecture *because of* ill health.

each other, one another. Careful writers distinguish between *each other* (referring to two persons or things) and *one another* (referring to more than *two*).

enthuse. *Enthuse* is a "back formation" from the noun *enthusiasm* and is used in colloquial English as a convenient short cut for "become enthusiastic" and "move to enthusiasm." Similar back formations, like *reminisce* from *reminiscence,* have become generally acceptable. *Enthuse* still has a long way to go.

etc. *Etc.,* the Latin abbreviation for "and so on" or "and the like," often serves as a vague substitute for additional details, examples, or illustrations. Furthermore, *ect.* is a common misspelling; "and etc." and "such as . . . etc." are redundant and unnecessarily reveal the writer's ignorance of Latin.

farther, further; all the farther. A traditional rule required *farther* in references to space and distance ("We traveled *farther* than we had expected"), *further* in references to degree and quantity ("We discussed it *further* at our next meeting") and in the sense of "additional" ("without *further* delay"). *Further* is now widely accepted as appropriate in all three senses.

All the farther in the sense of "as far as" ("This is *all the farther* we go") is variously classified as colloquial, nonstandard, or dialectal.

fortuitous, fortunate. "Fortuitous" changes are accidental, unplanned developments that often are, but don't have to be, fortunate.

full, fulsome. *Fulsome,* except when used by people who are confused by its similarity with *full,* means "offensive, disgusting." "Fulsome praise" is offensively exaggerated or insincere.

gentleman, lady, female. In nineteenth-century, and especially British, use, *gentleman* and *lady* identified people whose manners and social rank set them apart from the uneducated. Now both terms are usually used as polite equivalents of the blunter *man* and *woman*. Since they suggest refinement, they sometimes sound pretentious or ridiculous when used in comparatively unrefined situations. *Female* is biological and impersonal; it is overused as a condescending humorous term.

get, got, gotten. The verb *get* is used in many idiomatic expressions. Some of these are colloquial:

have got (for "own," "possess," "have available")
I *have got* ten dollars; she *has got* blue eyes; you *have got* ten minutes.

have got to (for "have to," "must," "be obliged")
I *have got to* leave now; we *have got to* think of our customers.

get to (for "succeed")
I finally *got to* see him.

get (for "understand")
Get it?

get (for "arrest," "hit," "kill")
The police finally *got* him.

get (for "puzzle," "irritate," "annoy")
What really *gets* me is that he never announces his tests.

Some grammarians commend the use of *get* in sentences like "He *got hit* by a truck" as an emphatic and unambiguous alternative to the ordinary passive, formed with *be, am, was, were* ("He *was hit* by a truck"). This use of *got* is still widely considered colloquial.

In American English, *have gotten* is an acceptable alternative to *have got,* except when the latter means *have* or *have to.*

hadn't ought to. *Ought,* unlike some other auxiliaries, has no form for the past tense. Forms like *had ought* or *hadn't ought* are nonstandard.

NONSTANDARD: You *hadn't ought* to ask him.
FORMAL: You *ought not to have* asked him.

human, humane. Not every human being is "humane"—that is, kind, compassionate, sensitive, or refined.

if, whether. Conservative readers object to *if* when used to express doubt or uncertainty after such verbs as *ask, don't know, wonder, doubt.* The more formal connective is *whether.*

FORMAL: I doubt *whether* his support would do much good.

in, into. Formal writing often requires *into* rather than *in* to indicate direction: "He came *into* (not *in*) the room."

infer, imply. In formal usage, *imply* means to "indicate or suggest a certain conclusion"; *infer* means "to draw a conclusion on the basis of what has been indicated or suggested." A statement can have various implications, which may lead to inferences on the part of the reader.

it's me, it is I. Traditional grammarians require *it is I* on the grounds that the linking verb *is* equates the pronoun *I* with the subject *it* and thus makes necessary the use of the subject-form. Modern grammarians recommend *it is me* on the grounds that usual English word order (he hit *me;* she asked *me*) makes the object-form natural. *It's me* is freely used in informal speech; other pronouns (*us, him, her*) preserve a more definitely colloquial flavor:

COLLOQUIAL: I thought it was *him.* It couldn't have been *us.*

judicial, judicious. A "judicial" decision is a decision reached by a judge or by a court. A "judicious" decision shows sound judgment. Not every judicial decision is judicious.

kind. Agreement requires "*this kind* of car" or "*these kinds* of fish." "*These kind* of cars" and "*those kind* of cars" are colloquial.

later, latter. "Although both Alfred and Francis were supposed to arrive at eight, the former came earlier, the *latter later*."

learn, teach. Except in nonstandard speech, the teacher *teaches* (rather than *learns*) the learner; the learner is *taught* (rather than *learned*) by the teacher.

leave, let. In formal usage, *leave* does not mean "allow" or "permit"; you do not "leave" somebody do something. Nor does *leave* take the place of *let* in suggestions like "Let us call a meeting."

less, fewer. *Less* is often used interchangeably with *fewer* before plural nouns. This use of *less* is widely condemned. The safe practice is to use *less* in references to extent, amount, degree (*less* friction, *less* money, *less* heat) but not in references to number (*fewer* people, *fewer* homes, *fewer* requirements).

***like* as a connective.** In informal speech, *like* is widely used as a connective replacing *as* or *as if* at the beginning of a clause:

INFORMAL: Do *like* I tell you.
FORMAL: Do *as* I tell you.

INFORMAL: The patient felt *like* he had slept for days.
FORMAL: The patient felt *as if* (or *as though*) he had slept for days.

However, *like* is generally acceptable as a preposition introducing a noun or a pronoun:

The girl looked *like* her mother.

luxuriant, luxurious. A "luxurious" house may be surrounded by "luxuriant"—that is, profusely growing—vegetation.

moral, morale. We talk about the "moral" of a story but about the "morale" of troops. People with good morale are not necessarily very moral, and vice versa.

most, almost. *Most* is colloquial when used in the sense of "almost" or "nearly": "*Most* everybody was there" (for "*Nearly* everybody was there").

possessives with verbal nouns. A traditional rule requires that a verbal noun (gerund) be preceded by a possessive in sentences like the following:

FORMAL: He mentioned *John's winning* a scholarship.
FORMAL: I am looking forward to *your mother's staying* with us.

This rule is widely observed in formal writing. In informal speech and writing the plain form is more common:

INFORMAL: Imagine *John winning* a scholarship!

practicable, practical. A "practicable" plan seems capable of being put into practice. A "practical" plan, when put into practice, is workable or effective. Unlike things, people can be practical but not practicable.

preposition at the end of a sentence. Many laymen remember a rule requiring a writer not to end a sentence with a preposi-

tion. This rule has been considerably modified by most teachers of grammar and of writing. The preposition that ends a sentence is idiomatic, natural English, though more frequent in informal than in formal use.

IDIOMATIC: I don't remember what we talked *about.*
IDIOMATIC: She found her mother-in-law hard to live *with.*
IDIOMATIC: You know very well what I hired you *for.*

On the other hand, placing a comparatively unimportant word at the end of a sentence can make a sentence sound unemphatic.

EMPHATIC: Let us not betray the ideals *for* which these men died.
EMPHATIC: Do not ask *for* whom the bell tolls.

prepositions often criticized. *Inside of* (for *inside*), *outside of* (for *outside*), and *at about* (for *about*) are redundant.

Back of for *behind* (*back of* the house), *inside of* for *within* (*inside of* three hours), *off of* for *off* (get *off of* the table), *outside of* for *besides* or *except* (no one *outside of* my friends), and *over with* for *over* (it's *over with*) are colloquial.

As to, as regards, and *in regard to* are generally acceptable, but they can seem heavy-handed and bureaucratic when used as indiscriminate substitutes for briefer or more precise prepositions.

AWKWARD: I questioned him as to the nature of his injury.
PREFERABLE: I questioned him *about* his injury.

As to whether, in terms of, and *on the basis of* flourish in all varieties of jargon.

Per (a dollar *per* day), *as per* (*as per* your request), and *plus* (quality *plus* service) are common in business and newspaper English but inappropriate in a noncommercial context.

provided, provided that, providing. *Provided, provided that,* and *providing* are interchangeable in a sentence like "He will

withdraw his complaint, *provided* you apologize." However, only *provided* has consistently escaped criticism and is therefore the safest form to use.

reason is because, reason why. In informal speech *the reason . . . is because* often takes the place of the more formal *the reason . . . is that*. The former construction is often criticized as redundant, since *because* repeats the idea of cause already expressed in the word *reason*. Either construction can make a sentence unnecessarily awkward.

INFORMAL:	*The reason* that the majority rules *is because* it is strongest.
FORMAL:	*The reason* that the majority rules *is that* it is strongest.
LESS AWKWARD:	The majority rules *because* it is strongest.

Reason why, though equally open to the charge of redundancy is less widely criticized.

respectfully, respectively. *Respectfully* means "full of respect"; *respectively* means "with respect or reference to each of several things in the order in which they were mentioned" ("*Un* and *deux* mean one and two respectively").

shall, will. In current American usage, *will* usually indicates simply that something is going to happen:

> I *will* ask him tomorrow.
> You *will* find it on your desk.
> Mr. Smith *will* inform you of our plans.

The more emphatic *shall* often indicates that something is going to happen as the result of strong determination, definite obligation, or authoritative command:

> I *shall* return.
> We *shall* do our best.

Wages of common laborers *shall* not exceed twenty dollars a day.

Shall is also common in questions that invite the listener's approval or consent:

Shall I wait for you?
Shall we dance?

Formal English often reverses the relationship between *will* and *shall* in the first person; that is, after *I* and *we* but not after *you, he,* or *they*. "I *shall* see him tomorrow" then expresses simple, unemphatic future; "I *will* not yield" expresses determination. Questions would use the form expected in the answer: "*Shall* you see him tomorrow?" Current handbooks of grammar no longer require the observance of this convention.

should, would. In many uses, *should* and *would* are parallel to *shall* and *will*. "I *would* help you if I could" is parallel to "I *will* help you"; the formal alternative, "I *should* help you if I could," is parallel to "I *shall* help you." However, both *should* and *would* are also used with distinctive meanings of their own. *Should* may express obligation ("I *should* study more"), probability ("I *should* be able to finish it tonight"), or a hypothetical condition ("If he *should* resist, call me for help"). *Would* may express customary action ("He *would* listen patiently to my excuses").

split infinitives. Occasionally a modifier breaks up an infinitive; that is, a verbal formed with *to* (*to come, to promise, to have written*). The resulting split infinitive has long been idiomatic English and occurs in the work of many distinguished writers. However, a split infinitive can be awkward, especially if the modifier intervening after *to* consists of more than one word:

AWKWARD: He ordered us *to* with all possible speed *return* to our stations.
BETTER: He ordered us *to return* to our stations with all possible speed.

The words that most frequently spit infinitives are overused intensifiers like *actually, definitely, literally, really,* and *virtually.* Omitting these altogether often improves the sentence:

We expect the public *to* [literally] *overwhelm* us with orders.
Education may be able *to* [virtually] *eliminate* race prejudice.

superlative in reference to two. In informal speech and writing, the superlative rather than the comparative frequently occurs in comparisons between only two things. This use of the superlative is widely considered illogical and generally labeled inappropriate to formal usage.

INFORMAL: Which of the two candidates is the *best* speaker?
FORMAL: Which of the two candidates is the *better* speaker?

take and, try and, up and. *Take and* in "I'd *take and* prune those roses" and *up and* in "He *up and* died" are dialectal. *Try and* for *try to* in "I'd *try and* change his mind" is colloquial.

titles: Dr., Prof., Reverend. In references to holders of academic degrees or titles, *Dr. Smith* and *Professor Brown* are courteous and correct. *Professor* is sometimes abbreviated when it precedes the full name: *Prof. Paul F. Brown.* In references to a clergyman, *Reverend* is usually preceded by *the* and followed by the first name, by initials, or by *Mr.* (*the Reverend William Carper; the Reverend W. F. Carper; the Reverend Mr. Carper*).

too. The use of *too* in expressions like "He isn't *too* well off" is often condemned as vague or overused.

type, type of, -type. The practice of omitting the *of* in expressions like "this *type* of plane" is colloquial. *Type* is increasingly used as a suffix to turn nouns into adjectives: "an escape-type novel," "a drama-type program." Such combinations strike many readers as barbarisms, foreign to idiomatic, natural English. Often they are used to turn simple ideas into fuzzy, wordy phrases: "a subsidy-type payment" says no more than "subsidy."

unique, perfect, equal. It is often argued that one thing cannot be *more unique, more perfect,* or *more equal* than another; either it is unique or it isn't. Formal English therefore often substitutes *more nearly unique, more nearly perfect, more nearly equal.*

up. *Up* is often criticized as redundant in expressions like *finish up, heat up, hurry up, rise up,* or *sober up.* In other expressions it modifies meaning or adds emphasis: *buy up, clean up, dress up, speak up, use up.* Most of these combinations have a colloquial flavor. *Beat up* is slang.

used to, didn't use to, used to could. Formal English does not employ *used to* in questions or negative statements with *did:*

INFORMAL: She *didn't use to* smoke.
FORMAL: She *used not to* smoke.

Used to could is nonstandard for *used to be able.*

very and *much*. Formal usage prefers *much* or *greatly* to *very* before a verbal like *surprised* or *embarrassed* (past participle) if the verbal idea is still strong; that is, if the verbal has not yet become an ordinary adjective with little suggestion of action or process:

SOMETIMES CRITICIZED	SAFE
very surprised	*much* surprised
very embarrassed	*greatly* embarrassed
very astonished	*very much* astonished

where, where at, where to. In formal English, *where* takes the place of *where to* ("*Where* was it sent?") and *where at* ("*Where* is he?"). Both *where to* and *where at* are generally condemned as redundant.

Where used instead of *that* ("I read in the paper *where* a boy was killed") is colloquial.

-wise. The practice of converting a noun into an adverb by tacking on *-wise* is characteristic of business or advertising jargon. Use *grammatically* for *grammar-wise, linguistically* for *language-wise.*

without, on account of. *Without* and *on account of* are nonstandard or dialectal when they serve as connectives introducing a clause:

NONSTANDARD:	The landlord won't let me stay *without* I pay the rent.
STANDARD:	The landlord won't let me stay *unless* I pay the rent.
NONSTANDARD:	Dr. X was unpopular *on account of* he was strict with his students.
STANDARD:	Dr. X. was unpopular *because* he was strict with his students.

you with indefinite reference. Formal writing generally restricts *you* to the meaning of "you, the reader." Much informal writing uses *you* with indefinite reference to refer to people in general. Formal writing would substitute *one:*

INFORMAL:	In ancient Rome, *you* had to be a patrician to be able to vote.
FORMAL:	In ancient Rome, *one* had to be a patrician to be able to vote. (You, the reader, are definitely not a citizen of ancient Rome.)

10

GRAMMATICAL TERMS

NOTE: Use the index to locate fuller discussion of many of the grammatical terms listed in this glossary.

Absolute Construction. A word or phrase that is grammatically independent of the rest of the sentence. Typically, a verbal or verbal phrase:

> *The guests having departed,* Arvin locked the door.

Active. See VOICE.

Adjective. A class of words that can point out a quality of a noun (or noun equivalent). They occur characteristically as modifiers of nouns ("the *happy* child") and as predicate adjectives ("The child was *happy*"). They normally have distinctive forms for use in comparisons (*happier, happiest; more reasonable, most reasonable*).

Adjective Clause. A dependent clause serving an adjective function:

> The man *who had startled us* apologized.

Adverb. A class of words used to modify verbs, adjectives, other adverbs, or a sentence as a whole:

> He ran *quickly.*
> He was *strangely* silent.
> He sang *moderately* well.
> *Surprisingly,* he did not answer.

Many adverbs show the distinctive *-ly* ending.

Adverb Clause. A dependent clause serving an adverbial function:

When the bell ceased to ring, I opened the door.

Agreement. Correspondence, mainly in number, between grammatically related elements. Use of matching forms of a subject and its verb (the *dog barks*—the *dogs bark*); choice of a pronoun matching its antecedent ("*Each* member must be aware of *his* responsibility").

Antecedent. The noun (or equivalent) for which a pronoun substitutes:

Aunt Hertha fell sick soon after *she* arrived.

Appositive. A noun (or equivalent) placed as a modifier next to—usually after—another noun:

Mr. Brown, *the registrar,* proved most helpful.

Article. *A* and *an* (the **indefinite** articles) and *the* (the **definite** article), used as noun markers:

a book, *an* honest man, *the* door

Auxiliary. Helping verbs used in forming complete verbs: *be* (*am, are, was,* etc.); *have; shall* (*should*); *will* (*would*); *can* (*could*); *may* (*might*); *must; ought.*

Case. Inflected forms of nouns and pronouns, signaling certain grammatical relationships within a sentence: the **possessive** of nouns (*George's* friend), the **subject-** and **object-forms** of pronouns (*I—me, he—him,* etc.).

Clause. A subject-predicate unit that may combine with other such units in a sentence. **Independent** clauses are grammatically self-contained and can be punctuated as complete sentences:

I think; therefore, I am.
I think. Therefore, I am.

Dependent clauses are grammatically subordinate to an independent clause (main clause):

Arvin had a dog, *which barked all night.*
After the rain stopped, we went home.

See ADJECTIVE CLAUSE, ADVERB CLAUSE, NOUN CLAUSE.

Collective Noun. Group nouns that are singular in appearance but may require a plural verb:

SINGULAR: The jury *votes* tomorrow. (thought of as a unit)
PLURAL: The jury *are* out to lunch. (thought of as individuals)

Comparative. The form of adjectives and adverbs that is used to indicate relative superiority:

Blood is *thicker* than water.

Complement. A sentence element completing the predication of the verb. The complements of action verbs are called **objects**:

Arvin called *the sheriff* (**direct** object).
She wrote *my father* (**indirect** object) *a letter* (**direct** object).

The complement of a linking verb is a noun or adjective describing the subject (**subjective complement**):

Her father was *a businessman* (**predicate noun**).
The girl looked *pale* (**predicate adjective**).

After some verbs, an object is followed by a description of the object (**objective complement**):

The editorial called the project *a failure.*
Arvin labeled the charges *ridiculous.*

Conjunction. See CONNECTIVE.

Conjunctive Adverb. See CONNECTIVE.

Connective. Words connecting sentence elements or clauses: **coordinating connectives** (*and, but, for, or, nor*); **subordinating connectives** (*if, when, because, though, whereas*); **adverbial connectives** (*however, therefore, consequently*).

Coordinate Adjectives. Two adjectives describing different qualities of the same noun, with a comma taking the place of *and:*

a *noisy, unruly* crowd

Correlatives. Pairs of connectives coordinating sentence elements or clauses: *either . . . or, neither . . . nor, not only . . . but also, whether . . . or.*

Elliptical Constructions. Constructions in which missing elements are supplied to facilitate grammatical analysis:

The paintings [*that*] he collected filled a large room.
When [*she was*] interviewed, the actress denied rumors of an impending engagement.

Expletives. The *it* or *there* used as mere introductory words in *it-is, there-is, there-are* sentences.

Finite Verb. A term used to distinguish a complete verb from a verbal, which cannot by itself function as a predicate.

Function Words. Words whose major function is to establish grammatical relationships within a sentence: articles, connectives, prepositions.

Gender. The quality of nouns and pronouns that determines choice between *he, she,* or *it;* between *actor* and *actress, alumnus* and *alumna, fiancé* and *fiancée.*

Gerund. See VERBAL.

Idiom. An expression that does not conform to general grammatical patterns but is established by usage as the habitual way of conveying a given meaning:

> bear in mind, have a mind to, keep in mind

Infinitive. See VERBAL.

Inflection. Changes in the form of words to reflect changes in grammatical relationships. For instance, the plural *-s* of nouns; the *-s, -ed,* or *-ing* of verbs; the *-er* or *-est* of adjectives.

Intensifier. Words that modify adjectives or adverbs and express degree; also called **intensive adverbs**:

> *very* hot, *quite* calm, *rather* young

Interjection. A grammatically independent element used to express attitude or emotion: *Ah, oh, ouch,* etc.

Linking Verb. See VERB.

Modifier. Words, phrases, or clauses that develop or restrict the meaning of other sentence elements or the sentence as a whole (see ADJECTIVE, ADVERB). **Restrictive** modifiers contribute to identification and need no punctuation; **nonrestrictive** modifiers provide additional information not essential to identification and are set off, normally by commas:

RESTRICTIVE: The man *who returned my wallet* was a complete stranger.
NONRESTRICTIVE: Mr. Norton, *who found my wallet,* is an old friend.

Mood. The classification of verb forms as **indicative** (plain or factual: *I am ready*); **imperative** (request or command: *Be* *quiet*); and **subjunctive** (hypothetical or contrary to fact: *I wish he were here!*).

Noun. A class of words that name or classify people, animals, things, ideas. They occur typically as subjects of clauses or as objects of verbs and prepositions. Their appearance is often signaled by noun markers like the articles (*a, an, the*). Many nouns add *-s* to the plain form to form the plural: *dogs, cars, houses, colleges.*

Noun Clause. A dependent clause taking the place of a noun:

> *That he was late* does not surprise me.

Noun Equivalent. Sentence elements grammatically equivalent to nouns: pronouns, infinitives, gerunds, noun clauses.

Number. Choice of appropriate forms to express **singular** (one of a kind) or **plural** (more than one).

Object. See COMPLEMENT.

Object-Form. See CASE.

Participle. See VERBAL.

Passive. See VOICE.

Past. See TENSE.

Perfect. See TENSE.

Person. Choice of appropriate forms to express the person speaking (**first person**: *I know*); the person spoken to (**second person**: *you know*); or the person spoken about (**third person**: *he knows*).

Phrase. A group of related words, typically a preposition or a verbal accompanied by its object or other related material.

PREPOSITIONAL PHRASE: Irene sat *at the window.*
VERBAL PHRASE: Father gave up *smoking cigars.*

Predicate. The second basic element of the typical written sentence, making an assertion about the subject. The predicate consists of a complete (finite) verb and its possible complements and modifiers.

Preposition. A class of words that relate a noun (or equivalent) to the rest of the sentence

Arvin left *after* dark.

Present. See TENSE.

Principal Parts. The basic forms of a verb: simple present (*know*), simple past (*knew*), past participle (*known*).

Progressive Construction. Verb forms expressing action in progress:

Fred *was lighting* a cigarette.

Pronoun. A class of words taking the place of nouns, classified as **personal** (*I, you, he*); **possessive** (*my, your, his*); **reflexive** or **intensive** (*myself, yourself, himself*); **demonstrative** (*this, that*); **relative** (*who, which, that*); **interrogative** (*who, which, what*); and **indefinite** (*one, anyone, everyone*). See CASE.

Relative Clause. A dependent clause related to the main clause by a relative pronoun:

The article *that I mentioned* begins on page five.

Restrictive. See MODIFIER.

Sentence. A grammatically complete and self-contained unit of thought or expression, set off from other such units by end punctuation. The typical written sentence contains at least a subject and a predicate (*Birds sing*). The most common exception is the subjectless request or command, in which the subject is said to be understood (*Show him in*).

Sentences combining two or more independent clauses are called **compound**. Sentences combining an independent and one or more dependent clauses are called **complex**. A combination of the two types is called **compound-complex**:

COMPOUND:	He hummed, and she sang.
COMPLEX:	He hummed when she sang.
COMPOUND-COMPLEX:	When they heard the news, he hummed and she sang.

Subject. The first basic element of the typical written sentence, about which the predicate makes an assertion.

Subject-Form. See CASE.

Subjunctive. See MOOD.

Superlative. The form of adjectives and adverbs used to express absolute (rather than relative) superiority:

Fred is the *fastest* runner on the team.

Tense. The system of verb forms expressing primarily different relationships in time:

PRESENT:	I know	PERFECT:	I have known
PAST:	I knew	PAST PERFECT:	I had known
FUTURE:	I will (shall) know	FUTURE PERFECT:	I will (shall) have known

Transitive. See VERB.

Verb. A class of words that signal the performance of an action, the occurrence of an event, or the presence of a condition. Verbs appear in typical verb positions ("Let's *leave*." "The boys *left* the scene"). They typically take an *s* in the third person singular of the present tense (*asks, leaves, condones*). They use characteristic **auxiliaries** in forms consisting of more than one word (*have left, was asked, will be leaving*). **Action verbs** are modified by adverbs; **linking verbs** are followed by adjectives:

ACTION VERB:	He *responded* quickly.
LINKING VERB:	His response *seemed* quick.

Regular verbs use the same form for the simple past and the past participle:

REGULAR:	I *laughed*	I have *laughed*
IRREGULAR:	I *knew*	I have *known*

Transitive verbs normally require an object:

TRANSITIVE:	He *raises* chickens.
INTRANSITIVE:	He *rises* early.

See TENSE, MOOD, VOICE.

Verbal. Forms that are derived from verbs but do not by themselves function as predicates: the **infinitive** (*to* form), **present participle** (*ing* form used as an adjective), **gerund** (*ing* form used as a verbal noun), **past participle** (*ed* form in regular verbs, irregular in others). Verbals appear as noun equivalents, modifiers, and *parts* of verbs.

INFINITIVE:	He liked *to dream*.
PRESENT PARTICIPLE:	Her *dreaming* look entranced him.
GERUND:	*Dreaming* got him nowhere.
PAST PARTICIPLE:	He had *dreamed* of childhood days.

Voice. The two sets of verb forms that show typically whether the subject is acting (**active**) or acted upon (**passive**):

ACTIVE: Eileen *feeds* the children.
PASSIVE: The children *are fed* by Eileen.

APPENDIX: LETTERS

Correspondence creates special problems of manuscript form. In writing or answering a formal invitation, you will do well to follow forms suggested in a book of etiquette. In writing a personal letter, you may allow yourself considerable freedom, as long as you observe the elementary courtesies of keeping your handwriting legible and using presentable stationery. Between these extremes of formality and informality is the kind of letter that you may have to write to a teacher, to a college official, or to a future employer. In applying for a scholarship or for a job, you will do well to follow a conventional letter form.

The following specimen letter illustrates one of several styles widely used in business correspondence. You may use it as a model for spacing, indention, and punctuation. Notice especially the following points:

(1) Study the arrangement and relative position of the address of the sender and the address of the receiver, the former followed by the date. When you are writing to a group or to a firm rather than to one of its members, "Gentlemen" or "Dear Sirs" replaces the usual "Dear Mr. Brown" or the more formal "Dear Sir."

(2) The "complimentary close" may range from the formal "Respectfully yours" to the simple "Sincerely." A married woman may put (*Mrs.*) in front of her typed name.

(3) The letter should be typed on one side of standard typing paper, with ample margins. Balance the material on the page. Avoid crowding a short letter into the upper half of the

138 South Third Street
San Jose, California
January 12, 1964

Mr. Ralph J. Clark, Jr.
Personnel Manager
San Rafael Independent-Journal
185 Washington Street
San Rafael, California

Dear Mr. Clark:

I should like to apply for a job with your newspaper. My interest lies in general reporting, a field in which I have had some working experience as well as college training.

During my last summer vacation I worked on the Santa Clara Journal for thirteen weeks within the internship program of the Journalism Department of San Jose State College. I did general reporting and some photography.

As a student at San Jose State, I was a general reporter and feature editor of the Spartan Daily, the college newspaper. I will be graduated February 1 of this year.

The following persons have consented to furnish references:

Dr. John Williams
Associate Professor of Journalism
San Jose State College
San Jose, California

Mr. Thomas Bigelow
General Manager
Santa Clara Journal
Santa Clara, California

Mr. Richard H. James
Editor
Los Angeles Examiner
Los Angeles, California

I am available at your convenience for a personal interview.

Yours truly,
Mary Ann Johnson
Mary Ann Johnson

page; double-space the body of a short letter for more balanced distribution of text.

EXERCISES

A. Write a letter of application for a position in which you have at one time or another taken an interest. Observe conventional letter form.

B. Find a project or recent development that merits publicity or support. Write a letter about it to the editors of a newspaper or magazine, to a legislator, or to a responsible official. Observe conventional letter form.

INDEX

GRAMMAR

DICTION

SENTENCE STYLE